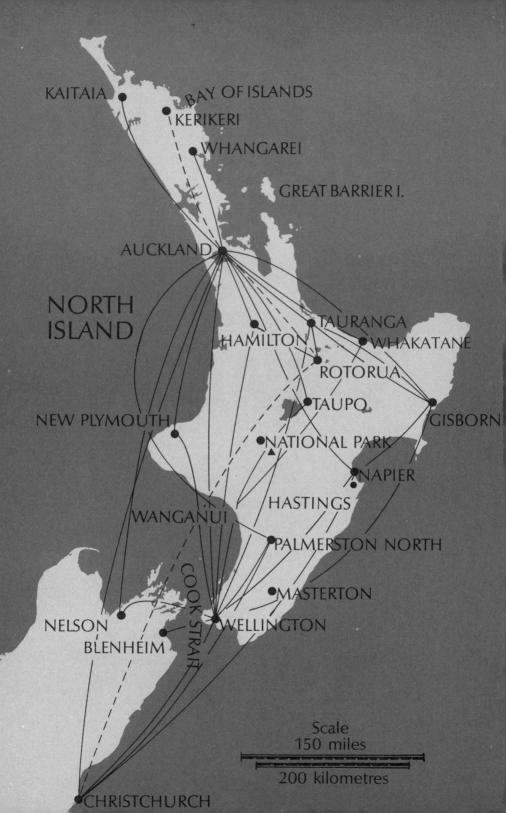

KAITAIA
BAY OF ISLANDS
KERIKERI
WHANGAREI

GREAT BARRIER I.

AUCKLAND

NORTH
ISLAND

TAURANGA
HAMILTON WHAKATANE
ROTORUA
TAUPO

NEW PLYMOUTH
GISBORN

NATIONAL PARK
NAPIER

HASTINGS

WANGANUI

PALMERSTON NORTH

COOK STRAIT

MASTERTON

NELSON WELLINGTON
BLENHEIM

Scale
150 miles

200 kilometres

CHRISTCHURCH

How To Get Lost And Found In Upgraded New Zealand

First Publication, 1986-87
Orafa Publishing Company, Inc.
1314 So. King Street, Suite 1064
Honolulu, Hawaii 96814
U.S.A.

Copyright © 1986 John & Bobbye McDermott

Library of Congress Cataloging in Publication Data

John and Bobbye McDermott
HOW TO GET LOST AND FOUND IN UPGRADED NEW ZEALAND
Includes Index
1. New Zealand—Description and travel—1986-87 Travel Experience Books.
I.B.L. Hughes. II. Title. III. Series
86-62291

ISBN: 0-912273-11-9

Typeset by Crossroads Press, Hawaii
Printed by Fairfield Graphics, Fairfield, Pennsylvania

Previous books in Series

HOW TO GET LOST AND FOUND IN NEW ZEALAND
HOW TO GET LOST AND FOUND IN FIJI
HOW TO GET LOST AND FOUND IN TAHITI
HOW TO GET LOST AND FOUND IN THE COOK ISLANDS
HOW TO GET LOST AND FOUND IN AUSTRALIA
HOW TO GET LOST AND FOUND IN CALIFORNIA
    AND OTHER LOVELY PLACES
HOW TO GET LOST AND FOUND IN NEW JAPAN
HOW TO GET LOST AND FOUND IN OUR HAWAII

How To Get Lost And Found In <u>Upgraded</u> New Zealand

By John & Bobbye McDermott

ORAFA Publishing Co., Inc.
Honolulu, Hawaii, U.S.A.

Dedication

To Berney and Rita Bookman and
Michael and Angela Brett
for advice, good and bad,
for food and wine, always good,
and for ten years of unceasing help
which went beyond mere friendship

How To Get Lost And Found In Upgraded New Zealand

A new look at their favorite country is the theme of *How To Get Lost and Found in Upgraded New Zealand* by veteran travel writers John and Bobbye McDermott whose popular first book on Kiwiland went through five editions and 135,000 copies.

Theirs is a voyage of rediscovery.

"We retraced our steps from the Bay of Islands in the Northland to Stewart Island in the Southland and found the dominating news story to be the increased amenities offered to visitors in the cities and the country.

"We found new hotels, new restaurants, new attractions and new friends," write the McDermotts.

The real experiences of the couple make a highly amusing and enjoyable armchair experience for the reader and an indispensable seat companion for the visitor to New Zealand. Prowling through cities, staying on farms, fishing for the fabulous trout, skiing, tramping, touring gardens and museums...the McDermotts do it all and share their first-hand knowledge with the future visitor.

"New Zealand seems to have discovered the virtues of tourism at the same time the international tourist market has discovered New Zealand. The upgraded facilities on all fronts will make the visitor's stay that much more satisfactory," they say.

Since first writing about New Zealand, John McDermott and Bobbye, the "Lady Navigator," have gone on to write seven other *Lost and Found* books on Pacific destinations.

"We return almost annually and compare our favorite country with the rest of the world. It's New Zealand by three lengths," say the authors.

Contents

List of Maps

Our Favorite Country
(An Introduction)

For the last eleven years the Pacific Ocean has been our private bathtub.

During that time we have explored and written books about the islands that make up the Polynesian triangle: New Zealand, the Cook Islands, the islands of French Polynesia—Tahiti, the Marquesas, the Australs, the Tuamotos—and our own islands of Hawaii.

We traveled and wrote about the shores of Japan and the shores of California and the shores of Australia.

We recorded our impressions about Fiji and learned from first-hand experiences something about Tonga and Western Samoa.

In between getting "lost and found" in the Pacific we traveled frequently to Europe, to Asia, throughout the United States, Mexico and Canada.

One result of our travels is the most common question "What is your favorite country?"

To which we answer: "Excluding Hawaii, our home base, our favorite country is New Zealand."

"Why?" always follows.

"Why? Because New Zealand is the most beautiful country in the world. Everywhere you look there is beauty. There are pure lakes and rushing rivers and snow covered alpine peaks and rugged coastlines and forests and endless miles of green pastures. And the beauty is undisturbed.

"There are only three million people in New Zealand and they are beautiful, too—laid back, kind, witty, friendly."

All of which is true. New Zealand is a country without tensions. Nicely old fashioned in some ways. Basically, it is still very much an agricultural society with the unaffected honesty of a farm upbringing. Strangers and neighbors alike are treated with the same common courtesy.

The increased importance of tourism has created changes, but the changes are all positive. The beauty of the country remains

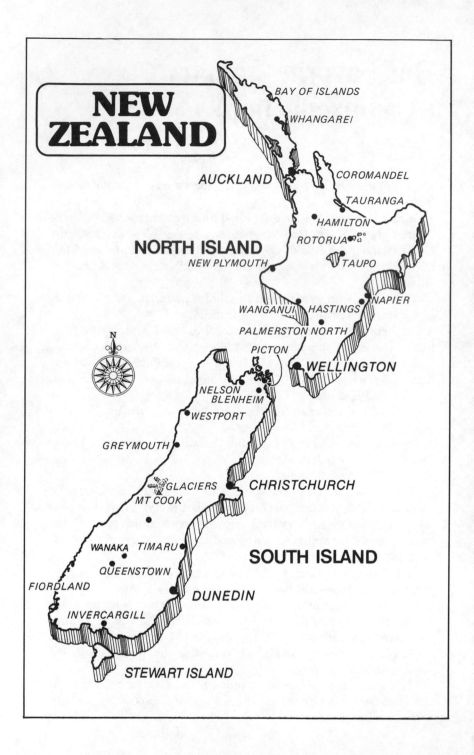

intact. The people remain the same.

The changes include, for example, more organized ways to get you into the heart of the country.

You can take four-wheel-drive safaris into the back country, camp out with Maori guides, stay overnight at sheep stations, meet the New Zealanders on their farm turfs.

Ten years ago there was virtually no river rafting. Today, there are fifty professional rafting companies.

You can take helicopter tours to high country to fish and hunt and hike and ski.

You can charter a yacht and explore the many bays and coves and islands of New Zealand coastline.

Getting into the beautiful wild country doesn't necessarily require machines.

New Zealand is famous for its organized walks: the Milford Track, the Routeburn, the Hollyford. New walks have been organized: the Wanganui River Walk, the Lake Waikaremoana Track, the Greenstone Track.

Equally well-known are some non-guided, independent walks such as the Heaphy and the Tongariro Track.

In 1975, the New Zealand Walkway Commission was established to create a network of tailored trails throughout the country to complement the existing tracks. By 1986, a total of 118 walks had been established.

You can pick up maps detailing local walks of varying length, their estimated walking time and an honest appraisal of their difficulty at any city and district public relations office. It's an easy way to experience the famous New Zealand bush country nose-to-nose.

Another wrinkle of growing importance is the increasing availability and variety of "caravans" for rent. These rolling homes—RVs in America and campervans in New Zealand—are available in every major city.

We took a four-berth Newmans camper in Auckland, stored our ton of luggage in the over-the-cab double bunk and traveled 6,500 kilometers, from the Bay of Islands in the North Island to Invercargill in the South Island, and left the lovely vehicle in Christchurch six weeks later to fly home.

Prices for campervan rental have many variables. You should

know that there is a low season from May to October (winter and early spring) and a high season from mid-December to the end of January (summer). A shoulder season offers a third rental rate.

A minimum hire is for four days. A substantial reduction is made for vehicles kept over 21 days except during the low season.

My estimate is that you could hire a pop-top for a 21-day swing through New Zealand for little more than a standard vehicle and have the added luxury of having a refrigerator, a range, and an inside table to eat at, and, if you wanted, a bed for the night. Bloody marvelous.

More Good News For Visitors

The hospitality of the Kiwis is as generous as ever. But there are more ways to meet more New Zealanders.

Home visit programs are just budding but farm stays are in full flower with many new organizations bringing new farms into networks of available working farm homes of every description. In our last visit we stayed on a deer farm, a stud farm and visited an angora goat farm, all new in the farm-stay scene. Bed and breakfast stays are another part of the accommodation opportunities where visitors can meet New Zealanders.

Over the last ten years during frequent returns to New Zealand we have begun to see a swing in cuisines. For example, you could never find lamb on any restaurant menu. Restaurants were for New Zealanders and they ate "lamb" at home and on the farm and they didn't want to go out "for a meal," as they say, and eat lamb. ("Lamb" is in quotes because at home they ate hogget—a two-year-old lamb also called "two-tooth" or mutton. More flavorful, they say.)

Today, thanks to tourism, lamb can be found on most menus.

Today, partially but not entirely due to tourism, there is a plethora of new restaurants throughout the country offering every sort of cuisine—even vegetarian in this meat-producing country. There are small restaurants with blackboard menus, ethnic restaurants, a growing number of seafood restaurants where there were none before—none in a country surrounded by ocean. (You still have trouble finding lobster, actually clawless crayfish, because it is all exported to North America.)

New Zealand always did have the highest quality of produce and meats but, in the farm kitchen tradition, everything was

cooked to the point of disintegration.
This is not true today. You can get a rare steak and crisp vegetables. Not everywhere, and not all of the time, but your chances are improving.

Wine has always been a part of the New Zealand heritage but there has been a dramatic improvement in the quality of New Zealand vintages.

In Christchurch we attended a wine tasting of the ten top table wines awarded at the national wine competition and were told by Terry Dunleavy, the executive officer of the Institute: "We've made a century of progress in the last ten years. In London we are considered the most exciting of the New World wine countries.

"Our distinctive style is a result of our cool climate. Our wines are similar to German wines in style, being low in alcohol with an intensity of fruit and varietal character."

We learned the virtues of the Alsatian-type white wines like Muller-Thurgau and Gerwurtztraminer because they can be drunk comparatively young.

There are some excellent New Zealand red wines but, in restaurants, they are usually immature. If you like good reds, go to a wine shop and buy a good bottle and take it to a BYO restaurant.

Upmarket Places To Put Your Head

The 100 percent growth in New Zealand tourism has resulted in every sort of new accommodation.

Bright new major hotels, small hotels, many new motels, and a host of sporting lodges in beautiful settings.

Many overseas visitors like the major hotels. They like to have an on-premise choice of several restaurants and they like to have shops where they can browse and buy gifts for family and friends back home.

Major hotels and chains like Sheraton, Regent International, Hyatt have come on stream and others are on drawing boards, particularly in the primary tourist centers of Auckland, Rotorua, Wellington, Christchurch and Queenstown.

THC, a government-owned but independently operated chain of hotels, has gone through a major expansion and renovation program including the addition of suites and villas to keep in step with the progress of New Zealand tourism.

New motels, small and not-so-small, are also part of an improved travel scene today.

I don't think we went into a city, town or village where we didn't see at least one new motel.

New Zealand motels, now more than ever, represent one of the best travel bargains in the world, particularly, we have found, if it is a small four- to eight-unit complex run by the owners. It will be immaculate and meticulously operated.

A motel awarded four stars by AA will give the independent traveler a living room with a color television set, a separate bedroom with electric blankets, a full-sized kitchen and a full bathroom.

Our only complaint with most accommodations—the exceptions can be counted on one hand—is the lack of decent reading lights. There aren't any. You have to go into the bathroom to read the evening newspaper.

Travelers like to read. They read brochures and time tables, reference books and menus. They like to relax in bed with a mystery or a current magazine. New Zealand hotel and motel owners do not know this.

We enter this plea to the New Zealand Hotel/Motel Associations: "Please, on behalf of your reading clientele, appoint a Save-the-Visitors' Eyesight Committee, get a bulk rate on floor lamps and bedlamps and install them immediately. Oh, yes, and please don't use 25-watt bulbs."

One caveat: farm stay opportunities have grown tremendously and they are very satisfactory as long as you have the right farm. Too many farmers are getting into the hospitality trade without the necessary qualifications—and sometimes, adequate facilities—to satisfy overseas visitors. Make sure you know what you are getting.

We stayed at two farms, for example, which the booking organizers had never seen.

In Auckland we were impressed with Graham Caldwell of Farmhouse and Countryhome Holidays who has been in the business many years. His company has 320 host homes and farms, including 30 homes in Wellington and Christchurch.

"We inspect every house and farm for cleanliness and comfort, of course, but more importantly, we go to meet the hosts. The quality of the home is not as important as the people. We look for genuineness in the hosts."

His company is at P.O. Box 31250, Auckland 9, New Zealand.

Bigger And Better Odds And Ends

The highways in New Zealand are better. Not bigger, but better. More highways are sealed or resealed for smoother driving. The highways are still only two lanes except for "motorways" going in and out of major cities.

Speed limits have been increased from 80 kilometers an hour to 100 kilometers an hour. Do not expect to pass anybody but a hay wagon at 100 kilometers an hour—and then the haywagon had better be going uphill.

New Zealanders have always driven 100 kilometers an hour. Now they drive 120 kilometers an hour.

Kiwis are good drivers. Given to tailgating so they can pull out and pull in quickly on the two-lane roads, but you get used to it. They also have a breathtaking penchant for passing on curves. However, we never saw an accident and we finally believed that they could see around mountains.

The wearing of seat belts is mandatory. Buckle up.

Self-drive tourists will find many rest areas along the route, usually in pleasantly scenic spots, and well-marked 400 meters in advance.

Historical markers need work. They are too small. Seldom well done.

Highway information is excellent, particularly from AA, the automobile club, which you can join in New Zealand if you aren't an AAA member at home.

AA supplies members with free maps, strip maps, brochures on attractions and accommodations and offers discounts on travel-oriented books.

Our favorite travel reference books have been the two-volume *Mobile Guide* books by Diana and Jeremy Pope. The books do not make easy armchair reading but they are solid for at-the-site information.

Another permanent addition to our library which we read along the way is the Readers Digest's *Wild New Zealand*. Mainly concerned with the most scenic areas of the country, the book contains excellent four-color photography.

The AA can also make bookings, a New Zealand word for reservations, at hotels, airlines, etc.

Another source of information—and bookings—is the New Zealand Tourist and Publicity Office, formerly the Government Tourist Office. Renamed, it has also been redirected toward making a profit, like the government-owned hotel company, THC.

The operation seems to be blessed with a new sense of purpose. NZTPO certainly was most helpful to us.

NZTPO has offices in Auckland, Rotorua, Christchurch, Dunedin, Queenstown and Wellington. Actually, Wellington has two offices, one regional, the other national.

Not only do they have every brochure printed in New Zealand but the organization also has more than 1,000 sightseeing excursions, attractions and participatory adventures computerized, enabling them to print out any activity that interests you.

Over 1,000 sightseeing excursions and attractions! I have to go back and reread the number. It reflects the dynamic growth of tourist-oriented activities in New Zealand. Upgraded New Zealand.

The biggest problem the visitor faces in New Zealand is choosing among those 1,000 activities which can be fitted into the time period available. Or shaping your own.

Physical ability is not a criterion for falling in love with the country.

To the student of flora and fauna, New Zealand offers a kaleidoscope of new and old friends in the many miles of bush. Eighty-four percent of New Zealand flowering plant life cannot be found in any other country.

To the horticulturist, New Zealand is a constant delight because of the abundance of botanical gardens, public and private.

If the study of different cultures appeals, the civilization—past and present—of the Maori people is an absorbing experience.

To the camera lover, New Zealand is a film devourer. Great scenic shots at every turn in the road.

For the sportsman, the outdoors person, the problem of selection is multiplied.

New Zealand is synonymous with trout fishing.

Zane Grey, in 1926, made the deep-sea fishing of New Zealand as famous as trout fishing.

Trophy game hunting lures hunters from far-away Europe.

Golf? There are 325 registered golf courses in a country two-thirds the size of California.

When the skier in the Northern Hemisphere is looking at oiled bodies on beaches but dreaming of snow on high mountains, he can enplane to new ski slopes, new chair lifts, new helicopter skiing on both the North Island and the South Island.

Remember, New Zealand is the home country of Sir Edmund Hillary and you can indulge in alpine climbing on the same craggy peaks on which he trained.

There are oceans of yachting.

There is magnificent salmon fishing from January to March and surf-casting the year around.

Tennis courts are everywhere, as is the gentler game of lawn bowls. Many squash courts.

Rafting down wild rivers is a new national industry.

If you like spectator sports, learn about the national hobby of mayhem called rugby. It is a thriller.

Horses? You can ride them or bet on them. New Zealanders are not given to bragging but they do savor the wins set by New Zealand horses in Australia's prestige races, especially the Melbourne Cup. (It's the lime content in the New Zealand grass, they tell you.)

Or if your sport is just having a drink in a cool pub, there is a lot of that, too.

Prices

New Zealand prices have increased at least ten percent per year for the last ten years, following a worldwide trend, *but these prices are in New Zealand dollars.* To the overseas visitor, particularly from the United States, who receives exchange rates as favorable as those of 1986-87, that is almost two New Zealand dollars for every one US dollar.

New Zealand is one of the great travel bargains in the world.

For the sake of simplicity, all prices quoted in the book are in New Zealand dollars unless specified otherwise.

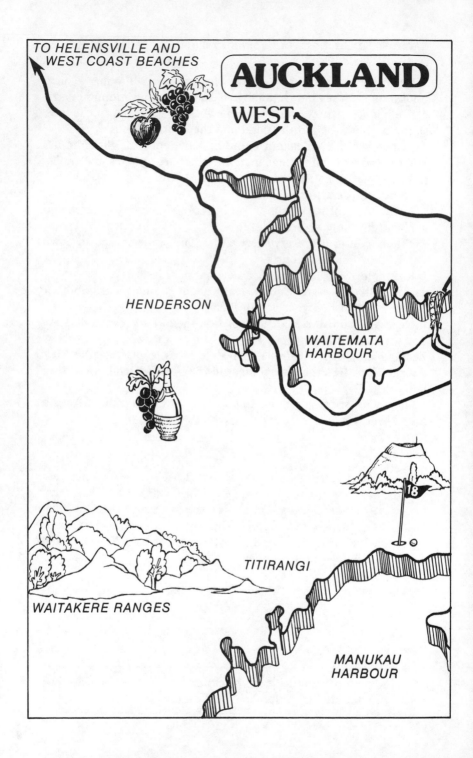

1. Look What's Happened To Auckland!

New Hotels . . . New Attractions . . .
New Restaurant . . . New Shopping

Who would have thought ten years ago that dear little dead Auckland, a dull duckling of a tourist city, would change into such an darling duchess?

Ten years go, in the first edition of *How to Get Lost and Found in New Zealand,* we wrote the line "What do you do on a rainy Sunday in Auckland? You cut your throat."

Ten years ago Auckland was a commercial and transportation center with Victorian railroad station architecture, few restaurants and hotels for visiting businessmen and prosperous sheep farmers. The shops on Queen Street bordered on the dowdy.

No longer. Over the years we've watched Auckland turn a corner. Today it is an excellent destination area in itself.

Don't be misled by yesterday's reputation—or our first book—and come in from the airport for one night's sleep and head off the next day to the Waitomo caves and Rotorua.

Auckland, along with the rest of New Zealand, discovered the importance of international tourism at the same time that international tourism discovered the charms of New Zealand.

In ten years the number of overseas visitors has doubled.

Fortunately, the tourist facilities have expanded in quantity and quality to satisfy the sophisticated expectancies of the new arrivals.

We date the initial breakthrough from the opening of the 427-room Sheraton in 1983. Its stunning beige marble and brass lobby with an elegant indoor fountain would win applause anywhere.

And, my dear, there was an indoor/outdoor swimming pool with a Jacuzzi bath, saunas, and exercise rooms on the second floor!

In New Zealand, it was all revolutionary.

So were the room decorations. They even had bedside lamps you could read by.

So were the room rates. They were considered astronomical.

1

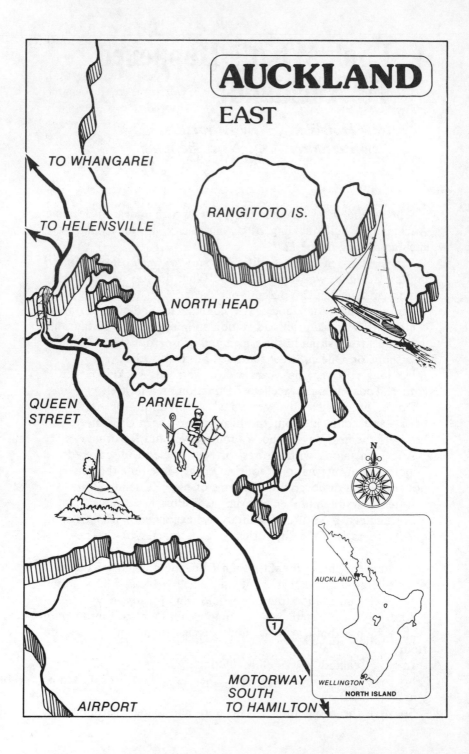

But overseas visitors came and paid the rates—actually lower than most metropolitan cities. When Sheraton prospered, it became evident to the most casual observer that a new age had dawned.

Sheraton continues to upgrade. In 1986, they created a shopping mall open seven days a week and a new nightclub, and renovated their ever popular swimming pool-exercise complex.

And then came the Regent.

The Regent hotels in Sydney and Hong Kong and Fiji and New York and London have always set the highest standards of elegance in decor, in service, in attention to detail.

The Regent of Auckland hired no one with hotel experience—a shocking idea—adhering to a policy that it is easier to train an entirely new staff to Regent standards of service than rid an experienced staff of bad habits. The new hotel spent over a million dollars on training. A shocking amount of money.

When the Regent opened and poured 3,000 bottles of French champagne for its invited local guests, it set a new tone for Auckland, and the entire country.

Its expansive black marble lobby backed by a recessed quiet lounge where afternoon tea was poured impressed. So did the glamorous marble bathrooms with luxurious terry cloth robes to wear during a stay. "Mom, they even have a telephone next to the loo (toilet)!" was overheard at the gala opening.

(We once stayed in a suite of a Regent hotel in Chicago that had nine telephones. That really impressed.)

Don't you love to watch the behavior of people?

Go to the lobby of the Regent and watch the magical effect the elegant decor has on the guests.

I have a vintage Rolls Royce 1958 Silver Cloud I which I keep in pristine condition. When first-time riders regally step—not crawl—into the back seat of "My Fair Lady," it is fun to witness the "to-the-manor-born" loftiness that overcome them.

The marble lobby in the Regent has the same effect. Facial and body gestures of the "bored hauteur" is the instant reaction, even among the T-shirt-clad ladies.

Incidentally, the staff at the Regent is probably one of the most handsome group of youngsters you'll find anywhere. One look at general manager Andrew Thomson's wife leads you to believing that picking a mate and hiring employees with that wow-now look is part of his talent.

Meantime, down the road, Hyatt Kingsgate had taken over the

International Hotel on a hill overlooking the harbor and poured $6,000,000 into a refurbishing program. Looks smart.

A new Travelodge opened at the entrance to the airport.

Other accommodations of all price levels have come on the market to meet the influx of visitors.

New buildings are popping up in the city like jack-in-the-box glass cubes. From our window on one side of the Regent alone, we counted eight building cranes whose job is to change the city skyline dramatically. Add the new chic shops, the new attractions and the action centers and a visitor is looking at a fine city in a new dress.

This is a new, upgraded Auckland.

Auckland By Sea

Auckland, with 800,000 residents, is by far New Zealand's largest city and the country's industrial heart and most important port.

You see few apartment houses for a city of such a size. The New Zealander way is to own his on home, his own plot of land with room for a garden. The resultant urban sprawl spreads out in every direction and wraps around all shores of the magnificent harbor.

Actually, there are two harbors. (In New Zealand it is spelled harbour.) When you drive from the airport, you cross over part of Manukau Harbour that leads to the Tasman Sea.

When you reach downtown Auckland, the expanse of water you see is the deep-water Waitemata Harbour which leads to the Hauraki Gulf and eastward to the Pacific Ocean. One of the visual pleasures of the city, it separates downtown Auckland from the North Shore.

Today, there are power launches and sailboats offering visitors sightseeing cruises along that 85 miles of shoreline. Sail among the islands of the Hauraki Gulf Maritime Park aboard the giant catamaran, *The Pride of Auckland,* a sweetheart of a ship, or motor to Rangitoto Island, a scenic reserve, on the new $500,000 *Manu.* As part of the *Manu's* half day tour, you ride—or walk—to the summit, passing black-backed sea gulls nesting on the shores and forests of pohutukawa trees.

We took both cruises.

Both ships sail from the dock adjacent to the Ferry Building which is at the foot of Queen Street.

The Pride of Auckland is 60 feet long with a 28-foot beam. Even in the strongest wind it heels only four or five degrees. The catamaran carries 80 passengers and a crew of four: the captain, a mate, and two pretty hostesses.

There is a two-hour morning cruise, a luncheon cruise, a two-hour afternoon cruise and a dinner cruise. The captain told us he is proud of the galley.

We had a calm sail under light breezes along the coast, beside the *Rainbow Warrior,* the famous Greenpeace ship which was blown up by the French in an unprecedented act of international terrorism by a Western nation. The ship was being stripped of all gear to be towed offshore and sunk as a diving memorial.

We sailed underneath the Harbour Bridge that connects Auckland to the North Shore. Before the advent of the bridge all commuting was by ferry. The passenger ferries still run and are another way to get out on the harbor.

When bridge traffic increased beyond its capacity, a plan was devised to suspend lanes on either side of it. A Japanese company won the contract to attach the prefabricated lanes in an operation that became known as the Nippon Clip-On.

Down wind, the jazzy blue-and-white striped mainsail and genoa spread over the water.

From the deck we could appreciate the new skyline of Auckland, the cliffside homes on the North Shore and islands floating on the horizon. A pleasant, relaxing morning.

"Anybody wanting to take the helm may do so," said the captain.

Who could resist?

Standing behind the shiny steel wheel and feeling the 60-foot beauty respond to the slightest turn was a king-of-the-mountain sensation.

I'd crew on her for nothing.

Co-owner Jim Edmonds said, "We are determined to provide year-round service. If only one person turns up we will take the boat out. In winter we will provide wet weather gear for those who want a fun sail on a blustery day."

What do you do on a rainy Sunday in Auckland? Go yachting of course. It's so much healthier than cutting your throat.

The Charter Cruise Company, owner of *The Pride of Auckland,* also operates 3- and 7-day Hauraki Gulf cruises, and bareboat or with-crew charters.

We tried to engineer enough time to take the short cruise but couldn't arrange it. The idea of spending three days and two nights on the island-studded Hauraki Gulf sailing, diving, beach barbecuing, and all that sounded like good fun. And the price was right. Next time.

The other major harbor experience is aboard the luxury motor launch *Manu* which offers a variety of cruises: morning cruise, luncheon cruise or afternoon tea cruise. Or a five-hour sea-and-land adventure on a scenic reserve island.

The *Manu,* meaning "Seabird," is licensed to carry 150 people but limits its passengers to smaller numbers for comfort. Our cruise, as example, had no more than 20 passengers, half of whom were cruise-only patrons.

We elected to do the "Volcanic Island" cruise which includes a ride to the summit of Rangitoto Island on something called "The Magic Bus" and a buffet luncheon on board on return.

The morning was ideal. Sparkling waters, clean air, just cool enough for a light sweater.

The *Manu,* like *The Pride of Auckland,* glided along the waterfront, past the *Rainbow Warrior,* but ducked into Westhaven Yacht Basin, home for a fleet of yummy yachts. They inspired the city's adopted slogan, the slogan, "Auckland, the City of Sails."

There is a common phrase used by New Zealanders explaining their economy to visitors: "We don't have any rich people but we don't have any poor ones either."

One look at some of the sleek craft moored at Westhaven gives rise to the impression that if there are no rich people there are some people who do quite well. Quite well indeed.

As the *Manu* went under the bridge, the loudspeaker commentator repeated the Nippon Clip-On story and we headed east for Rangitoto Island at the mouth of the Hauraki Gulf.

The island is one of 47 dots of land comprising the Hauraki Gulf Maritime Park.

Two other national maritime parks are in the Bay of Islands and the Marlborough Sounds.

Rangitoto is a "new" island having been built by basaltic lava eruptions, the last of which occurred 250 years ago.

The island was bought by the Crown in 1854 for £15. Not a bad buy but then you have to remember that the land for the new settlement called Auckland was purchased from the Maori for £55 plus assorted blankets, clothing, axes, pots, pipes and tobacco and bags of sugar and flour.

Today Rangitoto, about four miles wide, is a recreational area honeycombed with walking trails for nature lovers and for packs of small kids whose brave leaders have taken them on mischief-letting, energy-diminishing outings.

There is no overnight camping.

At the principal wharf are restrooms, an informational kiosk, barbecue areas and a saltwater swimming pool.

The "Magic Bus" wasn't there. Finally a yellow thing, similar to a St. Mary's Grammar School bus I rode in Colorado Springs a thousand years ago, wheezed and clanked into view. The "magic" of the bus was the fact that it ran at all.

"How old is this charming contraption?" we asked.

"Thirty-six years." We would have given it fifty.

The handsome young Maori driver, Malcolm Hita, was as gracious as the bus was unique. He told us about the island as we bumped and jangled along the trail to the summit.

"This trail consists of fifteen kilometers of road built by prisoners who used crushed lava rocks and packed them together. The project started in 1925 and went on until 1936.

"Before the Pakehas came, the island was used as a burial ground and as a lookout for enemy war canoes.

"At one time near the end of the 19th century a plant was set up to manufacture salt by evaporation but the idea failed. You can still see the salt pans.

"The trees are mainly pohutukawa, called the Christmas tree because they blossom in December with beautiful red flowers attracting bees. We collect forty tons of white honey which has an unusual flavor. It is said that Queen Elizabeth gets pohutukawa honey every Christmas."

A small alarm system went off in my head saying that we were going to be offered the rare chance of buying pohutukawa honey before the end of the journey.

We passed through a pretty glen of kidney fern plants and slowed down at Flax Point where thousands of black-backed sea gulls come to the nest in October and November.

At the sight of a couple of beaten up cabins Malcolm said,

"There are less than half a dozen left on the island and they cannot be sold or improved. When the leases expire the government will take back the property.

"We now have an animal population control program because the opossums, wallabies and fallow deer destroy the delicate vegetation. The animals are being trapped and eliminated."

The Magic Bus groaned its way to the 850-foot summit . . . almost. We walked the last 200 yards. From the top of the concrete block observation post left over from World War II we could see the entire coastline of the island, Auckland in the distance, and the isthmus which connects Rangitoto to Motutapu, another uninhabited protected island.

What I found interesting was the shape of the island. The perfect "cone" we had thought Rangitoto to be, in fact, is a "shouldered" silhouette. From the top of the more recent cone where we were standing, we could look down on the outer rim of an earlier volcano.

Rangitoto is called "The Coat Hanger Island" because these shoulders give it the profile of a clothes hanger.

It was a short descent to Yankee Wharf on the isthmus where a teahouse and honey shop await passengers awaiting their boats.

Manu appeared shortly and during the cruise back to Auckland a cold meats lunch was served. Cold beer or other refreshments were available at the bar.

Lunch was terrible but the trip was most worthwhile.

The Captain Cook Cruises, also known as the Blue Line Boats, has various other outings.

Both harbor cruise companies occupy the same pier sales office opposite the airline terminal and the Travelodge. Or contact Captain Cook Cruises at P.O. Box 448, Auckland (Telephone 774-074); *The Pride of Auckland,* P.O. Box 3750, Auckland 1, (Telephone 734-557).

Another different—and inexpensive—way to cruise the harbor is a Sunday-only outing aboard the *William C. Daldy,* one of two steam tugs left in New Zealand. The hand-fed, coal-burning antiquity departs on morning and afternoon hour-and-a-half tours, weather permitting, from the Marsden Wharf. That's two piers down from the Ferry Building.

The boat was saved from the breaker's yard by a society of steam engine buffs who restored the vessel.

Steam engine buffs are in a category by themselves. When a steam engine is huffing and puffing, their little old hearts tend to huff and puff in rhythm. If you are one of those, the *William C. Daldy* is for you.

Mark it down: another Sunday activity.

Auckland By Land

Three major and several minor attractions have been added to Auckland's upgraded menu of diversions.

One of the most unusual is Kelly Tarlton's Underwater World. Showcases of the ocean depths from municipal aquariums to multibucks and multifaceted attractions like Sea World, Sea Life Park, or the Monterey Bay Aquarium have become a standard part of water-oriented tourist destinations. The newer attractions tend, for the most part, to be highly innovative, expensive developments. The Auckland attraction can take its rightful place among the front ranks for imaginative, creative effort and most satisfactory viewing results.

Basically what Kelly Tarlton did was build the world's first upside-down aquarium. It's the damnedest aquarium you'll ever, ever encounter!

The man took three abandoned municipal sewage holding tanks, linked one to the next with a continuous gigantic Plexiglas tunnel, filled the tanks with sea water and an exotic array of New Zealand fish.

Have you ever studied the underbelly of a free swimming shark directly over your head?

The only time I saw a free swimming shark that close was in Rangiroa in French Polynesia and I had no interest in its color, texture or who its mother and father were. I was only interested in returning to the safety of the diving boat as quickly as possible.

But let's go back to how Underwater World began and its creator, Kelly Tarlton, a singular character who lived for the underwater world. He led many diving expeditions in the South Pacific, formed a diving company, specialized in underwater photography and salvaging wrecks.

The list of his successful diving ventures includes finding diamonds and sapphires and gold and historical cannons and anchors, including a Captain Cook anchor off of Tahiti Iti.

In one expedition he brought up jewels from the Rothschild family lost in a 1897 shipwreck off the Australian island state of Tasmania.

He created a Museum of Shipwrecks aboard the barque *Tui* at Pahia in the Bay of Islands which is still a major tourist attraction.

Tarlton's greatest challenge was to bring his Underwater World into reality. He did it most successfully, overcoming every sort of financial and physical problem, only to die in his sleep shortly after greeting his 100,000th visitor just seven weeks after his exciting monument opened in 1985.

Typical of Kelly's ability to get a job done was creating the see-through underwater acrylic tunnel. The basic material, 33 one-ton sheets of Perspex 2.7 inches thick, had to be bent and cut into proper shape to fabricate the water-tight walls of the tunnel. The best offer was $1 million from a Japanese company.

Kelly's innovative resources took over where his financial resources could not reach. His solution was to do the work himself in an old slaughterhouse.

The result offers the visitor a rare experience at the submerged aquarium in Okahu Bay two miles east of the Ferry Building.

You descend by stairs or elevator at the waterfront location into a spacious gift shop foyer where numerous static exhibits are featured.

Beyond the gift shop, you are introduced to the history of the Underwater World by an audio-visual presentation in the complex's 80-person theater.

You then descend a short flight of stairs to the beginning of the 395-foot tunnel onto a slow but constantly moving conveyer belt or to a footpath alongside it.

The first tank, the wave tank, lets you pretend you have entered the ocean beneath the surf that laps at beaches. Overhead simulated waves churn and surge, froth and bubble, flow in and ebb out. Now you are beyond the ninth wave, into calmer waters.

The surf melds into a reef. Verdant seaweed and kelp curtains provide a leafy camouflage for kingfish and snapper and their colorful kinsmen.

Farther on, the green underwater forest gives way to a sandy bottom sea, the classroom for schools of flounder, the ballet studio for graceful stingrays. At times the rays nap directly overhead on top of the tunnel.

The sunshine atmosphere of the clear sea dissolves as the conveyer takes you into a dimly lit section to deeper ocean where reef caves conceal all but the peering snouts of eels and where crayfish wiggle antennas in a cheery hello.

And then you enter the shark tank. Small dogfish swim along the bottom, not anything you'd want to take home but much friendlier, it seems, than the cold-eyed, fish-eyed monsters in torpedo suits that swoosh by just overhead, never stopping, always looking for a spare leg to munch on.

I never really had a great affinity for sharks and here they are in all of their underwater Mafia glory.

A hired scuba dive will cost no less than NZ$25. Here at Kelly Tarlton's Underwater World you get all of the same thrills at a fraction of that—and you don't even have to dry off.

It's a fine seven-day-a-week addition to the Auckland scene. Rack up another Sunday option.

Suggestion: Go early or go late. It's also popular with school groups.

For an overview of what the "Land Of The Long White Cloud" is all about head southeast of central Auckland to Heritage Park, another major attraction opened by the prime minister in December 1984.

You really shouldn't miss it. The essence of New Zealand is displayed in the 30-acre theme park: Maori dancing, carving, the animals, plants, birds, fish of the islands—all done in a first-rate fashion.

The high level of professionalism at Heritage Park is characteristic of most of the new attractions we found in upgraded New Zealand. USA Theme Park Consultants designed the facility against criteria set by the founding company.

Divided into three separate "worlds" (Natureworld, Agriworld, Cultureworld), each theme is dramatized with a variety of displays.

For example, Cultureworld centers on New Zealand's Maori heritage and what could be a better way to initiate the visitor to the excitement and the sophistication of the Maori than through his dance and song.

In the Tasman Theater we saw eight bright young men and women in a superb 30-minute concert. They started with the *haka,* a rhythmic posturing dance historically associated with a war. Stomping, yelling, pounding, gesturing, face-making—and best of all—sticking out of tongues (that is supposed to frighten) raises the heartbeat of the audience.

The kids were wonderful. They were trained in a rigorous, ten-month, government-sponsored program, the first of its kind. They are the only full-time Maori dance troupe in New Zealand. (There are many Maori dance troupes in New Zealand but none except the Heritage Park troupe is full-time.)

Note the carved Maori portal over the Cultureworld entrance. You are looking at the twelve different styles of Maori carving found in New Zealand.

Inside, Maori carving, flax weaving and other ancient skills are demonstrated. Adjacent is a theater with an audio-visual presentation of the history of the country.

In the open-air theater of Agriworld the audience is given a chance to enjoy a condensed animal show at the funny farm starting with a blindfolded demonstration of sheep shearing, a national industry. There are some 10,000 professional shearers in the country and any one of them can shear 400 sheep in a day. Think about that—400 in a day.

The speed is made possible by the shearer's technique of sitting the animal on its hind end, locking it between his legs and keeping the sheep immobile throughout the shearing. A work of art.

Jacky, the magnificent one-ton Hereford, was brought out, followed by Daisy, the Jersey dairy cow.

A milking demonstration takes place with a visitor invited from the audience to try hand milking. Our guest milker was a cute young Japanese who would most tentatively pull a teat and then cover her mouth, look into the audience and blush and giggle.

Squealing pigs followed Daisy. I learned that the Maoris rendered the fat from the pigs and poured it over meat to preserve the food.

In back of the Barn Theatre the visitor finds agricultural plantings: vineyards, young timber trees, fruit trees. There are recreated sawmill, gum-digging and gold-panning sites.

And a pavlova bar where you can add your own topping of fresh fruit. Pavlova is the national dessert. It is a crusty and crispy meringue with a soft chewy inside that does instant things to your waistline.

Natureworld features some 30,000 native plants. If your time in

New Zealand is limited, here is your chance to see the nocturnal national bird, the kiwi. Behind glass lit by an infrared light so you can see it but he can't see you, the kiwi goes after worms and grubs planted in the soil. Unusually "authentic."

An impressive aviary is part of the park near a lake containing 2.2 million gallons of water. Mirrored trout pools allow you to see rainbow and brown trout from above and below the surface.

The park goes on and on. Simulated swamplands, picnic areas, a children's playground. Even a miniature golf course outside the main entrance.

Of course there is a restaurant and nightly *hangis,* the New Zealand luau with Maori entertainment. The gift shop has quality made-in-New Zealand merchandise. No gimcrackery, Taiwan plastic.

Oh, yes, I inspected the restrooms and they are of a Disneyland standard. Immaculate.

Heritage Park, according to its own literature is "ten minutes from Auckland city."

You'll find after a time in the country that everything is "ten minutes" away.

Our rule of thumb, based on years of experience and exposure to the Kiwi time syndrome, when we hear "ten minutes" is don't walk but take a bus.

"Ten minutes and just a bit farther on" translated to "rent a car."

"Thirty minutes" . . . line up a Boeing 747.

Fortunately, the easy-to-get-lost-and-never-found visitor can catch a shuttle bus from any in-town hotel or the Downtown Airline Terminal for Kelly Tarlton's Underwater World, Heritage Park or Victoria Park Market for a small charge.

The shuttle bus is not really necessary for the young or the fit to get to Victoria Park Market, an easy fifteen-minute walk from central downtown. Notice that I didn't say "ten minutes."

Take Victoria Street West off Queen Street for half a dozen blocks and you are there. You can't miss it; on your right will be Victoria Park, playground for winter rugby and summer cricket. Opposite the park is the smokestack of the Market.

The landmark reflects its history.

At the turn of the century it was discovered that waste deposits were seeping into the city water system. Being as clean water and refuse disposal were both desirable city attributes, a study was made of overseas operations and an English-designed waste disposal facility called "Destructor" was commissioned and completed in 1905. The mayor at the time—I love this as evidence that there will always be a PR man—was hauled in a bosun's chair to the top of the 125-foot chimney to lay the last brick. Hurrah!

The Destructor served the city for almost a half century, including a period when it also furnished the city electricity. Its demise came when faced with expensive major repairs and complaints about soot and smoke.

The threat of dismantlement was turned aside by imaginative planners who proposed a permanent marketplace with small vendors selling everything from avocados to zircons . . . with the kitchen sink as an option.

Fresh fruits and vegetables, a bakery, meat market, game butchery and a fish shop are included in addition to a dozen tenants in the Foodhall with all sorts of snackies offered. I noted down fish and chips, pizza, of course, lasagne (NZ$3.50 a slice), Cantonese fast-food, roast sandwiches: beef, lamb, pork, bacon, seafood, hot or cold, (shrimp roll NZ$1.90), pita bread sandwiches, Cafe Latino hot dogs, hamburgers, lamburgers, etc.

Rick's Cafe Americaine offers a blackboard menu and the chance to chomp on lobster and swill chilled Chardonnay. Also, fish of the day, chicken salad. The choice of the licensed restaurant goes from a house white to something called Long Island Ice Tea.

"What is Long Island Ice Tea?" we asked the waitress.

She said "It is Bacardi, tequila, vodka, gin and cointreau topped with Coke."

In addition to Long Island Ice Tea, the Victoria Park Market offers the merchandise of over a hundred cart traders—especially on the weekend.

The open-on-Sunday policy is one of the great attractions of the Market. When you think that downtown Auckland is suffering from a nuclear bomb scare, you can walk the few blocks to the Market and be surrounded by happy people delighted to have a chance to rub shoulders and munch and browse and shop for Sunday night dinner.

The Lady Navigator bought two hand-knitted sweaters but, for details, I refer you to her shopping chapter, Found and Treasured.

Tours to take you into the best of New Zealand in and around Auckland are numerous today, tours and tourist activities that didn't exist ten years ago.

But let us stop for a minute because I found a page in my notebook which I think it typical of what one finds today in upgraded New Zealand.

After spending part of the afternoon in the Victoria Park Market, we went for dinner that night at Chatterley's on Ponsonby Road.

Here are a few of the imaginative items found on the menu: marinated lamb with kiwi fruit served with a sesame dip. Mushroom morel filled with pine nuts, baked in garlic butter and served in a tomato and basil sauce. Chicken breast with grape stuffing topped with a sauce of white wine and Stilton cheese. Quail with lemon and currant stuffing served with a tamarillo glace. (Tamarillo is a tart, deep red fruit found in New Zealand.)

We'll explore more restaurants later but the point I want to make now is that such refreshing, imaginative menus are not untypical of the New Zealand restaurant scene today, and such welcome improvements go along with what is happening on all fronts affecting tourism.

Another easy and recommended recreation on weekends is bicycling along the Mission Bay coast road. Beyond Underwater World there are bicycle rentals and six miles of level road offering a wealth of people watching opportunities: windsurfers and yachties, sun bathers and picnickers in the park.

Buy a hamburger. Eat on the beach.

We counted three weekend bike operators who rented tandem bikes, children's bikes, racing bikes. Costs were reasonable.

Incidentally, if serious bicycling is your thing, we found The Bicycle Touring Company which offers 15-day cycling holidays on the North Island and 18-day tours of the South Island. Prices include accommodation options of hotel or camping, all meals, all fares on rail or interisland ferry, a good quality 10-speed bike, a support vehicle for luggage and weary bodies when necessary, plus accompanying staff. For more information write P.O. Box 23-215, Papatoetoe, Auckland.

Getting Into The Bush and The Vineyards

For something more active—and operating seven days a week—

consider a guided walk in the forest.

West of Auckland is the Centennial Memorial Park encompassing the Waitakere Range which contains a lovely variety of scenery from forest-covered peaks to rugged and peaceful coastlines.

In between are waterfalls, pretty gurgling streams, fern forests and spectacular beaches.

Now, do you want to stay in your room and watch Sunday television or do you want to come out in the world and breathe the perfume of trees and smell the salt of pounding surf?

Bush & Beach takes a small group of people of all ages for an easy hike along good walking trails through native forests and balances the green experience with the open coast experience of cliffs and beaches and tidal pools. Great contrast.

I was picked up at the hotel by Gaylene Earl who together with Brian Moorhead own and operate the tour company.

A blond travel agent from Germany, a young lady from Canada and another travel writer made up the small party. Groups never exceed ten people.

The Waitakere Range is just 45 minutes from downtown Auckland so in no time, after passing the Avondale Racetrack, we were in the mountains hearing the unmistakable trill of the bell birds and mistakable echo of its imitators, the tui birds.

The scenic drive cuts down a road to the beach resort town of Piha.

"I never bring a party here on the weekend because it is too crowded," said Gaylene, a compact fit young woman, tanned from her frequent expeditions.

The beach was empty.

"After lunch, when the tide is out, we'll come back."

Our destination was the Esk Valley, about a kilometer away, where we hiked into the bush to Kitekite Falls, swollen by the recent rain.

Gaylene began separating the trees from the forest, carefully breaking down into separate entities the green wall of fascinating trees, bushes and ferns.

For example, the noble kauri tree which furnished the British navy with straight, knotless spars and masts in the 19th century starts out as a spindly tree with multiple branches. As it gains its place in the forest, the bark takes on a birch-like appearance. Growing still taller and finally breaking out of the surrounding trees and lifting its head to the sun, it sheds its bark and sheds its branches and stretches straight up, the giant of the forest to live 600 years and longer.

A bush pigeon, one of the prettiest birds in the New Zealand bush, with a white breast under a brilliant green coat tinged with royal blue, crossed our path, its wings beating a loud noise. "To frighten off its enemies." Gaylene said.

At the foot of the waterfall, we sat in the sun sipping "morning tea," keeping to the New Zealand tradition of filling up the stomach six times a day. Morning tea consisted of fruit juice and cookies.

We then climbed a crooked, winding path to the top of the waterfalls and peeked over the tumbling waters edge.

The descent was easier and faster in the dappled sunlit forest and we were soon back at the van where Gaylene unloaded soft drinks, cheese and cold cut meats and breads and spreads. We each made our own sandwiches or salads while gossiping and exchanging experiences.

By the time we got back to the beach the ocean was at low tide permitting the view of the Piha landmark called Lion's Rock. We walked around the rocky edge of a cliff and out onto a large flat of sand, peered through a hole in the rock of Taitoma Island—its Maori translation means "snapper cave"—and fixed on the reflections of the tidal pools.

We climbed the cliffs for magnificent views of the coast and continued along a cliff path back to the car. A gorgeous, inspiring, write-an-ode-to-God nature walk.

Who would trade this for a television rerun of an ancient Hollywood movie?

One diversion was to stop on Scenic Drive on the way home at a mountain house given to the city by a meat-packing family where we had more panoramic scenes at our feet, this time of metropolitan Auckland.

By 4:30 we were back in the city. A memorable day.

Winters, when the days are shorter, Bush & Beach does half-day bush walks or, alternately, half- and full-day tours of the city.

Bush & Beach, Box 4, Greenhithe, Auckland, Telephone 4139261. Bookings can also be made at the Auckland Public Relations Office, Aotea Square, Queen Street.

Another reason for visiting the Waitakeres is the vineyards and wineries of Henderson Valley.

The all-day tour starts at 10am and finishes at 3pm and includes free wine tasting at two small wineries in the morning and a final tasting and lunch at Penfolds, a major New Zealand wine company.

If you have your own car, this is a tour you can do on your own because the Henderson Valley wineries encourage wine tasting and buying at the vineyard. The city promotional office at Aotea Square has winery location maps.

In 1983, fourteen prominent vineyards formed a promotional organization, Winemakers of West Auckland, and published a brochure/map briefly describing each winery and siting its location.

What you will find interesting are the variety of names: Babich, Collard, Corbans, Fredatovich, Spence, Nobilo, Ivicevich, Selak, Brajkovich.

For the most part these are family-founded and family-operated boutique wineries which deserve support.

We asked Peter Saunders, sommelier at the Regent who also writes a wine column for the *New Zealand Woman's Weekly,* about the country's wine industry. At six feet ten inches, he has to be the tallest sommelier in the world.

"The future is good. What we have to do is maintain the ongoing prosperity of small wine growers so that quality is not surrendered to quantity. It isn't enough to have one or two big house winemakers."

You can make a reservation for the guided wine tour at any hotel/motel desk or call 398-760. Address inquiries to A.G.M. Promotions, P.O. Box 21-255. Auckland 8.

The wineries are closed on Sundays. Sorry about that!

The Upgraded Familiar Attractions

While I was romping up to waterfalls and kicking sand on the beach with Gaylene, the Lady Navigator was on her own expedition taking part in a Fashion Factory Outlet Tour. She covers it in Chapter 16.

There are several "City Tours" for a visitor to choose from and we are of the opinion that they are good value, particularly if you are a firstime visitor.

One tour that we didn't take but caught our eye was the Kowhai Tour.

Its first advantage is that it is small—a maximum of seven passengers. Huge tour buses always tend to have three passengers who can't walk, two passengers who always get lost and one passenger who has to go to the bathroom just before the bus leaves. Always.

Also, Kowhai stops at a couple of places we've never visited which have special historic charms, the Ewelme Cottage built in 1863 by the Reverend Vicesimus Lush and occupied for 105 years by Lushes.

Then the Kinder House built in 1857 for Rev. Dr. John Kinder who was the first Headmaster of the Church of England Grammar School. You have Devonshire tea in the House of the Headmaster. Doesn't that sound so British proper?

A third home is the Highwic House built in 1862, the elegant abode for an Auckland merchant prince, Alfred Buckland. Here passengers have a light lunch.

The tour also takes in the Domain Wintergardens, Parnell Village whose architecture reflects the former colonial atmosphere and, for a slice of Maori culture, gives you a guided walk through the Maori Display Court at the War Memorial Museum. A final highlight is a drive to the summit of Mt Eden once a mighty impregnable Maori fortress, or *pa,* for a lofted view of the city.

The Kowhai tour price includes pickup at 9:15am and return by 3pm, tea and lunch.

The telephone is 275-8314 or write P.O. Box 53039, Auckland 6, New Zealand.

(The kowhai is the unofficial national flower of New Zealand and is notable for the gold cluster of flowers which blanket its branches in the spring.)

If you don't take an organized city tour, you should visit the Auckland Museum—its proper title is The War Memorial Museum—in the Domain which dominates the skyline from its hilltop position. (When you read "domain," as you often will in New Zealand, think "park.")

The Maori collection is outstanding which you will appreciate more if you do a bit of preliminary reading. The Pope *Mobile Guide* books previously recommended have an excellent section on the Maori society.

You'll be taken with the 82-foot Maori war canoe, *Taki-a-Tapiri*, built in 1836 and used in the Manukau Harbour. Also, there is an elaborately carved meeting house, a food storehouse and a gateway, authentic, important buildings in a typical Maori village.

The museum holds many South Pacific artifacts including a collection of native canoes from different island cultures, and an exhibit of the *moa* bird, an ostrich-like bird, now extinct, which was indigenous to New Zealand.

If you are into European antiques and beautiful furniture, you'll find a lovely collection on the second floor.

The museum's planetarium schedules demonstrations Saturday and Sunday afternoons. Counting stars is another thing that is better to do on Sunday than cutting your throat.

Or go to the open-on-Sunday Museum of Transport and Technology which has constantly upgraded its exhibits since opening in 1963.

I don't think New Zealanders ever, ever throw anything away. They run cars, ships, railroad engines, farm machinery twice as long as any manufacturer intended, or hoped. And when they finally replace the old for a new, they put the old in a museum.

MOTAT holds an immense assortment of fascinating junk. You'll find steam engines, running of course, a pioneer village, computers, telegraph stations, airplanes you're never seen and automobiles you've never heard of. It is endless.

One exhibit which held our attention centered around Richard Pearse, a farmer's son and himself a farmer and a tinker.

He built a sound-producing machine, a four-speed bicycle with reciprocating pedals, a motorcycle and a motorized plow.

Mind you, he had no workshop training but built his own lathe for machining engine components.

He had little, if any, communications or exchange of knowledge from the outside world but he built a four-cylinder engine for an airplane of his own design. The airplane successfully got off the ground and remained airborne for a few seconds before it crashed. Back to the old drawing board.

This happened in the same year the Wright brothers flew at Kitty Hawk.

Later, he conceived what would become the helicopter. His airplane had an engine that tilted vertically. The torque of the engine was offset by a rotor in the tail. Sound familiar?

Pearce lived from 1877 until 1953 and one wonders what he would have done if he had gone to school at Cal Tech.

To visit MOTAT's 30-acre outdoor/indoor airplane museum, the Sir Keith Park Memorial Airfield, take the double-decker bus from the main exhibit grounds.

One of the preserved aircraft is a flying boat that flew a route from New Zealand to Suva, to the Cook Islands, to Tahiti by TEAL, the airline which became Air New Zealand. Old-timers get misty-eyed when they recall the days of the 34-ton, 45-passenger Solent flying machines.

The Zoological Park has a magnificent setting if you collect zoos and is also open on Sundays. Animals are mostly housed in natural settings and it is another place with a kiwi house where you can peek at the national bird in his darkened sanctuary.

Go to Mt Eden if only to have an aerial look at Auckland and then to One Tree Hill for another viewpoint.

Both hills are volcanic cones softened by time and weather and ancient Maori fortifications. Fragments of the elaborate terracing and palisades can still be seen.

One Tree Hill is part of Cornwall Park which also contains Acacia Cottage, the oldest building in Auckland (1841) which was built by Sir John Logan Campbell, the "Father of Auckland." Approach the 300-acre park via Twin Oaks Drive and its stately entrance, a memorial befitting Sir John who willed the land to the city for the park. He lies buried beside the obelisk on top of One Tree Hill.

The Ever-Changing Food Scene

The first restaurant we found in Auckland which cracked the 20th century food barrier was Clichy's.

It was a blackboard-menu, French-provincial type of restaurant with imaginative dishes, sexy looking waitresses and a pleasant atmosphere.

We keep going back to Clichy's on every visit and have never been disappointed.

Another of my favorites is Tony's for steaks on High Street.

Grazing in Auckland today is a pleasure and while we often return to favorites (luncheon at Antoine's in Parnell is another habit), we enjoy the experience of trying new places.

I like Andrew Thomson's attitude. He was quoted in a daily Auckland newspaper as saying, "The only meal I want our guests to have in the Regent is breakfast. I want them to go out into Auckland and enjoy the many fine restaurants. But I want our dining rooms filled with local people. I want them to think this is their hotel."

He obviously had made converts because the Brasserie at lunch was filled with chic young Auckland matrons and they seemed to return to the Longchamp restaurant at night with their husbands.

(Longchamp is excellent. I had a delicate carrot mousse in a puff pastry served with an orange sauce that was made by angels. And the oven-steamed fresh snapper fillets topped with bread-crumbs and ginger and surrounded with parsley sauce was nothing short of purr-with-pleasure dining.)

The closest thing to a national magazine is a radio/TV guide called *The Listener*. It conducts a readers' poll and publishes the Best Restaurant Awards in cooperation with Montana Wines.

The honor as the 1985 best licensed restaurant in the country went to Hoffman's in Auckland. When we staged a thank-you dinner for two couples who have been guides, mail drops, golf partners, bridge enemies, sweater suppliers, reservation clerks and the best of friends since we first started to prowl the country, we wanted the very best New Zealand had to offer.

Actually located on Jervis Street in Herne Bay, Hoffman's could be considered part of the upmarket Ponsonby dining scene since it is just around the corner.

An old two-story brick house was beautifully refurbished to seat a maximum of forty people. If you are late claiming your reservation, Phillip, the owner, is *displeased*.

One of our benefactors, a wine writer and a wine snob, took charge of ordering the most expensive grapejuice in the house. I knew we had copious quantities from the frequency of my guest's reordering.

We had a merry time. So merry that I forgot to take notes. I do remember the dishes were unusually imaginative, the service impeccable, and the bill put old-man wrinkles in my American Express card when it was presented to me at the elegant upstairs bar/lounge where we were having after-dinner coffee.

You must have reservations. Closed on weekends.

Other restaurants I have on my list include Le Gourmet, Top of the Tower in the Hyatt, Number Five which is opposite Sheraton's sidedoor, Mails and Wheelers.

The De Brett Hotel in the middle of the city is a venerable establishment. Its main restaurant is Delmonico's, an art deco original, now well known for its Sunday brunch with eggs benedict. We had a pleasant lunch in the windowless room upstairs but enjoyed the informal wine bar downstairs at another lunch even more. Superb asparagus crepes. Asparagus crepes in Auckland!

Also recommended for breakfast was Olivers in Parnell.

BYO (bring your own bottle of wine) restaurants that we enjoy include the French Cafe, Harleys, Bagatelle, La Brie.

Ethnic foods include Me Kong for Vietnamese dishes; New Orient on Elliot Street is so popular on Sunday that you have to have reservations, Fairview for Szechuen seafood, Pearl Garden, all Chinese.

Italian: Italian Cafe in Parnell, Franko's One on the Side in Ponsonby.

For seafood we had previously recommended Pelorus Jack but we hear it has gone off. Sails at the Westhaven Marina is new but garish in the evening. Try it for lunch and enjoy the view.

A BYO in the Ferry Building is the Waterfront Cafe, a scruffy, ancient, lots-of-atmosphere pub. You can eat outside and look at the boat action. Never tried it but looks like fun.

Late at night the localites stop by the White Lady, a rolling eatery that pulls up into Shortland Street just off of Queen Street, and serves all sorts of edible junk. Such operations are called "pie carts" in New Zealand.

We didn't get back to old favorites like Raffles and Oblios, but the point is that Auckland today—next week, next month—is filled with exciting, innovative, pleasurable places to eat.

Another new addition to the Auckland food scene are upmarket delicatessens.

We shopped for a cocktail party at Lord Ponsonby's Deli on Ponsonby Road and bought, among other things, a good liver-champagne pate that was a great hit, as was the cream cheese stuffed with walnuts.

Another deli is the same mode is Food Glorious Food also on Ponsonby Road, open from 10am to 9pm, even on Sundays. In

Auckland! People from all over Auckland are beating a path to the shop run by David Williams where they are attended by a smartly uniformed staff. "No scruffy jeans and T-shirts," says Williams.

Customers find niceties such as Beef Wellington covered with a red wine glaze, a steaming lobster bisque, cherries in armagnac, Stilton cheese, or any number of other menu choices to take away.

Williams probably by now has executed his plan to open a small, informal restaurant next door.

Spectator Pleasures

One of our greater pastimes in Auckland, if we are lucky enough to be there on the right dates, is the Ellerslie Racecourse, a mere "ten minutes" away from downtown.

Watching beautiful horses whether they are standing, walking or racing is a sensuous pleasure in itself.

Betting is exciting, addictive to some people. Betting is not gambling in my case; I know I will lose.

The best part about Ellerslie is people watching.

You have to go to your best source in Auckland and inveigle them to get you a guest card to the Members' Stand. Here is where the horsey elite assemble and it looks like a call up from Central Casting. You have never seen so many lovely characters at one time.

The first meeting in Ellerslie was held in 1857 and some of the original Members are still there.

The men are proper. They wear coats and ties and, often, soft brimmed hats and are harnessed with binoculars.

The women are mostly in imported tweeds in winter and soft silks in summer, with proper hats and gloves. They are tailored and immaculate but anything but stodgy. They twinkle all over the place.

At a California track you can't tell the difference between the sexes since the advent of unisex apparel and punk haircuts . . . between the stable jock and the owner's wife since the fashion acceptance of denim on denim. It is sartorially boring. Ellerslie provides a tidy relief.

(There is also a Men's Bar where you can get roast beef sandwiches and draft beer for pennies and be removed from your wife's persistent question of why you made such a dumb bet on such an obviously dumb horse.)

The 30-acre park of Ellerslie is known for its gardens and is one of the prettiest tracks in the South Pacific. Slightly bowlish, lifted at both ends, the horses come slightly downhill off the last turn and give the spectator the impression of watching and hearing the Charge of the Light Brigade.

In some races there are so many horses entered that the race is divided into two divisions.

All races are run counterclockwise in New Zealand—except at Ellerslie.

Don't miss.

Rugby is the national sport.

The bruising, bashing, blood-running-down-the-face sport enthralls the New Zealanders and if you get a chance to go out to Eden Park and see a game, do go.

You may not appreciate the nuances of the game but the principles of the scoring is easy to understand as is the primary reason for the game which is to annihilate the opposition or, minimum, change the facial landscape of the opponents so they will be unrecognizable to their mothers.

That's the winter sport. The summer sport is cricket.

For the culturally inclined, don't overlook the fact that Auckland has a healthy theater scene with professional Kiwi talent.

The Mercury Theater is a good example. We went to a performance of "Two by Two with Sondheim" and had a most enjoyable evening.

The Mercury houses two theaters giving live performances and is well worth a visit.

The Maidment Art Center is another and the Theater Corporation is a third.

The big, visiting acts are usually booked into His Majesty's Theater downtown.

Aotea Centre, next to Townhall, is Auckland's bid to become a major convention center. Its 1988 completion of a 300-room hotel and a multifunctional performing arts center boosts the visitor industry to even higher levels.

Repeat: don't give Auckland the overnight treatment. Plan to spend a few days.—It's a fair bird of a city.

Meet The "Chilly Bin"

After an initial week of enjoying Auckland we were ready to hit the road.

Prior to our return to write a sequel to the New Zealand book we attended a travel writers' convention where the idea was born to tour the country not in a car, as we had planned, but in a sleep-in/cook-in vehicle. What is called a recreational vehicle in America, is a campervan in New Zealand.

A delightful idea. It would give us a whole new perspective of traveling in New Zealand and a chance to share the experiences of other campervanners whose numbers are steadily increasing.

We made arrangement before leaving Hawaii with Newmans Motor Homes.

Newmans built in 1985 a multimillion-dollar facility near the Auckland airport to house its fast growing campervan business. Here, they service a fleet of hundreds of vans in three sizes: two-berth pop-top vans, four-berth caravans and six-berth travel homes.

The facility includes a lounge area, changing rooms, showers and storage space for travelers who want to leave extra luggage behind. Nothing lacking.

We signed out in a shiny new four-berth van with a diesel engine—"Count to five after turning on the ignition and before starting the engine"—a refrigerator, a gas-burning range, a cold-water-only sink and a porta-potty which we never used.

The over-the-cab double bunk became storage space for a ton of "essentials" we cannot travel without: golf bags and tennis rackets, a portable computer and reference books, and, of course, the accessories appropriate to each activity.

The table at the end of the cabin dropped down to the level of the cushioned seats to convert into a wall-to-wall double bed. Luxurious. Linens were supplied, including six bedrolls which, when zipped open, became bed-sized quilts.

The vehicle was completely equipped with towels, dishes, pots and pans, electric toaster, carving knives, brooms and mops, and even a starter kit of salt and sugar, tea and coffee. Again nothing was lacking.

The touch we loved was the two empty milk bottles in the refrigerator. You see, in New Zealand, you still either pay for the bottle or leave an empty bottle when you buy milk in the small grocery stores you see at almost every corner. Some "dairies" will not even sell you milk without a return bottle. Nice touch, Newmans.

Optional rentals: a color TV set or a microwave oven. Took the TV; skipped the microwave.

Also supplied were maps and a book of discount coupons.

A basic requirement for any traveler in New Zealand is what is called a chilly bin—a "cooler" in America—a styrofoam hamper to keep beer, cheese, butter, pate, cold meats, beer, wine and other snack components chilled and ready for a roadside tea in the morning, picnic lunch at noon and for afternoon tea before one gets peckish.

We named our campervan the "Two-And-A-Half-Ton Chilly Bin."

After being briefed on operations by a ground hostess, we drove back to the city, pulled into the port cochere of the elegant Regent Hotel in our sparkling blue-and-white Chilly Bin and said "Park it." Without a quiver or a flicker, the doorman did.

The next morning we headed north.

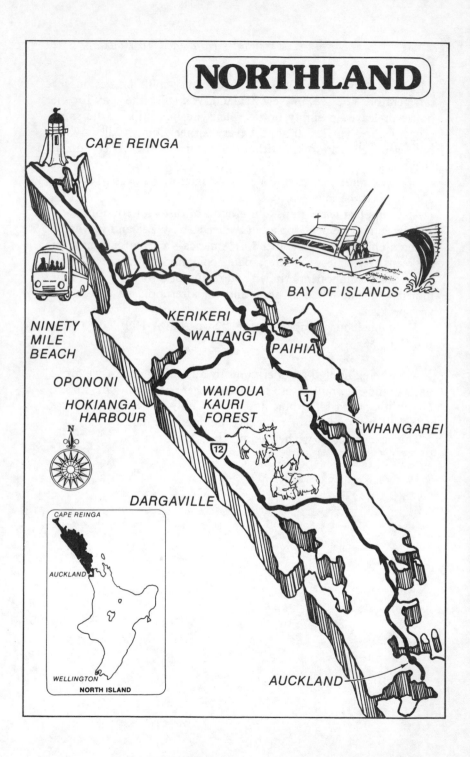

2. The Bay of Islands And The Northland

A City of Clocks . . . The Treaty House . . .
The Flagpole War . . . Ninety-Mile Beach

The "Chilly Bin" was rolling north in the spring sunshine after clearing the confines of metropolitan Auckland.

We had driven over the Harbour Bridge on Highway 1 as a steady stream of vehicles moved in the opposite direction flowing toward the center of the city.

There is a great feeling of smug-happy exuberance when you witness thousands of people driving to work in little cubicles while you are setting out on a new adventure. Happy that you are no longer one of those people doing what you have done for so many years and exuberant that there is an open road before you.

Hallelujah! We all should ride more merry-go-rounds and pick more daisies.

The open country in New Zealand in the spring looks like a gigantic golf course with lush fairways that are dotted with white balls. White balls that, on closer examination, turn out to be sheep.

The temptation is to keep one's foot down on the accelerator and just roll on and on and on—a bad habit learned over years of practice.

The cliche story in America is of the wife who turns to her husband while driving and says: "I knew we were lost but I didn't want to say anything because we were making such good time."

Fortunately, the morning before we had shared breakfast with Roger Miles of Rainbow Adventure Holidays. The young company started as a small boat charter operation in the Bay of Islands but was expanding in all sorts of directions including the packaging of tours for overseas visitors.

One of Roger's concepts that made his Rainbow Holiday Tours different was the Great Escape Accommodation Pass. The prepaid scheme allows the vacationer a wide variety of adventure choices in diverse accommodations encouraging him to do something different. He may stay at a hotel, motel, a farm or in a bed-and-breakfast facility. He may fly, drive, take a campervan . . . or a combination of all three. He can elect to sail a boat or captain a launch, fish in a stream or dive for coral in the Bay of Islands, play golf or ski.

"I want to give the vacationer a choice of options but he will have to pay for four. So he is *not* just going to *zip* through the country but will participate in at least four of New Zealand's attractions," Roger said.

We liked that: personal involvement for expanded enjoyment of the country.

The idea prompted the Lady Navigator to draw up a list for us. Or, more precisely, for people like me whose instinct is to *zip* through a country once I get behind the wheel of a vehicle.

"The Chilly Bin Non-Zip System" awards points to the free and independent driver for taking participatory action. We started with the a basic 10-point award for each of these deliberate take-a-break-from-driving activities:

1. Stopping for tea.
2. Stopping to read a roadside monument.
3. Stopping at a roadside park or a scenic lookout.
4. Assisting other travelers take "together" photos, using their camera.
5. Initiating a conversation with a New Zealander.
6. Exchanging addresses and telephone numbers with a New Zealander.
7. Visiting a museum or historic building.
8. Shopping for anything. (Picking your own fruit in a commercial orchard won an extra 10 point bonus.)
9. Stopping to taste a regional food or beverage specialty.
10. Picnicking in a scenic location.

Our self-assigned minimum goal per driving day was set at 50 points.

To extend the challenge to non-driving days, we agreed that up to 50 bonus points would be awarded for taking part in an active sport: a round of golf, a walk, a ski run, a sail. The number of points was determined by the time, effort and energy involved. Loosely.

The penalty for non-participation, that is, if the driver failed to pick up a single point over a period of three days, was drastic. He would have to turn in the car—or campervan—and leave the country on the next airplane.

At 10:30am, we stopped in Wellsford for tea. Ten points. (We always order scones, the fresh gently sweetened biscuits that you slather with butter. Sultana scones have raisins in them. If there are no scones—which is rare—go for bran muffins. Delicious.)

Farther along the highway, in Waipu, a roadside sign indicated an approaching monument. The "Non-Zip System" freshly implanted in my mind registered enough to overpower the temptation to roll on by. Brakes squealed. Out of the Chilly Bin.

The six-sided monument was dedicated to the six ships that left Cape Breton in Nova Scotia in the 19th century to carry the Scottish farmers whose farms had failed in Canada to Australia, first to Adelaide, then Melbourne, and finally to New Zealand at Waipu.

Gad, who was responsible for this nomadic story?

A little research later uncovered the chilling figure of the Rev. Norman McLeod, a man in his seventies who was a fierce, disciplined leader of the wandering farmers.

It was said he hacked off an ear of a disobedient boy.

McLeod was hated, feared and adored. When he died, his pulpit was pulled apart and distributed to his faithful who felt no other minister could replace him.

You could write a book about him.

"See," said the Lady Navigator, "You learn a lot by stopping at roadside monuments."

Whangarei is the most important city north of Auckland. You might say it is the only city north of Auckland. With an important harbor, the country's only oil refinery and an adjacent oil-fired power station which supplements the country's hydroelectric power during dry months, Whangarei is a prosperous city. Its parks and flower gardens reflect prosperity.

Its tourist attractions are limited, as far as we could detect, to an unusual museum, a museum devoted exclusively to clocks.

It started with an engineer named Archibald Clapham who financed his expensive hobby of collecting clocks from around the world and from past eras by an inheritance. He amassed over 400 different timepieces.

When he passed on, the Clapham clock collection became the

Clapham Clock Museum owned and maintained by the city council. The collection now numbers more than 800 pieces.

We had missed the museum on our first swing through New Zealand. Being as the Lady Navigator refuses to wear a watch and regards time only as an idea to be disregarded, I ordained the visit to the collection with her in the hope that complete immersion might result in the change of attitude.

A silly, non-productive idea, as it turned out, but the one-room museum is a kick.

A prominent picture of Archibald Clapham in the museum makes him look like a cousin of Jimmy Durante's. Apparently, he shared, along with the nose, the comedian's sense of humor.

A stuffed dog held by the museum guardian suddenly barks when a visitor pets it. The visitor always jumps ten feet. The dog was one of Clapham's favorites.

There is every sort of timepiece. Funny clocks, elegant clocks, curiosity clocks, alarm clocks, a wall of cuckoo clocks, grandfather clocks, water clocks, novelty clocks, ethnic clocks: French, German, English, Egyptian, Viennese. A different clock is a Japanese clock that shows only 12 hours. The six-hour day starts at sunrise and the six-hour night at sunset which is always six o'clock.

The most popular clock, according to the docent, is a Viennese clock whose face features thirty-three different hand-painted scenes and whose rose onyx stand conceals secret drawers.

There is an promotional clock whose slogan is "beer is best."

Another is the "Nark" clock which tells time in reverse, and time has to be read counter clockwise.

An enchanting clock is an example of French craftsmanship made about 1850 which features ten different birds, seven of which are in flight.

Variety is the key to the collection. A visitor could spend hours in the museum. A small admittance fee is charged.

When we left the museum, I tensed. When you've traveled with the same companion 100,000 miles a year for ten years, you know intuitively what that person is thinking and what that person is going to say next.

The Lady Navigator turned to me and asked, "What time is it?"

I knew it was a silly idea.

Northland's Bathtub

The Bay of Islands could well be called the Bays of Islands because it encompasses so many harbors and inlets and bays in protected waters about 45 miles north of Whangarei.

The sub-tropical weather makes it an ideal fishing and yachting center.

Naturally, the farther north you go toward the Equator, the warmer the weather becomes.

As we had failed to sail in the Hauraki Gulf, we were determined to have an overnight sailing experience in the Bay of Islands. To arrange it was one of our reasons for meeting Roger Miles in Auckland.

His Rainbow Yacht Charters maintains an extensive fleet of yachts for charter. Twenty-one sailing yachts between 20- and 38-feet and three 36-foot motor launches are kept for bareboat charter. Boats larger than 28-feet will accommodate six people. Three luxury boats are available for skippered, provisioned cruising.

The summer months, from Christmas to the end of January, produce hordes of Australian and vacationing Kiwis, and the Bay of Islands is bay-to-bay with people.

Mid-February to as late as mid-May are ideal sailing times for both visitors and Kiwis without children. The temperature stays around 64-degrees, the sailing conditions are good, and because the hordes have gone back to work, it is quiet, peaceful and more private.

We didn't plan to take a boat out by ourselves although we had enough sailing background, according to Roger, to qualify for a bareboat charter. The company has a thorough familiarization program including, if necessary, sailing time with an instructor.

Our experience was to be a crewed overnight sail aboard *Cheyenne,* a 38-foot Chieftan-designed sloop built in Christchurch. A solid, luxurious boat, it had sleeping accommodations for three couples, comfortably. The aft cabin had a double bed, the main cabin's lounge/dining area converted to a twosome (at least) sleeping quarters, and the forward cabin had two single bunks.

Our crew consisted of Ann Cambridge, the general manager of Rainbow Charters, and skipper Danny Ross.

We misunderstood directions to the boats and went instead to

Paihia. We should have gone to Opua. A one hour mistake that made us late getting away from the dock.

The sun was starting to set by the time we rounded Tapeka Point.

"We were almost pipped," said Ann. "We didn't know if you were going to show or not."

Pipped?

"Pipped. As in 'pipped at the post.' No? How about 'left at the starting gate?' You know that expression? Good."

There is no sensation quite equal to that of a small sailing ship being moved along by the dynamics of wind in the canvas and the counter corrective weight of the keel keeping the tilted boat on a straight and steady line.

You feel the force of nature in the balls of your feet and in the counter rocking of your body to that of the boat.

"Technically, the Bay of Islands covers some 500 miles of in-and-out coastline and includes 144 islands," said Ann. "It is ideal sailing for the independent sailor because there are so many islands and coves and secluded beaches.

"The majority of the visitors take the Cream Cruise because at one time, when this whole section of the country was known as the 'Roadless North,' the only way dairy farmers could get their product out and their supplies in was by boat.

"At the beginning of tourism in the Bay of Islands, visitors would go along on the boats as they serviced the outlying farms. They still go, on full day cruises, but the trips are more for tourists than farmers now.

"Mostly, today, boats go out to the Hole in the Rock, turn around and come back or stop off for a barbecue."

We sailed for just under two hours before reaching Opunga Cove, a shelter lined with white beaches and devoid of other boats. Danny Ross dropped anchor, reversed the engine until he was sure the anchor had caught and we settled down for the night.

Ann poured glasses of wine, busied herself at the galley preparing dinner and we talked. Cozy.

"We are curious about your questionnaire to people taking a yacht out on charter. Are they honest about their experience and ability?"

"Oh, yes," replied Ann. "If anything they downplay any expertise. When you are taking a 20- or 30-foot sailing vessel you don't know out into waters you don't know, it is not a time for bluffing or bragging."

"Have you ever lost a boat?"

"No, but we once had a very close call . . . but they were bank robbers."

"What!"

"Yes, I had two men come to the office and reserve a 36-foot boat for the next day. They were in business suits and carried briefcases. They paid cash in advance which was rather unusual. The next day they came back, still in business suits and took the boat.

"Well, they didn't return when they were supposed to but did call in and say they were one bay up the coast and would return the following day. The conversation was heard by a bartender who saw them get into a car and leave. Of course they never came back but we did recover the boat."

"Were they caught?"

"Oh, yes. They used false names at a hotel, skipped out on their bill and the police found them. Dumb.

"The other time that was unusual was when a catamaran from New Caledonia came in with a French crew. I talked to them for a long time because the Customs people had gone off duty and the visitors couldn't leave Opua Harbour until they had been cleared.

"Sometime later, it came out that the French intelligence agents involved in the bombing of the *Rainbow Warrior* were tied to the crew of the catamaran. The crew escaped and the catamaran was never found, probably scuttled at sea. We know the people in New Caledonia who chartered the ship. They got paid for the charter but they had just spent a fortune renovating the ship."

We had a delicious dinner including a pavlova which Ann said was fool proof. The Lady Navigator said she was living proof that there was no such thing as a foolproof pavlova.

"Try it. I'll give you the recipe but, more importantly, you have to have the right attitude about a pav. You mustn't be afraid of it."

"What are we going to do tomorrow?"

"Well, there is so much to do in just a day. Can't you spare two?" She paused, but seeing our negative gestures, she hastened on. "I thought we might go to Roberton Island; its Maori name is Motuarohia which Captain Cook found in 1769.

"And we'll stop by the scenic reserve island, Motukiekie, in the Bay of Islands Maritime Park. It has an easy walking track from one end of the island to the other which takes only half an hour. Beautiful views from the top through the Norfolk pines to the rocky shoreline.

"Then we might go to Pipi Bay and dig for pipis."

"Like in pipi at the post?"

"No, no. Pipis are small shellfish that were standard diet for the ancient Maori and found in old middens. We'll dig them out. . ."

"Wait. What is a midden?"

"A midden is a refuse heap left by an older civilization. Archaeologists consider middens to be significant sign posts. So we will dig the pipis out of the sand and steam them in wine and onion. Mild but delicious."

The Lady Navigator and I went on deck to bid goodnight to the stars that were sprinkled across a clear night's sky.

At four o'clock the next morning it started to storm. It rained for three days.

No island visits. No pipi digging. No summit views.

We sailed back to Opua having had just a nibble of what could be a great three- or seven-day experience.

Rainbow's finest yacht for pampered sailing is the 47-foot *Shalimar* with two private double or twin cabins, two heads and showers, and is licensed for six guests. Two convertible berths are in the saloon. Crew's quarters are separate.

Charter rates on request. Rainbow Yacht Charters, Post Office, Opua, New Zealand.

As promised, Ann dropped off her recipe at the Waitangi Hotel.

Never Fail Pavlova

5 egg whites
pinch of salt
1 cup sugar
1 large teaspoon cornflower
1 teaspoon vinegar
1 teaspoon vanilla
1 teaspoon cold water

Beat egg whites until stiff. Add pinch salt. Add sugar—slowly—beat well. Add cornflour & beat well. Add liquids and beat well. Place on wet greaseproof paper. Put in oven preheated to 200 degrees and then turn oven off.

Don't let it intimidate you.

The Cradle of the Nation.

The report of Captain James Cook in his journals on returning home to England from his first exploration trip of the Pacific detailed the finding of whale and fur-bearing seals around New Zealand which led to whaling and sealing expeditions from one end of the just discovered islands to the other.

In a period of a few short years the slaughtering of seals eliminated the herds but whaling remained part of the economy for more than half a century.

Headquarters for whaling boats was in the fine anchorages and the moderate climate of the Bay of Islands. Crews were either enlisted or shanghaied—from the resident Maori population.

It didn't take long for the ships' captains to find that the magnificent, branchless, arrow-straight kauri tree made the finest spars and masts in the world and that native flax woven into ropes made tough, durable hawsers and lines.

The incentive for bartering was simple. A Maori chief would supply a ton of woven flax for one musket because, with muskets, he could revenge and protect himself against a neighboring tribe.

As in all cases in the Pacific the native chief who was closest to the landfall of the Westerners and who first gained Western firearms became a dominating chief.

In the Bay of Islands the major tribe was the Ngapuhi whose chief was Hongi Hika. Hika was taken to England where he visited King George IV and, envisioning the power of a king, traded in his royal gifts for muskets in Sydney on the way home.

He then proceeded to mow down his enemies as far south as Wellington—over 550 road miles away and a lot longer by boat! His example and the need for revenge (*utu* by other chiefs led to a period of genocide almost without parallel. Nearly a quarter of the Maori population died—and was eaten—in internecine warfare.

What the muskets didn't eliminate, the diseases of the white man did as raging epidemics wiped out thousands of Maoris.

The nearest center of "civilization" to New Zealand was Sydney and there, as the Magistrate of New South Wales, was the Rev. Samuel Marsden, known as a tyrannical magistrate.

His reputation for brutality became a myth in New Zealand where he played a dominant role in esablishing the initial missions in the Bay of Islands.

He received permission from the Church of England to establish a beachhead of Christianity in the new country but was delayed by the massacre of the crew and the burning of a commercial vessel, the *Boyd*, in 1809.

In 1814, he arrived in the Bay of Islands with the first missionary recruits and conducted the first Christian services on Christmas Day on a hilltop overlooking the harbor. Nearby, he established the first mission.

Three important missions followed: Kerikeri in 1819, Paihia in 1823 and Waimate North in 1830. All are part of the visible history that, to some extent, visitors to the area can still see.

As you roam around the Bay of Islands the names and dates become more important.

For example, Paihia is the center of tourist activity in the Bay of Islands where there are motels, hotels, bed-and-breakfast facilities and restaurants. Here you catch the "Cream Cruise" out into the harbor. Here you hire a fishing boat. Here you can take the ten-minute ferry over to Russell.

In 1823, the first church in New Zealand was built in Paihia of indigenous materials by Henry Williams, later an archdeacon, who was joined by his brother, William. William, in translating the New Testament into Maori and compiling the first Maori dictionary, created the first written Maori language.

The brothers established a mission school for Maori children and built the first ship, the 60-ton *Herald*.

The present stone church, the Church of St. Paul, is the fourth on the site, and is a memorial to the Archdeacon Henry Williams and Bishop William Williams.

Joining the brothers in 1834 as the mission printer was William Colenso, a fascinating character. He produced an astounding number of publications under the most primitive conditions. The abilities of the Williams brothers and Colenso would prove valuable in times ahead when ungoverned and opposing forces were loose upon the land.

The Northland was the center of a major timber industry as forests of kauri were cut and shipped abroad.

The whaling industry was still at its zenith. Bar-and-brothel hell-raising and ship chandlery across the bay in Russell were other industries.

But there was no government.

The chaos of the pull-and-tug between the land-grabbing new-comers, the cultural shock of the Maoris, the protectionism of the missionaries, and the whooping and hollering of sailors in an exotic land created bedlam.

Britain was reluctant to get into the center of the maelstrom. Their attempted patchwork solution was appointing a British "resident," James Busby. He built a modest home on a hilly point at Waitangi just north of Paihia as Britian's Official Residency. But denied any military support, Busby could only fail.

The Maoris were torn between the white men who were exploiting them and the white men who said that they would protect them.

The exploiters didn't want the British to interfere with their fun and games for profit.

The missionaries' desire for an establishment of law and order went unappreciated by rioting whalers and blackbirders.

Finally, in 1840, the British Government appointed Captain William Hobson to negotiate with the Maori chiefs for the transfer of sovereignty with "the free and intelligent consent of the natives expressed according to their established usages."

The summit site was the modest home built by Busby. A tent was erected on the spacious lawn of the British Residency for a debate that lasted a full day. The Williams brothers had translated into the Maori language—and Colenso had printed—terms of treaty. By the next day, a contingent of Maori chiefs had decided "to walk with the Pakeha." Forty-five chiefs put their marks on the treaty on February 6, 1840 and copies were sent throughout the country for other influential chiefs to sign, a task that took five months.

Hobson named himself the first Lieutenant Governor—prematurely as it turned out—and reported to the Governor of New South Wales in Australia.

The former residency is now known as the Waitangi Treaty

House and remains as an historic museum of the birth of New Zealand.

The simple classic Georgian colonial house was preframed in Sydney and shipped to Waitangi in 1833. The nails were hand forged, the roof shingled. The verandah casement doors are cedar and the paving is dressed sandstone from Sydney.

Since we last visited the Treaty House, it has been graciously furnished with tables and chairs and beds of the period.

A new Visitor Centre was opened in 1983 by Prince Charles at the entrance to the Waitangi National Reserve.

Here you'll find pictures of the treaty principals including a portrait of Topeora, one of three women permitted to sign the treaty.

Every half-hour an audio-visual presentation documents the events surrounding the Treaty of Waitangi. (Its narration is very, very sensitively written—the author tiptoed through a mine field—because, even today, the circumstances which led to the Treaty creation and the understanding behind its signing are controversial.)

Also on display are copies of Treaty documents.

A walkway leads the visitor to the waterfront at Hobson's Beach where the Canoe House protects a magnificent war canoe created for the Centennial Celebration in 1940. It is not only the largest war canoe in the world, being over 100 feet long, but probably has the longest name in the world: *Ngatokimata-whaorua.*

The center section of the canoe came from one giant kauri tree. The bow and the stern came from a second giant kauri tree. The carved topside sections were carved from a third tree. A massive stump of one of the trees is displayed in the Canoe House. The canoe was completed two weeks before the celebration and carried 80 paddlers and 55 passengers.

Another Maori work of art built for the Centennial is the Maori Meeting House on the north side of the Residency. The Whare Runanga was started in 1934 and opened on February 6, 1940 and represents six years of elaborate carving.

The meeting house does not represent just the local Ngapuhi tribe but stands generically for all the Maori people; its carvings honor the ancestors of many tribes in the tradition of each tribe's style.

Hobson established the capital across the Bay at Russell where it was to remain for only nine months before being moved to Auckland.

Russell is a village today of about 600 residents where additional growth is limited by the ability to treat sewerage and the lack of water.

What remains of yesterday is the Duke of Marlborough Hotel which boasts of the oldest liquor license in the country, the old police station, and a church whose walls now proudly exhibit bullet holes as reminders of the Flagpole War.

Twentieth century peaceful Russell once was "the hell hole of the Pacific," its waterfront of brawling establishments magnets for the roisterers from the twenty or so ships that could anchor simultaneously.

In modern times, at Christmas, a hundred yachts can be found at anchor and the partying of yachties continue the ancient Russell tradition.

A popular postcard structure is the picturesque Pompallier House where Jean Baptiste Francois Pompallier (1801-1871) served as the first Catholic Bishop in New Zealand. The original building was not his residence but a simple printery. A classic Gaveaux printing press is on display at the house along with other memorabilia.

The garden rambles with rioting flowers framing the building in four colors. Out back of the house, on observation hill, you get splendid views of the harbor, Paihia and the island.

A museum near the center of town, the Centennial Russell Museum, exhibits all sorts of odds and ends: an antique apple corer, kauri tree gum that looks like amber and a sample of gum drawn thin to form "kauri silk." There's a stuffed kiwi bird with gigantic eggs beside it, at least one quarter the size of the bird.

Museum director: "The kiwi bird lays an egg only once a year."

Woman bystander, with feeling: "Oh, I'd hope so."

Also on exhibit is a quarter-sized reproduction of Captain Cook's *Endeavour* which sailed into these waters in 1769. A special room has been tacked on to the museum to accommodate the model.

And even tiny Russell has had a major upgraded facility added to its attractions: the headquarters for the Bay of Islands

Maritime and Historic Park.

The Park, established in 1978, does not consist of all waters and islands in the Bay of Islands but rather 38 selected scenic, historic and recreational reserves. The objectives are to preserve the past and guard the area for the appreciation and the enjoyment of future visitors.

Park Headquarters, adjacent to the Centennial Museum, is a handsome one-story building completed in 1981.

Here one finds an excellent selection of phamplets, charts and maps detailing areas for picnicking and camping, scenic views and nature walks, boat ramps and hydrography. The pictorial displays are exceptional.

We particularly liked the quote by John Gardiner on one exhibit wall:

"True conservationists are people who know that the world is not given to them by their parents but is borrowed from their children."

We found the audio-visual about the Maritime Park, like all the other presentations we screened in the new upgraded New Zealand, to be a fine professional job.

Annually, Park headquarters draws 75,000 visitors, many who come ashore from the more than 4,000 boats that cruise the Bay's waters.

The yachties would agree with Captain Cook who anchored at Motorua Island and wrote in his journal on Friday, 1st December (1769): "I have named it the Bay of Islands on account of the great number which line its shores, and these help to form several safe and Commodious harbours where is room and depth of water sufficient for any number of Shipping."

We later were told about a very successful bed-breakfast-dinner home in Russell operated by Kay Bosanquet who draws visitors from all over the world. P.O. Box 23, Russell.

We can't leave Russell without sharing one of the more intriguing chapters in the Bay of Islands history. Remember the church with the bullet holes still showing? This is the last physical evidence of the famous Flagpole War.

The Flagpole War

Hone Heke was a warrior chief who was the first to sign the Treaty of Waitangi. He was also the first to break it four years after the signing.

He was a chief of the Ngapuhi tribe and a descendant of the powerful chief, Hongi Hika. Besides being clever and attractive, Hone Heke possessed great *mana,* which, to the Maori, was not just an air of prestige but a true psychic force.

In his youth Hone Heke was a pupil of the Church of England and schooled with the missionaries at Paihia. It was a factor which probably saved the church in Paihia and the other church buildings in Russell.

An entrepreneur, Heke collected Customs fees, charging $5 a ship to berth in Russell. When the capital was moved to Auckland, and to discourage ships from utilizing Russell instead of the new capital, the British imposed their own Customs fee. The port business declined and so did Heke's income.

The situation became explosive.

Then an unlikely incident started a chain reaction which led to a war. A former Heke slavegirl, now the common-law wife of a white store owner, referred in public to Heke as a "pig's head." The remark was passed on to Heke who considered the insult a reflection on his mana. The mana would not be the same until the insult was revenged (utu).

He raided the white man's store, carried off the woman and in a final sign of rage, chopped down the hilltop flagpole above Russell which was used to signal ships. To emphasize his revolutionary act, Heke went to Paihia and performed a war dance before the surprised missionary bishop.

The British responded by bringing up the frigate *HMS Hazard,* along with 170 officers and men and two six-pounder cannon. A conference was called and Nene, the peacemaker of the Treaty signing, promised that the Europeans would be protected and Heke would be kept in order. The fumbling Governor FitzRoy who had replaced Hobson promised in turn to abolish the unpopular British Customs duty.

Heke replied by cutting down the flagpole again, putting an American ensign on the stern of his canoe and parading across the Bay singing war songs.

A third flagpole was erected and guarded by friendly Maori. So great was Heke's mana that he personally marched through the guards and cut down the flagpole the night after it was erected.

Heke: 3. Brits: 0

A fourth tree was prepared as a flagpole but an old chief claimed he had been born under that tree and he had his men steal the pole.

The British, probably weary by now of the whole exercise, bought a mizzen mast from a foreign vessel in the harbor, and erected it inside a blockhouse manned by British soldiers.

Successfully using a diversionary tactic, Heke drew the soldiers away from the blockhouse and cut down the flagpole for the fourth time.

Meanwhile, his colleague, another powerful chief named Kawiti, was carrying out an offensive against the town. British women and children were put aboard ships for safety. Then a workman's pipe accidentally ignited the military powder magazine and blew it up. Without ammunition the military cause was hopeless and they, too, abandoned the town.

The Maoris moved in, looted the stores and houses, and set fire to all the buildings except those belonging to the churches.

The exception was the partial looting of Bishop Pompallier's house. Heke was furious and was set to execute the thieves when they were saved by Pompallier who, hearing of the executions, marched three miles to Heke's camp and asked that the thieves be spared and only his goods be returned.

Heke agreed, and provided the bishop with an escort of thirty warriors back to his house.

To the British, it was war.

The governor offered £100 for Heke's head.

Heke offered £1 for the governor's head, saying that each man knew what the other was worth.

The Maori warriors had a sense of gamesmanship that was hard to match. One story of the Flagpole War was that Heke refused to intercept a British food line because he feared the British would be unable to carry on the game without their beef.

But the fun was soon over. A battle was joined at Okaihou where the British made an ill-advised frontal attack on an entrenched pa, losing fourteen men with forty-four wounded. A major defeat for such a small force.

The Maoris correctly assumed the British would bring up cannons and retreated to a stronger pa at Ohaeawai. This time the

British appeared with 500 soldiers and 18 sailors armed with two 6-pounders, two 12-pounders and one 32-pounder.

Again the British repeated their first mistake by making another frontal assault. The result was 40 British killed, 70 wounded. A catastrophe. The triumphant Maoris ceremoniously cannibalized one of the officers. It was the only such incident in the war.

FitzRoy's time had run out. He was sacked. In his place came George Grey, a military office who, at the age of 28, had been appointed the Governor of South Australia and quickly straightened out a chaotic situation there. He did the same in New Zealand.

His first and finishing battle took place ten miles south of Kawakawa where the chief Kawiti built a hilltop pa called Ruapekapeka or "Bat's Nest." It was a sophisticated fortress with double outer walls of tall timbers angled so that if the walls were breached, the enemy faced angled lines of fire. There was also a moat. Inside, bombardment-proof shelters and an internal water supply made it a tough fort to crack.

Governor Grey took personal command over 1,100 British troops augmented by 400 friendly Maori warriors. The fort's force numbered 500. The British arrived on New Year's Eve 1845. In ten days they erected earthworks and aligned mortars and cannons. On a Saturday they opened fire and successfully breached one wall.

Governor Grey was urged to charge but he continued pouring on the firepower. That night his offer of an armistice was turned down.

The Maoris now made a mistake. Having been baptized as Christians, they thought of Sunday as a day of rest and prayer and retreated outside of their pa for services. When the Maoris attending the British heard the hymns, they guessed correctly what was happening and informed Governor Grey who quickly ordered a charge. The pa was taken and the Flagpole War was over.

Grey pardoned Heke without conditions and sent the Maori warriors back to their families without punishment.

He played by his own rules. Over many years Governor Grey and the Maoris formed a mutual admiration society.

You can see a model of Ruapekapeka in the Waitangi Treaty House or visit the actual site ten miles south of Kawakawa, three miles off the highway.

Lady Navigator: "Is it really worth the trip?"
(This is an innocently phrased question masking a negative attitude.)
Answer: "If you are intrigued with history, it's worth the trip."

Another attraction is the Waiomio Cave, two and a half miles south of Kawakawa and a mile off the highway, where you'll find glowworm caves and interesting limestone formations. On a scale of one to ten, the caves rate about a five as an attraction, but ten points in the Chilly Bin Non-Zip Greater Appreciation Of The Country System.

Paihia, Boating And Fishing Mecca

Our overnight experience on the yacht was just a nibble of grandeur in an upgraded New Zealand compared to our Bay of Island digs.

We drove trusty Chilly up and out of Opua, past Paihia to Waitangi and to the Waitangi Hotel, the first of several inns we visited owned by The Hotel Corporation, (THC), a profit-prone government hotel chain whose properties are located in resort areas—sometimes remote resort areas.

Stuart Long, the manager, an acquaintance of ten years whom we first met as manager of the THC Te Anau hotel, greeted us with a Mine-Host graciousness bright enough to erase the rain.

I told him that we were driving a campervan and asked if we could park it near the entrance to our room, facilitating unpacking.

"Meet me at the side door," said Stuart.

We did and followed him to the second floor of a new wing, part of THC's new construction program, through a door and—my!

We were in a most splendid suite with wrap-around view windows looking out on the outlet of the Waitangi River and the Bay of Island. A telescope with which to sight the ever changing aquatic activities was poised ready for action. The pearl grey upholstered furniture accented with coral-pink was as soothing as a Mozart symphony.

The wet bar and its glass and mirror china cabinet equipped with Doulton china, sterling silver flatware and Waterford crystal glassware ranked a ten.

Crystal decanters contained an assortment of warming beverages.

In the spacious bedroom, an electric pants presser stood attentively. Of course the bathroom was marble.

And we thought the yacht had been luxurious.

The suite was the Bledisloe Suite. Who was Bledisloe, we inquired.

Viscount Bledisloe, while Governor General of New Zealand in 1932, purchased 568 hectares—over 1,000 acres—of reserve land which included the historic Treaty House and Treaty grounds and donated it all to the people of New Zealand as a national heritage.

Also included in the park are the THC Waitangi Hotel, the fine Waitangi Golf Course and club house—visitors welcome—a walking path that leads through a mangrove forest and a boardwalk over the Hutia Creek to spectacular Haruru Falls, the Bay of Islands Yacht Club, the Waitangi Bowling Club, much native bush and valuable coastline. All preserved and protected forever for the New Zealand public and its visitors.

Part of exploring the neighborhood includes visiting the Tui Shipwreck Museum, the only one of its kind in New Zealand and is the only one we have found in the world.

A creation of the late, legendary Kelly Tarlton, the founder of the unique aquarium in Auckland, the *Tui* is moored in the Waitangi River which separates the reserve from Paihia. The former lighter was transformed into a three-masted barque and actually sits on cradles in the river.

Below decks visitors will find artifacts and treasurers dug out of old wrecks explored by Tarlton during his many years as a diving prospector.

The popularity of the Bay of Islands—one million visitors a year with almost one quarter of them coming from overseas—has led to an upgraded marketplace.

Over seventy hotels and motels and fifteen campgrounds now accommodate the visitor in addition to many new bed-and-breakfast homes coming on line. And new restaurants too. Ah, new restaurants.

Our inquiries and requests for recommendations led us to the Courtyard Restaurant in the Beach Haven Motel next to St.

Paul's Church, a bring-your-own-beverage establishment. First rate.

We had prawns in cream and mushrooms wrapped in filo dough then baked as first courses, gypsy chicken and lamb supreme as main courses.

The unisex bathroom is themed to transport, circa 1816.

Paihia is the center for bay tours and land tours.

At the dock the visitors finds several cruises offered by Mt Cook and by Fullers, the best known being the "Cream Trip." (Fullers merged with Captain Cook Cruises in 1986.)

Beginning in 1919 a launch went three times a week to farms scattered among the islands in the bay picking up milk and dropping off mail and provisions, an operation taken over by Fullers in 1927 which still flies the Royal Mail flag.

A "Cream Trip" cruise leaves at mid-morning and returns mid-afternoon with an optional barbecue lunch at Zane Grey's fishing camp site at Otehei Bay.

The majority of cruises go out to the Hole in the Rock, at the head of the bay and come home again passing the historic islands on the way: Motorua where Captain Cook first anchored in 1769 and nearby Assassination Cove where, three years later, the French explorer, Marion du Fresne, anchored two ships. He put ashore with scurvy-sick seamen, set up a tent camp to gather wood for spars and masts. For some unknown reason, perhaps having unknowingly crossed into sacred forest areas or fishing grounds, two crews were massacred and eaten. One of the victims was the captain.

The French never did well in New Zealand. Jean-Francois Marie de Surville, probably passed Captain Cook around the northern tip of the island in a storm as he arrived in New Zealand in 1769. The French captain put into Doubtless Bay, just north of the Bay of Islands. A dingy was stolen by the Maoris and de Surville, over-reacting, burned a village and several canoes and kidnapped a local chief who died on board. Captain de Surville drowned later in Peru.

Another historic site pointed out by Cream Trip cruise directors is the cross on the distant hill where Marsden preached his first sermon.

To a large group of international visitors, the bay of Islands is a

mecca. These are deep-sea fishermen.

Zane Grey, the popular novelist and story writer of the Wild West, came to the Bay of Islands in 1926. It took him twenty-six days of sea voyaging to reach his destination.

He established a fishing camp at Otehei Bay and called it "The Camp of Larks."

Zane Grey caught marlin, swordfish, mako shark and tuna in large numbers and wrote about his exulting experience in a book called *Tales of the Angler's Eldorado*. The book established the Bay of Islands as one of the most productive game fishing waters in the world.

An international marlin fishing tournament is held annually in the Bay of Islands.

Two neighboring points of interest which shouldn't be missed are Kerikeri and Waimate North.

Kerikeri: Could This Be Southern California?

Kerikeri, site of the second mission, is where the first plow went into the ground in New Zealand. The name kerikeri, in the Maori language, means "dig, dig." When you come into this lush, southern California-type community overflowing with citrus groves and kiwifruit vines, you will appreciate that there has been a lot of kerikeri-ing going on.

Roadside stands sell fruit by the sackfuls.

Kerikeri is a likable place and has been found by Americans, South Africans, artists. Land is pricey.

The community, with a population of around 1,500, has seen a 200-percent growth in the last five years and will undoubtedly continue to grow at the same rate.

Most commercial tours stop at the Kemp House which is upriver from the Kerikeri inlet. This is the site to which Marsden returned with his second band of recruits in 1817, anchoring in a river basin just below a picturesque waterfall. A pretty, restful haven.

Here the missionaries completed a two-story frame house made of kauri wood in 1822. It is the oldest standing building in New Zealand.

Adjacent to the Kemp House is the Stone Store which was completed in 1835. In its time the Stone Store was to serve as living quarters, a library and an ammunition store house. Today it is half curio shop, half museum.

Across the waterfall is a reconstructed pre-European Maori village called a *kainga.* As opposed to a fortified pa, the kainga was the village where Maoris lived and farmed in peace. In the time of trouble they retreated from the kainga to the pa.

Waimate North

In 1830, the Reverend Marsden set up his next missionary station and the first inland station, believing that spiritual virtues of Christianity should be properly blended with the practical virtues of agriculture, a format for eternal salvation employed with great success by the Franciscans and the Jesuits in California.

At first the attempts at agriculture bore fine crops. When Charles Darwin visited the area on his voyage of discovery aboard the *Beagle,* he wrote of Waimate North, it had been touched "by an enchanter's wand."

Alas, the agriculture was to fail and the missionaries to lose their influence with the Maoris after the Flagpole War. Worse, British troops were stationed at the mission, destroyed the gardens and all but the central mission house and the church.

What remains, however, is delightful.

The Georgian-styled colonial building was erected by George Clarke out of an architectural book which is on display at the house. A "pattern" book, if you please. (He built a bridge out of the same design book.) A winding staircase to the second floor is a symbol of its ambitious, difficult-to-execute construction.

To one side of the downstairs is a dining room where Grey and Heke shared breakfast after the war. The mind instantly conjures up the scene of the English gentleman general and the Maori Christianized chief eating and talking together. Wouldn't you have loved to have been there? Behind it is an inside kitchen, and a master bedroom with a separate dressing room, both unusual for the time and place.

On the other side is a parlor is a guest bedroom and a den.

Bedrooms for servants, children and students are upstairs.

The Waimate North mission house is made entirely of kauri timber. It was here that we first learned to appreciate the golden patina, the fine grain and texture of the wood. It ages magnificently.

With the exception of the hearthstones and the blown pane glass windows which came from England, the entire structure was built by Maori carpenters.

Fortunately, the Historic Places Trust took over the house in 1959 and did an excellent job in restoring and refinishing the house to its original design and character. If you like the era, you'll envy the antique furnishings.

The little church next door, St. John the Baptist, is the third church to stand on the site.

Because the first bishop to come to New Zealand, Bishop Selwyn, established residency at Waimate North, the modest mission house automatically became the "Palace" and the little church the "Cathedral."

Cape Reinga & The Grandeur Of The 90-Mile Beach.

You should take a trip to the tip of Cape Reinga and come back via the 90-mile beach.

Take a tour by bus from Paihia. Don't take your car.

The trip takes almost a full day, the roads are narrow, and you should sit back and enjoy the scenery and the comments of the driver. If you tried to take your rental car to the 90-mile beach, you might lose it in quicksand. And lose fifty points in the Chilly Bin Game.

Cape Reinga is not the farthest point north in New Zealand. Kerr Point is.

Cape Reinga is not the farthest point north accessible by car. Hooper Point is, providing you have a four-wheel powered jeep.

But Cape Reinga is where the currents of the Tasman Sea and the Pacific Ocean meet visibly in a collision of spray.

Here also, according to Maori legend, the spirit of the deceased Maori descends the twisted roots of the pohutukawa tree to the ocean entrance of the underworld, to reappear on the largest of the offshore islands, the Three Kings, take a final look at the mainland and then journey to "Hawaiiki," from whence the Maori came.

The bus tour leaves Paihia about eight in the morning and returns about seven. Lots of stops along the way. Morning tea stop, luncheon stop, museum stops, Waimate North stop, afternoon tea stop, photo stop—take a cue from the New Zealander and Australians on the bus—relax and enjoy it.

We had an American on our tour to Cape Reinga who tapped

his wristwatch imperiously and said to the driver, "We are running ten minutes late."

The driver smiled gently and spread his hands, "What's time, Mate."

That remark became another weapon in the Lady Navigator's anti-time arsenal.

A nature and history lesson you learn on the Cape Reinga tour is the story of gum formed on the root of the stately kauri tree.

At one time kauri forests covered the north island from Hamilton, 80 miles south of Auckland, to the tip of Cape Reinga. When the trees died and collapsed, they left massive pools of kauri gum which, in time, were covered over with earth and became fossilized.

In 1819, the Reverend Marsden picked up pieces of gum exposed to the surface and sent samples to England as a curiosity. A piece was tested accidentally and found to have characteristics for making outstanding varnish, particularly fine varnish required by painters.

It led to a gum rush. By 1880, there were over 2,000 Europeans working in the gumfields of the Northland. Most of the gum-workers came from the area of Dalmatia, now included in the boundaries of Yugoslavia.

Like the goldrushes, the gumrush produced grog shops, gambling, shantytown living. The museums you visit in the Northland will invariably include relics from this rare chapter in New Zealand history.

The Dalmatians stayed after the gumfields were exhausted to become successful farmers and, in their tradition, to make sherry and port which was the basis for the successful wine industry today and the reason you still find Slavic names as part of the wineries around Auckland.

The visual characteristics of the first part of the tour is typical of lush New Zealand. Rolling green farmland, sheep inhaling grass, vistas of protective bays.

You pass Whangaroa Harbour where the *Boyd* still rests on the bottom and Doubtless Bay where de Surville landed.

Notice in the sheep country how landing strips for fertilizing airplanes are built into hilltops. Planes are loaded at the top and take off downhill like a ski jump. Erases a number of pilots who are less than skillful, we heard.

At the base of the Aupori Peninsula the character of the land changes to one of sand dunes.

You make a stop a third of the way up the peninsula at Houhora, a popular New Zealand vacation area. The bus will stop at the Wagener Museum, the one time homestead of a family of Polish nobility, the Subritskys, which has been restored by a descendant of the family and a modern 5,000-foot museum built next door.

Amber jewelry is made from fossilized resin and you can buy inexpensive pieces at the museum—but, beware, this amber shatters easily.

By early afternoon you are at Cape Reinga, and assuming you have a sunny day, you can understand why this is a favorite postcard subject.

The pristine white lighthouse, now unmanned, stands at the end of a rocky peninsula. Beyond the lighthouse you can see a line of foam in the ocean where the Tasman and Pacific currents fight for dominance.

On a clear day you can see the tips of the Three Kings Islands where Tasman tried to land and was prevented by heavy seas in 1642. He settled for naming the cape to the west Cape Maria van Diemen after the lady of the Batavian Governor.

As you can tell by the grungy cars with surfboards on top and the sun-bleached blonds inside, this is surfing country where the young lads and lasses chase the perfect wave and the endless summer.

The return trip down the peninsula turns west at the Te Paki stream bed which is the entrance road to 90-Mile Beach. The bed of the stream is quicksand. Not quick quicksand but slow quicksand.

The bus driver tells you several fear-building tales of past disasters and then turns the bus into the shallow stream bed and heads down through the water and the sandy banks. You feel properly nervous, just as he wanted you to feel.

If a car or bus stops, it will sink—but only up to its undercarriage.

Ninety-Mile Beach was named obviously by one of New Zealand's first advertising copywriters. (No one knows how it got its name.) It is fifty-six miles long. At low tide the beach is a hard, smooth, sand-packed superhighway—possibly the best highway in New Zealand.

There is not much to see but the sight of the curling ocean is soothing and many passengers promptly fall asleep.

"How was 90-Mile Beach, Mom?"

"Oh, I'll never forget it," will be the reply.

This area of coast is famous for *toheroa,* a highly prized shellfish which makes outstanding soup.

Returning to Paihia the tour bus takes Highway 1 through Kaitaia where a sign says "Hello" in Yugoslavian, through the Mangamuka Scenic Reserve, and past the Waimate North Mission House—a long but memorable day.

Note: the popularity of the Cape Reinga 90-Mile Beach tour makes reservations mandatory if you go in the busy summer season.

Return To Auckland Via The Big Trees

For a different look of scenery, plot your trip south along Highway 12 to the West Coast, then down through Dargaville to rejoin Highway 1 at Brynderwyn Junction.

When you reach the village of Omanaia, you get your first sight of Hokianga Harbor, a ragged stretch of water stretching half way across the North Island.

Historically, Kupe, the original Polynesian explorer, was said to have left from this harbor to return to Hawaiiki.

One of the first groups of settlers, the New Zealand Company, came here in 1827 from London to establish a planned settlement but the colonists gave up and moved to Australia.

The harbor attracted more than its share of characters. Cannibal Jack Marmon was perhaps to first to settle in the area and, it is said, became more Maori than the Maoris, including the participation in cannibalistic ceremonies.

Another even wilder character was Charles Baron de Thierry, a French expatiate who declared himself "Sovereign Chief of New Zealand." He had met Hongi Hika at Cambridge in 1820 when the Maori chief visited England. de Thierry claimed to have bought 40,000 acres of land around the harbor for 36 axes. He brought to New Zealand a band of colonists attracted by his grandiose dreams but the colonists deserted him when faced with the realities of carving a settlement out of forest land. The Maori chiefs denied the sale of the land and the kingdom collapsed.

As always in the Pacific, any French move was seen by the

English as a threat of territorial expansion and de Thierry was a big reason for the British Empire becoming involved in New Zealand.

Another character, more whimsical, was *Opo* the friendly dolphin who appeared in the waters of Opononi, a tiny seaside resort not too far from the entrance to Hokianga Harbor. For two summers, 1955 and 1956, Opo appeared at the beach and would give rides to the local children. The dolphin drew international attention and was the cause of two books and countless newspaper and magazine stories. He was killed needlessly and tragically the day before a law was to go into effect to protect him.

Opposite the local pub is the famous dolphin's grave and above it, a statue of a child riding the silken back of Opo.

The principal reason for taking the westward loop back to Auckland is to visit the Waipoua Kauri Forest.

The Waipoua Reserve is one of the few pockets of kauri remaining in what once was a noble forest. Before man scalped the land of her irreplaceable beauty.

The story of the rape of the kauri forests can only be matched by the shameless destruction of the California redwood forests.

Trees, hundreds of years old, were mowed down to make ship spars and masts, fence posts and cabins. The timber boom lasted into the 20th century when at last the land was depleted, the noble trees exhausted.

Fortunately, the Waipoua Kauri Forest saves forever the largest stand of mature kauri in New Zealand. Of the park's 29,000 acres, over 6,000 acres bear mature kauri.

Two magnificent trees create the awe and respect deserving of the kauri. The junior of the two is only 1,200 years old and has a mid-girth of 44 feet and reaches 170 feet into the heavens. Its name is Tanemahuta, meaning "God of the Forest."

The big brother is Te Matua Ngahere, "Father of the Forest," estimated to be 2,000 years old and 53 feet through the middle.

A second reserve of kauri timber is at Trounson Kauri Park, a short detour off Highway 12.

The road continues on to Dargaville, at one time an important shipping port for timber due to its location at the top of Kaipara Harbour. You don't believe this is a port because you are so far inland and you have to look at a map to see how far the harbor and the Wairoa River slice into the interior. When the Northland was known as the "Roadless North," Dargaville played an important transportation role in outbound kauri timber and gum.

A museum in Dargaville was first a stable built from bricks brought from China as ship's ballast. One curiosity in the museum is a 185-pound specimen of gum.

The Lady Navigator: "Is this loop road return worthwhile?"

Answer: "It is off the usual tourist track. But if you love noble trees, if you love the being-in-church feeling you get when standing in the middle of an untouched forest, you will enjoy the only kauri forests of their kind in New Zealand."

The Lady Navigator: "And pick up ten points."

Answer: "And pick up ten points."

3. The Fat Calf City of Hamilton

Golf at St. Andrews . . . A Stud Farm Stay . .
The Pretty Waikato River . . Glowworm Caves

We left Waitangi at dawn in order to make a rendezvous in the city of Hamilton, 80 miles south of Auckland, by three o'clock.

Pushing the right-hand drive, left-hand stick-shift Chilly Bin was not like driving an automatic-drive Cadillac. The four-berth vehicle was designed to get 26 kilometers per gallon of diesel. Excellent economy at the expense of significant power.

What you learn quickly is to anticipate the need for shifting down to a lower gear on hills, so that the van does not stall. In the up-one-side-down-the-other-side rolling topography between Waitangi and Hamilton, the driver gets a good workout.

Sometimes we crawled up inclines, traffic mounting behind us. We pulled over to the shoulder whenever possible to let frustrated drivers pass because, as campervans become more and more popular—and they will—more and more New Zealanders are going to be muttering naughty words about international tourists. It is up to campervan drivers to display simple courtesies of the road.

Not only on hills. We were perfectly happy to tootle along at 80kph on the open highway while the local traffic wanted to do 110kph. When we were in the way, we pulled off. Often there was an acknowledging beep of a horn and a wave of a hand. Better than being sworn at.

Before we left Newmans in Auckland we had been given a Stars-and-Stripes flag sticker to put on the back window. Visitors from other Australia and Canada were also offered replicas shaped like their country's flags. We felt it better diplomacy, considering our driving, to leave ours off.

The general flight pattern of overseas visitors is to see suburbs

57

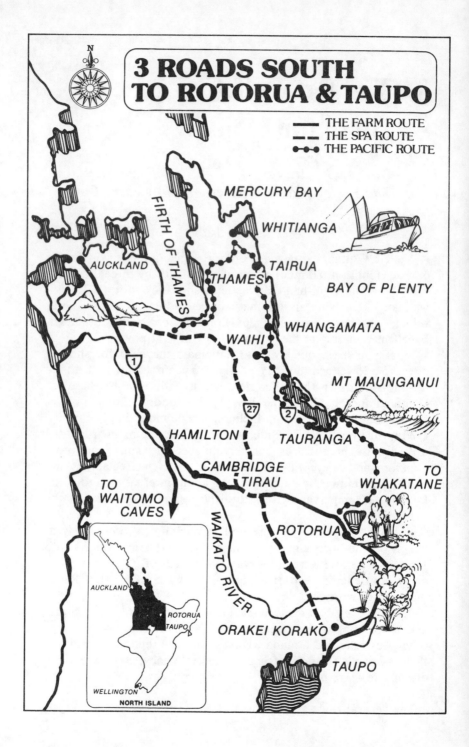

of Hamilton while driving 80 or 110kph toward the Waitomo Caves. Such a zip-zip itinerary misses one of the most pleasant cities in New Zealand.

Snaking through the green, lush Waikato Valley is the Waikato River, the geographic basis for the district's prosperity. The Waikato starts at Huka Falls just below Lake Taupo, 80 miles inland, and flows a distance of some 250 miles northwest before emptying into the Tasman Sea, the longest river in New Zealand.

For centuries, the river has deposited river silt on either side of its banks, building fertile agricultural lands for future crops and dairy farming.

Rich? There is more livestock per acre in a 50-mile radius of Hamilton than any place on earth.

We think the Waikato is one of New Zealand's most attractive rivers and yet the city of Hamilton has for years turned its back on it. Someone finally figured out that if the city treated the Waikato importantly, perhaps the rest of the country might slow down to enjoy both the river and the city.

Enter the Riverside Development Committee with inspired ideas such as maintaining a major riverside garden, night lighting the trees on the river bank, constructing several recreational jetties.

One of the most unique ideas we've ever heard suggests a Riverside Golf Classic. Of the thirteen golf courses ringing the city, six border the river and the idea is to stage a tournament pitting participants against three holes at each of the six courses, gliding between the courses, we assume, by boat. What a great tournament that would make.

Once, the river was a principal means of transportation, before boats were replaced by cars and trucks and trains and planes.

Until a couple of years ago there were no commercial pleasure boats on the river. Hard to believe. Now there are several river companies renting rafts, canoes, small jet boats and offering cruises on major tour boats.

The latest craft to come on the market is the *MV Waipa Delta,* a NZ$1,000,000 floating restaurant-cum-paddle steamer.

Actually, the ship is built on aluminum catamaran hulls and the main propulsion comes from jet engines, although the paddle wheels do supply an important element of power.

Almost 70 feet long, the *Delta* is licensed to carry 150 passengers for cruising, or 82 for dinner.

Three 90-minute scenic river tours are scheduled daily . . .

morning, afternoon and evening, the later voyage including dinner and a jazz trio for entertainment.

The present pastoral calm of Hamilton is in dramatic contrast to its beginning as a military outpost when the land was scrubby and undeveloped, the region swept by the Maori-Pakeha Wars, now commonly referred to as the Waikato Wars.

Today, Hamilton, with a population of almost 100,000, is known as the largest inland city in New Zealand. The city takes pride in its university, a teachers college and a farm animal breeding institute whose reputation for research is international.

The Lady Navigator: "I'm not thrilled by farm animal breeding institutes. What else do you do in Hamilton."

Answer: "You go out to Hamilton Lake and look at the birds. You visit the modern university campus and look at the girls. You—."

The Lady Navigator: "Hold it! Look at the girls?"

Answer: "Part of the charm of the new upmarket New Zealand is the new sense of style, the awareness of self among the young ladies. They are coming on chic, a great improvement over the last ten years. I report on these matters in the most clinical manner."

The Lady Navigator: "Uh-huh. I'm here to make sure you keep it clinical."

You appreciate the fountains of Hamilton. The city fathers call it the city of fountains.

There is a good amateur theater and excellent golf.

One of the advantages of revisiting an area is that you can tuck in activities that you missed on previous visits.

We wanted to play St. Andrews, the course of the Hamilton Golf Club. Arrangements were made for us to join the husband of a city council member, Peter Mowbray, whose home borders the course. (Madam Councilwoman was attending an open house at the city zoo—put that on your list, too.) We had a most enjoyable afternoon of pleasant conversation, fresh air and terrible, terrible golf. Why is it when you want to show your host a reasonable facility for a sport, you play like a robot that has blown its last microchip?

Just outside the city is a Clydesdale Museum next to another attraction called Farmworld where live animal shows are staged together with an audio-visual presentation. There is also a

Mormon Tabernacle, a first-rate race track, Te Rapa, and Frankton, the site of annual yearling sales.

Another reason we like Hamilton are the hundred or more stud farms that decorate the plains with their eye-appealing pastures, paddocks and show-ring ovals.

In our original New Zealand book we described our stay at a sheep station, Linden Downs, outside of Masterton. The letters and comments we received afterward from readers who also had enjoyed Linden Downs were so enthusiastic that we decided to expand our farm stay experiences in the sequel, tasting an assortment of agrarian lifestyles.

A stud farm was high on our list and, before leaving for the Bay of Islands, we called Agritour in Hamilton, an organization that specializes in agricultural, horticultural and 'countryside' tourism to arrange a two-night stay.

After several phone calls, and a bit of hedging, we were booked at a stud farm just south of Cambridge, about an hour's drive from Hamilton. There would be a small extra fee because this was the busy season, we were told, a statement which bothers the Lady Navigator to this day.

"If they are too busy, then we will find another stud farm," she challenged the booking agent.

They weren't that busy.

We drove about two miles south of Cambridge, a tree-lined village known for its antique shops and gentle air, to Kiteroa Stud Farm, a 134-acre spread with one new house, one old house and new stables. The fencing was immaculate and an entry road was being finished to the new stables, part of the window dressing of a modern stud farm operation. The appearance of prosperity and efficiency are essential elements of the farm's marketing package.

Pastures on either side of the long impressive driveway were filled with brood mares, mares that lifted their majestic heads in curiosity at this strange blue and white vehicle. What kind of horse was it delivering?

We stopped in front of the new house on a circular driveway of new gravel.

A redheaded bantam rooster of a man came to the door and motioned us in quickly, announcing The Caulfield was just about to start.

Our timing couldn't have been better—or worse. Australia's

Caulfield Cup is the last big race before the following week's Melbourne Cup, the most important race south of the Equator. The Melbourne Cup is the Kentucky Derby, the Grand National, the Arc d'Triomphe, and Santa Anita rolled into one.

We sat like obedient little children while our hosts glued their eyes to the color television set during the running of the race—the VTR dutifully recording it for later review.

Then we met our hosts, Keith and Bev O'Callaghan.

Keith, fifty-ish, had wirey, curling red hair tinged with grey. He habitually stood with hands on hips, balancing on his toes, like a lightweight boxer, alert, ready to move quickly to his right or left. He was faultlessly forthright, not given to braggadocio, and an excellent teacher for a visitor who wanted to know the details of stud farming.

Bev, his wife, gave the impression of towering over Keith. This handsome large-boned chain-smoking woman had a smile that broke all boundaries, dissolved any tension of newcomers entering a strange household.

"Take us like you find us," said Bev.

It was easy to do. They were basic, no-nonsense, happy, hard-working farm people.

The white stucco house was just being finished, part of the development of Kiteroa. The new O'Callaghan farm had been purchased a year before moving their operation from an older farm down the road.

A tour of the house revealed that Kiwis do not build new houses; they keep one wall of an old house and remodel the house around it. There is a strong tax advantage in remodeling. There is no tax advantage in building a new house.

The O'Callaghans had kept an exterior wall and built a California ranchhouse. An open kitchen and a large dining room were partitioned off from the sitting room by a half wall. Three bedrooms shared one bath and a shower located in the gum boot/utility room.

Because they entertained so many overseas clients, mainly Australian horsemen, Bev was considering adding a bedroom/bath unit to a building in back of the house.

We were the farm's first paying guests. (Agritour, we found out later, had never seen the property. The Lady Navigator still wonders if the O'Callaghans ever saw the higher "busy season" fee.)

The O'Callaghans had three children. An elder son, Colin, lived in Auckland pursuing a successful marketing career and raising a couple of horses on the side. A beautiful daughter, Carol Ann, had recently married a golf professional and they spent all spare time cleaning- and painting-up the original old farmhouse next door. Tubby, who didn't live up to his name at all, lived at home and was part of a good-natured partnership with his father.

A likable family.

The "factory" of the Kiteroa Stud Farm consisted of two stallions, Imperial Seal, an English bred thoroughbred and Le Monarc. The two stallions would "cover" 160 mares in a season, from August to January. Imperial Seal's stud fee was NZ$10,000 per service, Le Monarc commanded only NZ$2,000.

It was now October and the farm was at the peak of its busiest period. In addition to the breeding of the brood mares in the paddocks, the mares coming into foal had to be attended.

Mares, we learned, rarely foal in the daytime—and if they do, according to Keith, the foal has trouble with its eyesight. As the foaling time becomes imminent, the pregnant mare is moved into a pasture nearer the house along with four or five other mares approaching motherhood. A NZ$250 electronic beeper is positioned around their necks and, as each goes down in the night, signaling the start of a birth, the beeper touches the ground and sets off an alarm in the bedroom of either Keith or Tubby—they alternate nights. The person on duty gets to the pasture to midwife the birth of the foal within three minutes.

The night before we arrived, three colts had been born. The two nights we were there—I was going to send out the Lady Navigator—nothing.

The other part of stud farming is the breeding. Most of the mares in the pasture belong to other owners and are there awaiting their gestation period.

Every evening and every morning, Keith goes out into the pasture with a gelded pony on a long rope and roams among the mares. Mares coming into heat will approach the pony whose function is to tease, giving Keith the opportunity to determine if she is ready to be serviced. There's a bit of nipping and kicking and, if she urinates, the mare is ready and will be serviced the next day.

"Now, watch this," said Keith as a mare approached the pony, making advances as if she wanted to be serviced. When the pony began to get into position, the mare lashed out at him with vicious kicks.

"That's what we call 'spite showing' and you have to be careful that your teaser doesn't get caught off guard too often or he is going to lose his enthusiasm for his job and you have to start all over again with a new pony.

"Then there are mares who just turn into trollops. We have to get rid of them or they will exhaust your teaser.

"Others won't make any move as long as I'm around. Then I tie up the pony to this post in the middle of the pasture and hide behind those hedges and watch. Then the mare will make her move and I'll know she is ready."

"Is there a limit on how many mares a stallion can service?"

"Oh, sure. Imperial Seal is limited to 100 mares a season."

"At $10,000 a throw?"

"Yes, but you have to remember, to get a decent English bred stallion your starting price is a million New Zealand dollars—minimum. Imperial Seal, who is ten years old and can be good for another ten years, would cost you between three and four million dollars today."

I looked over to the three-acre enclosure where the rich bay horse with superb confirmation was peering over the fence, ears up, eyes bright. "Why isn't he in a private shed?"

"No need," Keith laughed. "He stays out there all year long. The closer you keep to nature, the better the horse will be."

The farmhouse food was awesome.

I remember having a beer or two before dinner, then thick slices of pork, three kinds of potatoes, delicious gravy, vegetables, white wine and a trifle desert laced with dairy cream. Bev was hurt if we didn't go back for seconds of everything.

Breakfast consisted of three huge free-range eggs together with half a plate of spaghetti and enough toast to feed a boarding school.

Awesome.

Bev, after breakfast, drove us over to Wexford Stables "ten minutes away"—more like 30 minutes—just outside of Matamata. It belonged to David O'Sullivan.

A compact, trim, former jockey, O'Sullivan started as a trainer at age 27 and today is New Zealand's leading trainer. He had 60 horses in his stables which, conveniently, is located next to the Matamata racetrack where his charges work out.

He has won everything in sight and, besides the race horses, has earned a fine reputation for training apprentice jockeys.

In addition to the horses his farm carries 200 Holstein bulls, 200 angora goats and, experimentally, fitches, a type of weasel raised for their fur. (Smelly little animals.)

He gets 10 percent of the winnings of the horses he trains. Jockeys get 5 percent. His goats cost almost $500 each. His farms produces 3,000 bales of hay and he has five children, the eldest daughter being a veterinarian surgeon. He breathes success.

Does he own any horses himself. Oh, no!

I asked New Zealand's leading trainer what he did with all of his money. "Hah!" said Mr. O'Sullivan. "I have 2,000 mouths to feed." I think he was counting the fitches.

He likes to play golf and said he'd call the next time through Hawaii and we'd have a game. Remind me to play for small stakes.

That night Carol Ann, the pretty daughter, and her husband, Ross, came to dinner and we watched video memories of their wedding, a social gala in the region that utilized vintage cars for the bridal party—good visuals. The wedding dress by Auckland's most expensive custom designer must have cost Imperial Seal a couple of days of real solid work.

We also watched tapes of past horse races because that's what horsemen do.

However, unlike the homes of other horsemen, the walls of Kiteroa were not decorated with blue ribbons and pictures of horses and their jockeys and trainers. Not yet, anyway.

The second morning, after a six-egg breakfast which Keith the Breakfast Chef cooked, Imperial Seal had a customer from outside the pasture herd.

As the mare arrived and was unloaded, Imperial Seal came to the near fence, ears up, whinnied and then retreated into the corner of his pasture. He knew.

The mare was taken into a separate shed along with the teaser pony who brought the horse up to proper heat and then she was led into the pasture with Imperial Seal. The mare was hobbled.

After Imperial Seal was positioned behind her, he mounted her, did his job like a highly qualified professional, dismounted and went back to his private corner to munch the green, green grass. It was a five-minute $10,000 ho-hum job.

"Who gets involved in horse racing?" we asked Keith.

"Doctors, judges, attorneys, manufacturers, professional people with money, people with reputations for clear, successful practices based on clear logical thinking. They go out of their minds when they get involved with horse racing. Crazy."

Crazy? Really?

Oh, yes.

Once upon a time the Lady Navigator gave me one percent of an Irish race horse in Dublin as a gag Christmas gift.

I couldn't get to Dublin fast enough to buy 50 percent of Flying Column. I was like a child buying the Brooklyn Bridge. Worse. I got 50 percent of another horse from the same stable. Danny Boy couldn't finish and Flying Column kept falling down.

Crazy. Feed bills and jockey bills and race entry fees finally stabilized my sanity. Never, never again.

Yet, when I wandered the pastures with Keith and he pointed out the differences in the animals and I saw the magnificent beasts stretching their graceful legs as they sprinted from one fence to another, a strong yearning came over me to play in the game, to take my silks out of their showcase on the wall, to stand in the winners' circle, to get my picture taken with him and, in years to come, say "Let me tell you about a horse I once owned."

We put the stud farm experience down as a five-star stay.

Six stars . . . if only I could afford a horse.

Keith & Bev, O'Callaghan, RD 4, Cambridge, New Zealand. They have since signed on with Town & Country Home Hosting, Victoria Street, Cambridge.

The Glowworm Caves of Waitomo

Heading south on Highway 3 we stopped at Te Awamutu, a pleasant farming center and shopped, had a picnic lunch on a hilltop overlooking a rain swept valley where the dairy cattle huddled together with their tails to the wind.

The bypass around the business core of Otorohanga, the next

town, also bypasses the entrance to the Otorohanga Kiwi House and Native Bird Park.

We visited the park shortly after it first opened and enjoyed the walk-through aviary—the largest in New Zealand at that time. The park is owned and operated by the Otorohanga Zoological Society, dedicated to the conservation of New Zealand's wildlife heritage.

Go, if you have time. A good ten-point stop.

A short distance south of Otorohanga, watch for the turn to the Waitomo Caves.

A lot of upgrading has taken place at Waitomo.

We checked in the Waitomo Hotel, a graceful hotel, a holdover from a gentler era, which has been modernized but not plasticized, repainted and remodeled but not bowdlerized. Too many decorators do not know what treasuries they are working with when assigned the redo of a charming yesteryear hostelry.

It gives us great pleasure to report that the Waitomo is still a place of charm amid quiet gardens with broad vistas and a tea-on-the-porch atmosphere.

Dating back to 1911, the Waitomo Hotel suggests the long history of popularity enjoyed by the Glowworms Caves.

A small but absorbing museum sits at the bottom of the hill leading to the hotel. Several of its exhibits used to be showcased in the corridors of the hotel.

Here the visitor finds the history of the caves since their discovery in 1887 by a Maori chief and a European surveyor who floated into the cave at the stream entrance using candles for light that was brave and followed the stream into a giant chamber whose roof was a mass of tiny stars, actually glowworms.

The two phases of the glowworm is also explained in the museum.

As a two-inch larva, the glowworm will exist for about nine months when it changes into a small mouthless fly. The fly lives only a few days, just long enough to reproduce eggs, most of which are eaten by other glowworms. The eggs hatch, produce young glowworms which spin a long tube of mucus from which 30 to 40 sticky lines will be suspended to begin the cycle of life anew.

The light organ in the tail of the glowworm shines brightly to attract small airborne insects. When food is entrapped on its sticky lines, the glowworm sucks up the line and devours the insect. It's a neat way of doing the grocery shopping.

A three-dimensional model of the caves, exhibits of the exploration equipment used from the candle and hob-nailed boot era through carbide lamps to the modern electric head-torches, and photographs of cavers, both historical and modern, are part of the museum.

The area around the Waitomo Caves is honeycombed with limestone cave formations.

An excellent slide presentation shows teams of cavers descending long reaches of rope through small holes in the earth surface to deep dark caverns. Very exciting.

You, too, can take an organized "off the beaten surface" caving excursion where you emulate the cavers in the slide show and go slithering through tiny cracks into unknown caves, wade through knee-high water by torchlight, face drops which come out in China. The operators of private adventure caving expeditions provide all of the gear. You have to bring your own nerve.

Just the idea makes my skin crawl with claustrophobia.

The musuem has a list of available guides.

Because the Waitomo Caves were developed as a government-sponsored tourist attraction requiring a nearby government-sponsored hotel, the Waitomo Caves continue to be managed by the THC. Bill Sheedy, the manager of the Waitomo Hotel, suggested that we visit the caves first thing in the morning "before the tour buses arrive." He arranged an interview for us with the caves manager.

You might fear that a remote hotel with a captive audience would be casual about food service. Does this sound like the work of an indifferent chef or general manager? Fried camembert and raspberry sauce as a starter, lamb chops cooked tenderly to just the right shade of pink, and a gooey dessert from a trolley that deserved a one-of-each taste test.

The next morning Waitomo Cave manager David Williams, a young, efficient, pleasant chap, met us at the new entrance to the Glowworm Cave.

The popularity of the caves has been ever increasing for almost 100 years and we were well advised to get there early. Avoid going mid-day. Either early morning or late afternoon. Another good reason for staying over at the Waitomo Hotel.

Since our last visit, two major improvements have occurred.

The first was the entrance itself, now enhanced with a new ticket booth, a pleasant gift shop and clean restrooms.

The other is that the final portion of the 45-minute tour is the boat trip to the Glowworm Cave proper. Your boat drifts downstream through the dark cavern with its overhead milkyway of tiny glowworm stars into the daylight of ferns and singing birds. A short walk takes you back to the entrance gate.

It is a much better finale.

Formerly, you retraced your steps through the different caves, side stepping incoming visitors. It was anticlimactic.

The first part of the conducted tour journeys through the upper caverns above the stream bed, through a former water passage. A vertical shaft called the Tomo links the upper portion of the cave to the dark caverns below and visitors are asked to be very quiet because disturbed glowworms turn off their lights.

The Banquet Chamber is the first major cavern you visit. Visitors of an earlier era who had struggled many hours through unlighted passages would rest and have a meal here.

Next is a "living" cave where water dripping down through the limestone ceiling is forming stalactites and stalagmites. Here you find the Pipe Organ, the largest living formation in the cave. It is 750,000 years old and still growing.

The largest chamber in the cave, the Cathedral, has a ceiling 45 feet high. The size and shape of the cavern and the texture of its walls make it an ideal—and unusual—recording studio. The Vienna Boys Choir, opera stars and musical groups have recorded music in the Cathedral.

"Would anybody volunteer to sing?" asked the guide. There was much tittering but no volunteers. Too bad.

On our first trip to Waitomo, a young lady stepped forward, laughed nervously and said she would try.

The first quavering of notes of "Some Day We'll Meet Again" lifted in the chamber and then, assured by the resonance of the chamber, the voice became stronger and sweeter. At the beginning of the second chorus the audience joined in, first tentatively and then in increasing numbers until, at the end, the entire crowd was singing and the chamber was filled with glorious music. It was tingle time.

The piece de resistance occurs when the guide takes you down darkened stairs and quietly loads you into a boat on an underground river to float through a cavern lit by countless tiny, twinkly lights overhead. This is the Glowworm Grotto. The few moments that you spend here will stay with you for the rest of your life.

You exit on the stream by which the explorers who discovered the caves entered. Waitomo means "water entering a hole" or, more aptly, "water passing through a hole."

David Williams then took us up the valley to two other prominent caves, Ruakuri, which was closed, and Aranui.

Ruakuri's experience, in addition to high caverns and glowworm caves, is a walk along an underground roaring river.

Aranui is a relatively smaller cavern but with beautiful formations.

A three-cave pass is sold at the Waitomo ticket office.

How popular are the caves? Williams said that estimates of the annual visitor count by the year 1993 approach 500,000.

The popularity of the caves has drawn two satellite attractions to the area. Both are on the branch road into Waitomo from Highway 3.

Merrowvale is a model Lilliput village depicting New Zealand life. Spread over three acres, its town center is surrounded by farms and pine forests. A built-to-scale model railway toot-toots through the village periodically.

The other attraction is Ohaki, a replica of a pre-European Maori Village.

Its purpose is to encourage the Maori to retain his own culture and to show other racial groups the ancient Maori customs.

The *kainga* is built on and around a small hill adjacent to an entrance house that sells modestly priced tickets and Maori-made souvenirs. Demonstrations of Maori handicrafts—weaving, flax making and the like—are conducted here also.

The ancient village would have been home for 100 to 150 people. Protected by a 10-foot staked pole fence, there are sleeping houses, lookout towers, a chief's house which is the center of the village, food storage houses mounted on poles as an anti-rat precaution, a hangi pit for underground baking, a kumara pit for storing potatoes, a round house for the priest.

A visit to a Maori cultural project is in keeping because you are in King Country.

In the mid-1850s, the Maoris attempted to protect themselves from the Pakeha settlers by establishing a unified "kingdom" of tribal groups. They selected a king and adopted laws prohibiting the sale of land to the Pakeha.

Much of the northern part of the kingdom, which formed the richest part of the North Island, was taken over by New Zealand government armed forces. But, for years, this central area was rebel territory— King Country—and the country around Te Kuiti remained an independent stronghold until 1885, when a railway was laid through the territory, over the king's objections, and the Pakeha moved in.

Six miles south of the Waitomo Cave cut-off on Highway 3 is the town of Te Kuiti, population 5,000. I always have the feeling in Te Kuiti that it is not a place where I will be comfortable going into a pub and having a beer. Even its name, a contraction of Te Huititanga, means "hemming in."

Sometimes instinct tells you it is better to keep your teeth rather than try and pick up ten points.

However, I, at least, slowed down before the splendidly carved Maori meeting house at the southern end of the town. It is said to be the finest example of old-time carving remaining outside of museums. Maybe your partner will concede five points. Mine did not.

The road south leads to New Plymouth but we cut across country east toward Rotorua.

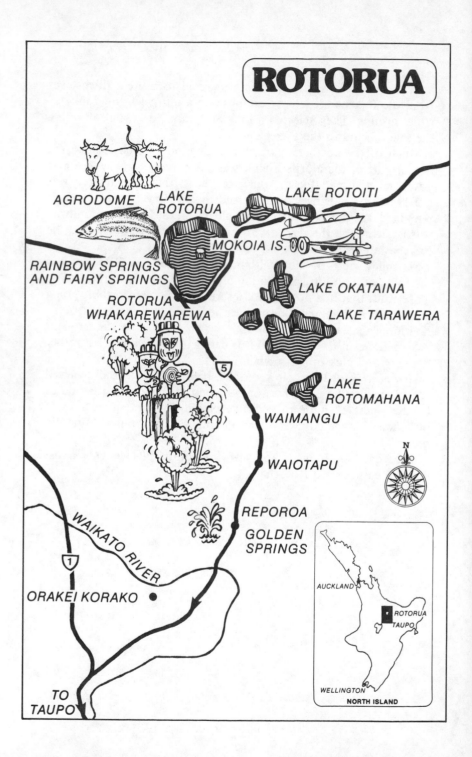

ROTORUA

AGRODOME

LAKE ROTORUA

LAKE ROTOITI

MOKOIA IS.

RAINBOW SPRINGS AND FAIRY SPRINGS

ROTORUA WHAKAREWAREWA

LAKE OKATAINA

LAKE TARAWERA

5

LAKE ROTOMAHANA

WAIMANGU

WAIOTAPU

N

REPOROA

GOLDEN SPRINGS

WAIKATO RIVER

1

ORAKEI KORAKO

AUCKLAND

ROTORUA
TAUPO

TO TAUPO

WELLINGTON

NORTH ISLAND

4. Upgraded Rotorua

Steambaths And Maori Culture . . . Sheepshow
Orchids & Herb Gardens . . . And Moose Lodge

Rotorua is on a roll.

Like the Waitomo Caves, Rotorua's popularity among overseas visitors continues to mount. For all kinds of reasons: improved facilities, added accommodations and attractions and upgraded attractions, new shopping opportunities, expanded outdoor activities.

Overseas visitors—and New Zealanders—for a hundred years have gone to Rotorua to 1) catch a trout, 2) take a steambath and a massage, 3) view the local thermal volcanic wonders.

Now tourists can 1) take an aerial tramway, 2) visit an herb garden, 3) visit an orchid garden, 4) sightsee by helicopter, 5) witness a resurgence of Maori culture.

The list continues to mount with Rotorua's popularity.

In one day you can pick up a week's worth of Non-Zip-Zip points for involvement.

The city, heading a district population of 50,000, a major number in New Zealand, sprawls along the south side of the lake of the same name.

It smells of sulphur. The scent of bad eggs might repel some but to the city fathers, whose prosperity has been built on the practice of humans ridding themselves of various bodily ills and warts and sins by frequent immersions in the evil smelling waters, the scent of bad eggs is that of violets in the spring.

An interesting contrast to the major centers of Maorism on each end of the city, as designated by carved Maori meeting houses, is the solid string of glittering modern motels that connect them. Private saunas and waterbeds are advertised enticements to attract guests.

For us, the theme building of Rotorua is the Tudor Towers in the Government Gardens, built to create the atmosphere of the posh European spas.

Surrounding Rotorua are half-a-dozen fish-filled lakes which in

73

turn are surrounded by lush forests.

Excellent golf courses are within the city limits and dotted around the periphery.

A sizable, bustling commercial center with banks, shops, restaurants and souvenir boutiques emphasizes the economic well-being of the attractive community.

The international magnetism of Rotorua dates back to the late 19th century and two principal attractions: the famous Pink and White Terraces at nearby Lake Tarawera, immense in size, were created by the build-up of silica laden streams fanning out like giant stillborn waterfalls at the base of Mt. Tarawera. (A small version of what the terraces must have been like can be seen at the Orakei-korako Valley.)

Then one night in 1886 the most terrible earthquake ever recorded in the region occurred when Mt. Tarawera erupted, splitting open like a giant pea pod spilling volcanic mud and pumice for miles around, destroying a nearby Maori encampment, the tourist hotel across the lake at Te Wairoa, and burying forever the lovely Pink and White Terraces.

One of the favorite tours today takes you past Blue Lake and Green Lake to Lake Tarawera and, by launch, to the foot of the mountain.

Another tour is to Waimangu Thermal Valley which was created by the Tarawera eruption.

Scenic flight tours abound in Rotorua. We have always wanted to take a float plane or a helicopter ride over Mt. Tarawera and look into its awesome craters but weather has hindered every attempt.

Another Tarawera frustration lies in its fish. The rainbow trout, I'm told, are giants. I wouldn't know, personally. I have had three lengthy tries at the lake, once with a professional guide and twice with lakeside residents, and have never had a nibble.

Today's main thermal attraction in Rotorua is within the city limits at the south entrance to the city on Highway 5 to Lake Taupo. The area is known as Whakarewarewa Thermal Area—sometimes just called "Whaka"—and encompasses hot mud pools, a model pa, hot springs, the Pohutu Geyser, the largest geyser in the country which can spout up to 100 feet. A Maori village is part of the area where the inhabitants still use the steam vents for cooking.

Also part of the complex is the Maori Arts and Crafts Institute, where the art of Maori carving and other crafts are taught to Maori students.

It has to be remembered that there was no written language in Polynesia and that the history of the tribes was passed down through chants and through carving. The Maoris of New Zealand brought to the art of carving in wood and in jade a degree of sophistication not found elsewhere in the Pacific with the possible exception of the Marquesas in what is now French Polynesia.

In 1985 a major exhibit, "Te Maori," opened at New York's Metropolitan Museum of Art. Organized by the American Federation of Arts, the exhibit consisted of 200 sculptures and carvings from all New Zealand tribes, some dating back to 1200 AD. It was a smashing success subsequently traveling to St. Louis, San Francisco and Hawaii.

Because the exhibit was acclaimed by the art world, it generated new awareness and appreciation for Maori carving, and, more importantly, it brought a renewed sense of pride to the Maori people.

Posters from the exhibit are on the gift shop walls.

Also on exhibit is the stern piece of a war canoe. According to the legend, the helmsman and navigator could look up at different stars through the carved holes in the stern piece and triangulate his position.

A major change in New Zealand today is the growing importance of the Maori culture as exemplified in Rotorua.

We called to chat with Howard Morrison, a major entertaining talent, whom we had met in Hawaii and who had become a leader in the Maori movement.

He met us in a lakefront parking area near the Maori village of Ohitemutu which is near the center of Rotorua.

Howard is a strapping Polynesian with a genial, at-peace face but commanding in presence.

Our question was preceded by a backgrounding statement: "As you know, in Hawaii, Polynesian entertainment is a major part of tourism, not only giving tourist pleasure but also giving thousands of dancers and singers and musicians solid employment. Do you think the overseas visitors to New Zealand will witness more Maori entertainment in the future?"

The answer took about two hours. We talked at length in the Chilly Bin. We drove in Howard's car into Ohitemutu and strolled through the Maori village where Howard lives. We talked in his private thermal bathhouse while the rain pelted down on the tin roof. We talked in his home over tea and coffee and a snack of smoked trout on crackers.

In summation Howard said, "Yes, but there is a lot more at issue than just the entertainment of tourists.

"A lot has happened in recent years to emphasize the importance of the Maori culture. First, there was a campaign launched to increase Maori pride called *Tu Tangata*, or 'stand tall.'

"That resulted in the establishment of language nests, *Kohanga Reo*. We anticipated five nests opening the first year. Instead, 120 sprang up. By early 1985, the number had increased to 334 and continues to mushroom.

"Not only will there be more evidence of *Maoritanga* —things Maori—but there will be more Maori participation in activities where Maori land is concerned. In the past, Maori land has been leased to entrepreneurs who have established attractions without Maori involvement. I think you'll see more Maori executive involvement when these leases run out.

"We find visitors who want to spend a night in a meeting house, in the Maori manner. That is going to happen. A fine example is the success of the Te Rehuwai Safari, a five-day trek through private lands of the Tuhoe Tribe where there is dual emphasis: natural beauty and true Maori culture.

"Another example is the development of Okawa Bay Lake Resort where Lake Rotorua and Lake Rotoiti join. This project is on Maori land and will involve Maori management."

Howard's village of Ohitemutu is a popular tourist spot that predates the coming of the European . . . and the tourists. Steam vents and thermal pools surround the compound.

The principal tribe in the area is the Arawa and the most important sub-tribe is the Ngati-Whakaue which occupies Ohitemutu.

The meeting house facing the village compound is Tamate-kapua, the most important meeting house of the Arawa tribe.

When other tribes were committed to fighting the government forces in the Waitomo Wars, the Arawa pledged its loyalty to the Queen—Queen Victoria.

Their loyalty was rewarded with a present from the Queen, a bust of the royal figure which now occupies a space between the meeting hall and the church.

The Tudor-styled St. Faith's Anglican Church is on the lake side of the compound. To the left of the church entrance is the grave of the American minister, Seymore Mills Spencer (1810-1890), a founder of the church who traveled widely throughout his mission area, always carrying a large umbrella which he frequently used as a tent.

He became known as "the parson with the umbrella" and in the chapel window above the organ he is depicting preaching to a Maori group with a unfurled umbrella by his side.

Another important grave in the cemetery to the right of the church entrance is that of colorful Captain Gilbert Mair (1843-1923) who twice saved the local community from annihilation from enemy tribes with his government troops. He was the only European to be made a full chief of the Arawa tribe.

Inside the church are the ancient battle flags carried by the tribal warriors. Unique is a window in the right hand chapel with a sandblasted figure of Christ wearing a Maori cloak. When you are seated in a pew facing the chapel, it appears that the figure is walking on the waters of Lake Rotorua seen in the background through the glass.

The eruption of Tarawera with international publicity was a setback to the development of Rotorua.

To regain the lost popularity a major development was created in the grand Elizabethan-styled Tudor Towers built in the Government Gardens in 1906 together with a Bath House. The style was copied from the great spas of Europe.

This ancient and quaint structure should be approached from Hinemaru Street through the ornate, wrought-iron Princess Gate because that entry captures the charming visual Victorian flavor of the building and gardens.

On a sunny weekend when the lawn bowlers are out en masse on the front lawn of Tudor Towers, men on one lawn and women on the other lawn, all in immaculate whites, it is one of the great photo opportunities of New Zealand. Don't miss it.

Lawn bowling will be found throughout New Zealand. We always enjoy the scene of the code-garbed figures in pristine white trousers or skirts, white shirts, sometimes jackets, and white hats seriously rolling the black balls from one side of the green lawn to the other.

Presently, the Tudor Towers holds a restaurant, a museum and art gallery . . . and needs a good facial.

The Government Gardens site also houses the Polynesian Pools—a labyrinth of pools in varying sizes—some steamy hot and evil looking, some chokingly smelly, but also a large outdoor pleasant pool. The circular entrance, lobby and gift shop were new to us. Swept up.

On a quick tour of the premises, we saw saunas and "Aix Massage."

What, I asked, is an "Aix Massage?" It is a massage with jets of hot water beating down on the recipient while the body is rubbed down with oil.

You should have a thermal bath before you leave Rotorua.

While you are in the area, duck into Rotorua's downtown Fleur Orchid Gardens and Aviary, an inspired combination of exotic flowers and birds in two hothouse buildings.

Walking through the Temperate House and the Tropical House is a sensual experience of exotic blossoms, of earthy pungent odors associated with wet greenery, of appealing sounds of water tumbling gently down perfect waterfalls into reflection pools.

The attraction is first rate, well-designed for easy strolling along graded curving paths and over little rustic bridges that cross shallow streams and lotus ponds.

Night tours, too, until 10pm.

A pleasant addition is the Greenhouse Tea Garden where you can have a light snacks including beer or tea.

The most visual addition to the Rotorua scene is the Skyline ride which is about three miles outside of the city on the highway to Auckland.

Swiss manufactured four-place enclosed gondolas take riders to a tearoom terminal on the slope of Mt. Ngongotaha overlooking the lake and the surrounding countryside.

It is a pleasant place—on a cloudless day—to lunch and pick out landmarks surrounding Lake Rotorua.

The operation is owned by the same people who have the Skyline gondola in Queenstown.

Next door was something we had never seen. The Luge Run, it was called. Plastic sleds slide down one kilometer of mountain on a curving, banked concrete path. A sign forbids riding with bare feet or thongs, and children under four years of age. (And no adults over 30, I thought.)

At the foot of the Skyline is another new attraction, the Hillside

Herb Gardens. It is enchanting.

Opposite the Herb Gardens is the well-known Rainbow and Fairy Springs which, like much of Rotorua, was under major renovations during our surveillance trip.

Its basic attractions are the thousands of rainbow and brown trout swimming free (but protected) in natural pools and streams throughout the gardens marked with woodsy walking paths and an occasional waterfall. Twenty-four million liters of clear water bubble up in the Fairy Springs every day.

To further attract visitors, management added a large display of New Zealand birdlife, including the inevitable kiwi house, and hoofed wildlife of the ilk of deer and wild pigs. Just as at any of the tourist attractions, you can depend on finding a restaurant.

Continue north on Highway 5 leaving the shoreline of Lake Rotorua behind, cut inland toward Hamilton to the Agrodome, one of the more successful attractions in Rotorua. It will be on the right hand side of the highway.

Since our first visit, the "dome" has been rebuilt and substantially expanded. The show is the same (two shows in the morning and one in the afternoon): the sheep of New Zealand on display and the shearers of New Zealand demonstrating their skills. It is an easy and entertaining way to learn about New Zealand's most valuable industry. (It is difficult to comprehend that at lambing time there are about 130 million sheep in New Zealand.)

The rams open the show. Their pen doors open and, on signal, they scramble around the stage madly seeking their particular spot marked by a familiar can of grain meal.

A shearer demonstrates the art of shearing—and it is an art the way he immobilizes the sheep between his legs and defrocks the animal in two minutes or less. His sharp shears move over the sheep's body rhythmically and smoothly, releasing the full pelt without hurting the sheep. Oh, there'll be an occasional skin nick, but nothing serious.

Another demonstration, conducted outside, has a working head or "eye" dog and a huntaway sheep dog. These dogs are so keen, so alert, so alive that you want to introduce yourself. Dog demonstrations never last long enough.

If you continued on the shoreline road, past the Highway 5 turnoff, you'd come to Taniwha Springs, a recreational area, and

Hamurana Springs which includes a nine-hole golf course, a stand of California redwoods, a new "tree" walk and what looks like a new subdivision of vacation homes.

Organized tours are a way of life in Rotorua. Big, air-conditioned buses roll continually through the streets and line up in fleet fashion before every major tour stop.

One of the non-bus tours is the launch trip to Mokoia Island.

Mokoia Island is in the middle of Lake Rotorua, the Maori stage for the traditional Romeo-and-Juliet love story found in most countries' legends. Here Hinemoa (Juliet) who lived on the shore loved the prince of another tribe, Tutanekai (Romeo), who lived on the island.

The couple planned to elope but their get-away canoe was stolen. Frustrated but undaunted, Hinemoa made waterwings of six calabashes, the native gourds, and swam to the island and found Tutanekai's servant at the island's spring. She insulted the servant who returned to tell Tutanekai. He grabbed a club swearing utu and went to the spring to revenge the insult to his mana. And out of the bushes came his lover. They played kiss-kiss instead of club-club and lived happily ever after.

Part of the island trip is to swim in the lover's pool.

Daytime Sports

The leading attraction of the Rotorua area is fishing.

There are a dozen or more lakes to choose between. The most famous are Rotorua, Rotoiti, Okataina and Tarawera, and less than a hour's drive south, the never-fail-to-catch-a-trout, Lake Taupo.

Stream mouths and streams are reserved for fly fishing in a season beginning October 1, ending June 30. Fishing is generally allowed in the Rotorua and Taupo lakes all year long.

The national authority for all hunting and fishing in New Zealand is located at the NZTPO at Fenton and Haupapa Streets. He can give you the latest word on fishing and hunting guide costs, equipment and what is being caught or shot where with what.

There is a season on birds in the area and open season on pig and deer.

There are two excellent golf courses side by side. One is the 18-

hole par-70 Rotorua Golf Club called Arikikapakapa. Free lift if you hit in a volcanic mud pot.

The other is the Springfield Golf Course.

An interesting observation: New Zealanders dress in every costume imaginable on the street: high fashion, yesterday's fashion, no fashion, gum boots, bare feet, overalls and torn sweaters, three-piece suits and jump suits. But on the New Zealand sports field you will dress according to the rules . . . or you don't play.

Like the immaculate whites on the bowling green.

A sign at the first tee at the Springfield Golf Club warns "Prohibited Dress. Men: No blue denim jeans, joggers, walking shorts with short socks. Women: No blue denim, short shorts or sun dresses."

River rafting is big in the area.

New Zealand River Runners' Neil Oppat claims to have taken 45,000 people rafting on 13 different rivers, "and we expect that number will double over the next few years."

Favorites around Rotorua are the Wairoa River, the Rangitaiki, the Tongariro, and the Motu. Rafting adventures can last an hour-and-a-half to four days, depending upon the number of thrills you want to tuck in.

The Grade 5 runs which, in North America, are defined as very dangerous are promoted because they want participants to know that this is an exciting trip—not dangerous, he claimed, but exciting.

Places to Eat and Places to Stay

If you ask around Rotorua about new and different places to eat, you are steered towards the Aorangi Restaurant on Mt Ngongotaha overlooking the lake. We passed up the idea of taking our under-powered Chilly Bin up a mountain on a rainy night and went instead to the second recommendation, the Landmark Restaurant. (I must say I was tempted by the sign of the downtown "Chez Bleu Bon Appetit French Hamburger Restaurant.")

The Landmark Restaurant is on Fenton, the main thoroughfare of Rotorua, south of town near Whakarewarewa.

It is a former "mansion" built by a successful timber mill owner in the late 1800s. The finest rimu was used in constructing the two-storey house and its lookout tower.

The tables are set well apart in the spacious rooms with fresh flowers, lace table clothes, wine buckets, linen napkins—items missing a few years ago in Rotorua when the *best* restaurants offered only paper napkins.

There is still room for improvement. The young waiter pulled the plastic from around the cork of the wine bottle and stuck it into his pocket, pulled the cork and put the cork in his other pocket.

The food unfortunately matched the service. Maybe it was one of those nights. Never condemn a restaurant on a one-shot basis.

New places to stay abound in Rotorua.

Fenton Street is one long line of motels, many with private spas.

The international chains, Sheraton and Hyatt, have hotels in the city now. We gave Hyatt good marks for its exercise facilities and emphasis on fitness programs.

Travelodge has been refurbished and upgraded.

The pioneer and traditional hotel in Rotorua is the THC Rotorua International, redecorated periodically to keep its guests returning. It is the venue of the most popular hangi in town, that traditional baked-in-the-ground feast of Polynesia.

Bus loads of visitors had come to feast from the groaning boards of kumara, potatoes, salads, chicken, lamb, pork, ham on the bone, venison casserole, mussels, sashimi, even the salty local muttonbird.

Johnny, the emcee, introduced everyone by nationality. There were even two tables of people from Hawaii.

Maureen Kingi, the gracious mistress of ceremonies, led nineteen dancers through several Maori dance routines including, predictably, an audience participation number. I always get picked and I hate it—absolutely hate it. There should be an optional lapel tag for tourists like me reading *"I will not go on stage."*

Pressing noses together, *homi* or "the exchanging of the breath of life," is a Maori custom—part of the on-stage dance drill. Somehow I'm not comfortable rubbing noses with strangers.

Other hotels, slightly envious of the International's full house hangis, try to emulate the success with their own hangies, but not with the same results.

Weighty Problems

We had been on the road two weeks and I was suffering from pavloitis, the stretching of the belly that comes from eating too much cream-filled meringues topped with ice cream.

I really needed four weeks in the desert in a tent but, instead, we were going to move from the luxury of the Rotorua International to one of the most famous estates in New Zealand, Moose Lodge.

There is a growing movement in New Zealand of taking country homes and turning them into small, intimate, luxurious—and relatively expensive—country inns.

My file for years has contained a color brochure for Muriaroha on the Old Taupo Road outside of Rotorua. It shows a Victorian frame home, gracious with antiques and chintzy bedspread, a huge stone fireplace, green gardens, swimming pool, private launch. That sort of thing. The last tariff sheet I saw was NZ$150 per person. All meals, activities, wines, spirits included.

Never visited Muriaroha.

While researching our first book, we had passed the gates of Moose Lodge, famous then even as a private residence because of royal family visits, first Queen Elizabeth and her prince in 1953, and, in 1972, the Prince of Wales, Charles, and Princess Anne.

The lodge and its 17 acres of trees and gardens had been created by millionaire Sir Noel Cole, a successful contractor, who entertained international personalities frequently in his idyllic haven overlooking Lake Rotoiti, one of the most beautiful lakes in New Zealand.

The Moose, the estate's 28-foot launch, carried the royal family on a lake tour and was the only privately owned vessel in New Zealand to fly the royal pennant.

When Sir Noel died, the estate was bought by a farmer who gradually let the lovely house and grounds run down, a steady deterioration witnessed by Noeline and Errol Officer en route to and from their vacation house down the lake road.

They took over the estate, spent six months with a corps of tradesmen renovating the house and grooming the grounds, and opened the lodge as a country resort and executive retreat in April, 1985.

"You are ten minutes from the airport," Errol Officer told me over the telephone.

Another New Zealand ten minutes. I wondered about setting up emergency rations of hot coffee and sandwiches for the drive from Rotorua to the lodge.

Shockingly, ten minutes after we passed the Rotorua airport, we were at the gates of the lodge. It was the first and last honest "ten minutes" we were to hear in New Zealand.

Our weather had not been the best. Miserable, would be the better word. Now, suddenly, the sun came out as we drove down a long driveway on two concrete tire paths under an umbrella of pink cherry blossoms. As we made our way uphill to the house, falling petals fluttering around the Chilly Bin making a pink snowfall in the dappled morning light.

It was a royal entrance.

As we pulled into the white courtyard, Noeline, the manor house major-domo, came out to greet and escort us inside.

If first impressions set the tone for a resort, as the cherry blossoms had done, the immediate view on entering the mansion doubled the pleasure.

It couldn't have been better. We looked straight through the entry hall to the cozy living room framed by the rain-freshened, sun-lit, magic blue waters of Lake Rotoiti.

Errol Officer is an in-shape, middle-aged former financial officer who enjoys inn-keeping. I never saw him outside when he was walking. He was always running.

The Officers walked us through their project, explaining how they had gutted the inside of the lodge, added a breakfast room, a modern kitchen, two suites on the ground floor and had completely refurbished the building.

The interior decorator had retained the spirit of the 1930s.

Our room was a large corner room with a four-poster bed, our own bath. It was the suite occupied by the Queen and later by Princess Anne.

(There was no pea under the mattress.)

There were seven other double rooms but we were the only guests and had the pleasure of inspecting them all. On the lower ground-floor level is also a billiard room, a handsome, masculine den with a full-size table. Very posh, just the place for cigars and port.

A bungalow on an adjacent knoll had been converted into three luxury suites, an executive conference center was added next to the main house and a tennis court built by the lake.

The house has its own soda bore which is utilized for heating and for filling the open-but-roofed hot water pool, the "Wharekai," located at lakeside. The pool area is also a barbecue area for outdoor activities.

Nearby, *The Moose* rests in a boathouse. The yummy kauri launch, a throw-back to another, more gracious age, was being stripped and redone, hopefully with cane chairs on the afterdeck where men will be required to wear straw boaters and white flannels and women must don flowered frocks and sun hats with pale blue ribbons.

The Wharekai was dedicated to Te Rangi Hiroa, also internationally known as Sir Peter Buck, a famous anthropologist and pre-war managing director of the Bishop Museum in Honolulu.

Peter Buck, half Maori, wrote in one of his books that he had "inherited a mixture of two bloods that I would not exchange for a total of either. My mother's blood enables me to appreciate a culture in which I belong, and my father's speech helps me to interpret it."

Activities at the lodge include fishing from a runabout, which Errol and I did the following morning.

We trolled back and forth in front of the lodge which is a favorite feeding ground for the local rainbow but didn't scare up a bite. We then zoomed to the other side of the lake and cruised along the shoreline, pretty, pretty country uncluttered by vacation houses. Also uncluttered by any fish.

"We can offer guests golf in Rotorua. We keep a full set of Ping clubs at the lodge. Or helicopter trips into the backcountry to hunt or fish with a guide. Deepsea fishing is only an hour's drive away at Whakatane.

"But for busy people who want the best, we offer the tranquillity and the quality which make for a recharging of batteries and a renewed sense of living."

Our dinners were served in a family-type dining room with wines which were better than those offered by most restaurants. Breakfasts were served in a sun porch overlooking the lake with hot coffee and fresh juices on the sideboard and the morning newspaper at the plate. Eggs and bacon to order.

The refinishing of *The Moose* has been completed and is afloat in all of her former glory.

Moose Lodge accommodations and meals run about NZ$250

per person, plus drinks and wines.

We hated to leave and would go back anytime.

For more information write Moose Lodge, RD 4, Rotorua, New Zealand.

5. The Many Choices of The East Coast

Coromandel Peninsula . . . Golden Beaches . . .
The East Cape . . . Hawkes Bay
Wine & Earthquakes

The popularity of the Hamilton-Waitomo-Rotorua circuit has one drawback. It deprives visitors the pleasures of the East Coast.

If you can't squeeze the East Coast in on a return-to-Auckland drive, come back to New Zealand and include it in your next trip.

To enjoy the best of it, you should have your own car—or Chilly Bin. And review the rules of the Chilly Bin Non-Zip Contest because there are many delightful places to stop.

Awaiting you will be the variable beauty and gold-mining history of the Coromandel Peninsula, the bounty of the Bay of Plenty, the adventure of the East Cape, the abundance of wines and produce of Gisborne and Napier and Hastings.

The Lady Navigator: "Aren't we going to tell them about the East Cape?"

Answer: "Yes."

The Lady Navigator: "We flunked the East Cape, you remember. We didn't pick up five points on the East Cape."

Answer: "Yes, but we tried. You get twenty points for trying."

The Lady Navigator: "You keep making up new rules."

South from Auckland you take Highway 1 going through Bombay Hills whose roadside stands of fresh farm products are famous, then take Highway 2 cross country to Highway 25 which leads to the town of Thames, the gateway to the Coromandel Peninsula.

(See "Three Roads South" map on Page 58.)

When you fly into Auckland, you often get a good view of the peninsula off your left wing. You are looking at one of Aucklanders' favorite get-away-from-it-all playgrounds. Here the city citizens go to swim, play golf, deep-sea fish and hunt for pigs, hunt for gemstones, eat the crayfish, surf, sail and sleep in the sun.

Geographically, the peninsula starts in Thames and stretches farther north than Auckland. The Firth of Thames and the Hauraki Gulf form its western border, the Pacific Ocean its eastern border. The Bay of Plenty slides off to the east from its base.

Captain Cook landed here and explored the interior along what is now the Waihou River by longboat. He named the river Thames as well as the bay. The name of the river was later changed but the name Firth of Thames remained. Cook wrote that if colonization were considered he would recommend the Bay of Islands and the River Thames.

The peninsula's modern history started in the 1850s when the government offered a £1,000 reward to any person finding a "workable mineral find." It was an official attempt to restore population stability caused by residents rushing to the goldfields of Australia and California.

In 1851, a Coromandel lumberman dipped into a nearby stream for a drink of water, saw flecks of gold in the stream-bed and the riches of a $1,000 reward in his future. With samples from the river, he went to Auckland to claim his prize. Over 2,000 miners flooded the area immediately but no great strikes were recorded. The miners disappeared and the reward was denied.

Some fifteen years later, W.A. Hunt stumbled on a riverbank and dislodged dirt revealing a rich vein of gold. The discovery led to a payoff of bank bulging dividends for almost 100 years.

The fever rose again. Thames saw its population balloon to 20,000, twice that of Auckland which was already denuded by the transfer of government personnel to the new capital in Wellington.

Alluvial gold in the streams was quickly exhausted but rich ore-bearing quartz was found and the hills were honeycombed with mine shafts. The earth bounced to the rhythm of quartz-smashing batteries.

The batteries have long since gone but you can still see evidence of the goldmining era like the sign pointing to the Duke of Edinburgh mine. In a ten-year period, the Edinburgh paid the equivalent of half a million dollars per share of stock.

The 1980s Thames is a small quiet town with a population of

about 6,000 and the Thames Mineralogical Museum. If you are a rockhound, you shouldn't miss it.

Driving up the west coast of the Peninsula brings you to the tiny town of Coromandel, past dairy country, where there is another Coromandel School of Mines Museum in a small two-room bungalow with all sorts of odd knickknacks dating back to the original goldrush days. An unusual ten-point stop.

Country roads crisscross the peninsula for adventurous drivers but the best road is from the base of the peninsula, Highway 25A, leading across to Tairua, a holiday town featuring girls in bikinis, sun-bleached kids with surfboards, roadside stands selling crayfish and deep-sea fishing boats. Across the harbor is the new resort town of Pauanui with a golf course, holiday homes and its own little airport.

Farther north is the popular seaside resort of Whitianga at Mercury Bay, well-known among overseas anglers for its superb deep-sea fishing. Whitianga has two advantages. Its proximity to Auckland and to the high yield big game fishing grounds off Great Mercury Island. It is possible to leave Auckland in the morning and be tied into a marlin or mako shark or yellowfin tuna just off Great Mercury Island by mid-afternoon.

The 800-member Mercury Bay Game Fishing Club holds several world records. For a few dollars you can be a member.

The season is January through March. Reservations for a boat during peak season have to be made well ahead of time.

For information regarding golf, squash, bowls, skeet shooting, boat charters and dozens of white sand beaches—miles of them—check the Public Information Office on the main street.

A small passenger ferry shuttles visitors to the other side of the harbor where walks can be taken to Front Beach and Cook's Bay. Here the good captain anchored in 1769 to take a sighting on the planet Mercury, giving the inlet his name after the occasion.

His log of Saturday, 4th November 1769 reads in part: (sic)

"My reasons for puting in here were the hopes of discovering a good Harbour and the disire I had of being in a convenient place to observe the Transit of Mercury which happens on the 9th Instant and will be wholy Visible here if the day is clear."

On the southeastern tip the peninsula, another seaside resort, Whangamata, mushrooms every summer, led by the surfers.

You leave the Coromandel Peninsula at the little town of Waihi, the last gold producing town in New Zealand. Its famous Martha Mine, one the world's richest gold mines, closed down in 1952. During its 65-year history the mine produced $360 million in gold. As late as 1909 it was producing $5 million annually and paying 80 percent of that to its investors.

Today the mine shafts are flooded.

Plenty of Beaches In The Bay of Plenty

At Waihi you pick up Highway 2 and enter the Bay of Plenty, so named by Captain Cook because provisioning his ships in 1769 was so easy by trading with the abundantly supplied natives. It is interesting to note that Captain Cook estimated a local Maori population of about 10,000 people.

It is still a Bay of Plenty for the vacationer.

The entire coastline is a series of beautiful beaches enhanced by marvelous temperate weather and soft air. There is a tinge of a semitropical atmosphere here, both in weather and vegetation, and especially in the city of Tauranga's wide, palm lined streets.

The city is proud of its many gardens: The Strand Gardens, Robbins Park, Memorial Park, Tauranga Domain, among many.

The countryside grows all kinds of fruit. We stopped at a roadside stand before entering Tauranga and bought nectarines as big as peaches and peaches as big as cantaloupe. We then had a fruit salad lunch, a game of backgammon and a wee nap by a riverbank. No wonder it is such a desirable place to retire for many New Zealanders.

One special place we discovered is The Elms. The gardens are open to the public but the buildings can be seen only by making a private arrangement.

The Elms is a former mission residence, one of the oldest in the country, its chapel and a one-room library set in an expansive garden facing the harbor.

The main building was erected between 1838 and 1847 and, seen from the front, its white classic colonial lines, perfectly framed by majestic green trees, is simply an irresistible visual to photographers.

In one corner of the property is an English oak planted in 1838 and, in another corner, two towering Norfolk pines which were used by sailors as navigational aids when entering the Tauranga

Harbor. The trees were known as the "Archdeacon's Sentinels."

A poignant story revolves around the folding table on display in the chapel. The head of the mission hosted dinner for a number of officers on the eve of their battle of the Gate Pa. He buried all but one of them within the next few days.

Not far from The Elms is an old military cemetery which was built on an ancient Maori fort overlooking the harbor. Buried here are many of the dead from the Maori Land Wars including Captain John Faine Charles Hamilton after whom the city of Hamilton was named. The cemetery seems very old in the shadows of the surrounding trees. Very quiet. Sadly peaceful.

Gaiety and youth, however, are not far away.

Across the harbor from Tauranga is Mount Maunganui—known simply as The Mount—and the scene of glistening, oiled bodies, loud music, surfers and the smell of salt air mixed in with grilling hamburgers.

It is one of the most popular beach resorts on the North Island, partially due to the miles long, golden sands of Ocean Beach.

The Mount itself was a former Maori fort and, like Mt Egmont at New Plymouth, is the track for a traditional New Year's Eve dash to the top. The walk—or dash—to the summit is rewarded by superlative views.

In back of The Mount are golf courses, tennis courts, a marineland, launch trips to nearby Motiti Island and, far out, Mayor Island, another deep-sea fishing mecca.

A new addition, since our last visit, is Tauranga Historic Village, a recreated colonial town to be toured by horse and carriage clip-clopping along cobblestone streets.

On "live days" the village's 1877 locomotive is fired up for steam train rides.

The village covers 14 acres and includes a gold mining area, a Maori pa, barracks and a landlubbered war veteran, the steam tug *Taioma*. Village tearooms, of course.

Whakatane, about 60 miles south of Tauranga on Highway 2, was a landing site of early Maori explorers.

Kupe, the original Polynesian explorer, was said to have landed here yet the city took its name from the legend of a courageous chief's daughter. The story goes that the women were left on board one of the original migration canoes while the men investigated a cave in the river mouth.

The canoe lost its anchorage and started to drift out to sea. Now, the giant paddles were tapu, forbidden, to women but Wairaka, the chief's daughter seized a paddle in desperation saying, "Ka whakatane au i ahua" ("I will be a man"). The other women followed her example and they brought the canoe back to shore.

Whakatane, meanly manly, became the name of the subsequent Maori center. A statue to Wairaka is on top of Whakatane Heads. And we thought women's liberation was a 20th century phenomenon!

We left Moose Lodge for the two-hour drive to Whakatane early in order to beat the Saturday noon closing of the supermarkets prior to a three-day New Zealand holiday. It meant going back to the old style of zip-zip driving.

A rich stretch of forest known as Hongi's Track separates Lake Rotoiti and Lake Rotoehu.

It was along this route that the infamous chief, Hongi, came on a mission of revenge for the murder of a nephew.

Hongi portaged his war canoes through the forest, fought the Arawas in a bitter battle where, it was said, his life was saved by a metal helmet given to him by King George.

Watch for a fenced off tree on the north side of the highway about halfway through the track. The tree was planted, it is said, by a Maori chieftainess in honor of the place where she met her husband. If you stop and make a speech in honor of the tree and leave a fern branch as its base, you can go on your journey protected against evil spirits.

That should be worth twenty points.

Rather than miss our groceries in Whakatane, we missed the bonus.

Rotoma is the last in the series of roadside lakes, a quiet area, sparsely sprinkled with vacation homes.

The drive into Whakatane is through timberland, orchards and, of course, pastureland nourishing thousands of sheep and cattle.

The first time we drove into Whakatane we saw an island offshore dramatically bellowing white clouds of steam into the heavens.

"Heavens!" indeed, then asked the first person we saw "Does this happen all the time?"

No, not all the time, but with some regularity. White Island anchors one end of a volcanic rift that extends 120 miles from noble Mt Ruapehu at the south end of Lake Taupo through Mt Tarawera, the towns of Rotorua and Whakatane and beneath the Pacific to its offshore terminus.

It had erupted just an hour-and-half before our arrival. Captain Cook must have seen the same type of eruption because he named it White Island.

An attempt was made to mine sulphur but the effort was aborted in 1914 when an eruption blew ten miners out to sea.

You can drive to the Puketapu Lookout from which there are spectacular sweeping views of the Bay of Plenty. It is a sacred place to the Maori and you are asked to behave accordingly. The local Rotary Club has mounted a plaque reminding visitors that the ocean in front of them is called Pacific, meaning peaceful, and asking them to pray that the many countries bordering the Pacific Ocean will live in peace.

A variety of ten-point Non-Zip activities are offered the visitor.

Check into the local Public Relations office for information on trout fishing in one of the four nearby rivers, jet-boat trips up the Rangitaiki River, big-game fishing charters, available hiking tracks, and sightseeing flights over White Island. You won't believe the small airport; it looks as if it were designed for Disneyland.

Our mission, after shopping for the holiday weekend, was a trip which had been on our "hit list" for a long time.

While researching the first book, we played a name-your-favorite-scenic-drive-in-New Zealand" game with local Kiwis.

A strong favorite was always "The East Cape."

The Lady Navigator: "Are we really going to write this?"

Answer: "We must."

The East Cape, they had said, was still relatively "natural," meaning undeveloped. The road around the peninsula had been paved only a few years and we would see a part of the North Island that is still rugged and wild, our friends said.

Now that we were about to embark upon the East Cape escapade it would also mean sleeping in the Chilly Bin for the first time. No suites. No fruit from the manager. No bottle of wine

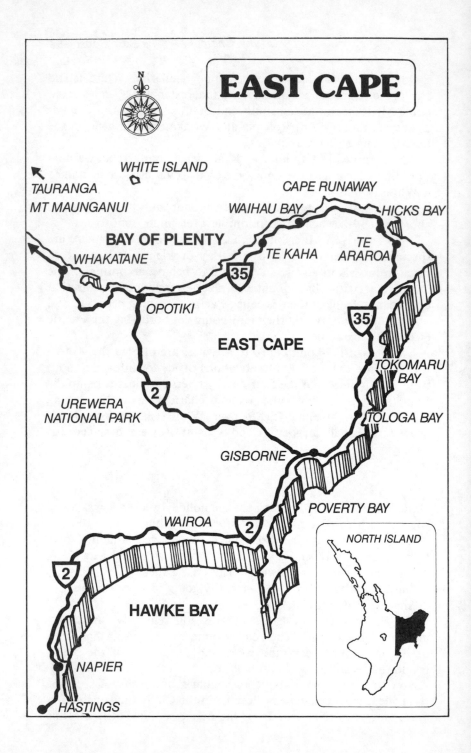

and cheeses. No crystal decanters of sherry.

We plotted caravan parks on our Newmans map as potential stopping places, laid in a $100 stack of groceries and another $100 worth of liquids—we were looking at a three-day weekend, remember—and headed out into the wilderness in our trusty Chilly Bin.

Opotiki, on Highway 2 between Whakatane and Gisborne via the Waioeka Gorge, is the northern gateway to the East Cape. A pretty farming town with a pretty golf course on the approaching outskirts.

We pulled into the main street looking for a restaurant. Being after twelve on a Saturday afternoon, nothing was open. Church Street, the main street, was lined with three Victorian hotels freshly painted. It looked peaceful . . . and empty.

It was all very much in contrast to the ghastly tragedy that took place in 1865. In 1859 a Lutheran minister came to Opotiki to establish a mission. His name was Carl Sylvius Volkner.

During a Maori uprising of a violent warring sect, the Reverend removed his wife to Auckland but made the mistake of returning to his parishioners. He was taken prisoner by the chief of the rabid sect and was subsequently hanged. His eyeballs were gouged from his head and eaten by the rebel leader, the blood from his severed head filled the chalice and the cup was passed among the frenzied warriors.

The Lady Navigator: "Charming. I think I'll throw up."

The church of St. Stephen the Martyr stands now tranquilly in the middle of Opotiki. The blood-stained chalice, Volkner's Bible and his colleague's book are on exhibit. Also, by the font are photographs including a bust shot of Kereopa, the sect's leader, who was ultimately captured and hanged in Napier.

The more pleasant aspects of Opotiki are long stretches of beach safe for swimming, surfing, spear-fishing and skin-diving.

The Lady Navigator: "Don't forget the rain."

After we left Opotiki, gusting winds slanted wild rains nearly horizontally across the road as we made our way along the shoreline of the East Cape. Our Chilly Bin rocked in the storm.

When the weather is terrible, you tend to lose your appreciation for sightseeing.

I can't remember much of the road except for the ancient, gigantic pohutukawa trees which were showing off their spring finery with red blossoms many of which were on the ground, victims of the strong winds.

We passed through the Motu Hills, eventually passing over a bridge crossing the Motu River and looked down on a river raft which had just completed what was probably a two- or four-day trip to the Pacific. Terrible weather for rafting.

We were relieved to reach Te Kaha, a former whaling village, and pull into an outlying caravan camp—NZ$11 per night—equipped with electrical "hot points." When I plugged into the hot point, all of the electricity in the Chilly Bin immediately switched over from the van battery to the 230-voltage national electrical system.

I then opened a side compartment on the van and turned on the valve which connected one of the two small butane gas cylinders to our range.

The water gauge inside of the cabin indicated we had sufficient fresh water.

The New Zealand caravan parks do not have plumbing connections for sewerage or fresh water.

An on-premise concrete block house provided showers, toilets and sinks. It was not the Bledisloe Suite. It was not even sparkling new but it was clean enough. I showered and shaved and remembered army days. (I preferred the Bledisloe Suite.)

We also hooked up our color television set, pan fried a "chuck" and listened to the wind howl. Over a glass of after-dinner port, we settled down to read the Australian Reader's Digest book, *Wild New Zealand*, one of our favorite reference books of the journey. Even if we couldn't see the scenery, we enjoyed reading about it.

The first Maoris, we learned, came to the Cape in three canoes. One canoe, legend says, returned to Tahiti to bring back kumara (a type of sweet potato), the staple root plant of the Polynesia people. The canoe distributed the plant among the tribes already in the Bay of Plenty.

The Maoris did not encourage the early European settlers who were not encouraged either by the ruggedness of the Raukumara Range, the backbone of the East Cape, or the thick underbrush of the Urewera Forest. Without roads, land communication was impossible.

The East Cape Maoris, however, quickly adopted the European

techniques of agriculture and were soon supplying Auckland and other settlements with maize and wheat delivered aboard native vessels.

The principal tribe of the area was the Ngati-Porou, an isolated, tough tribe. They refused to sign the Treaty of Waitangi, government forces had to be brought in to protect the whalers and the tribe fought the government troupes until 1865 when a peace treaty was signed.

Today the Maoris own about 27 percent of the East Cape and form half of its rural population. You see carved Maori meeting houses throughout the peninsula.

Severe deforestation of the land by the few early European settlers who came to the Cape led to erosion of the soil and that part of the Cape facing the Bay of Plenty is considered as marginal agricultural land.

The interior country abounds in wild game: red deer, wild pigs and goats, possum and many birds.

The next morning a chilled wind was still blowing but the sun was battling to come through and warm our path ahead.

We drove up to Whangaparaoa Bay, once known as the "Bay of Whales." At the foot of the bay we left the highway and cut back into Waihau Bay to inspect a tiny enclave consisting of a pier and boat ramp, one general store and post office and a nine-room hotel, the Waihau Bay Lodge, with a licensed restaurant. It was just about as far away from the world as you could get. I bought two six-inch lobsters from the proprietor for NZ$9 and got back on the highway.

The Whangaparaoa River enters into the bay of the same name. That morning muddied waters extended almost a mile from shore, the result of the heavy rains.

The cape we would see in the distance was Cape Runaway so named by Captain Cook after he encountered five large war canoes approaching him with ready-to-fight occupants as he rounded the cape. The steady Captain ordered a charge of grapeshot fired in front of the canoes. When the cannons thundered and black smoke rose from their mouths and the water rippled with scattered shot, the Maoris—witnessing magic—turned to shore paddling furiously to save their lives.

It was Sunday and there was a great deal of activity around all of the Maori communities we passed through that day, including teams of rugby players preparing for warfare in their own way.

One thing was obvious to us, the occupants of the only campervan on the road, and that was the fact that we were not surrounded by members of the chamber of commerce. When we waved and smiled at the local Maoris, no one smiled or waved back.

Perhaps the attitude is consistent with the history of the Cape and the antagonism the Maori had toward the European.

The road cuts inland to emerge again at the north extremity of the cape at Hicks Bay—named after the lieutenant on Cook's *Endeavour*—which is a popular summer camping area with surfing and fishing to occupy the vacationers.

We thought we would spend the night at Te Araroa, the next seaside village but it was not yet noon and the town was closed. We pushed on through but not until we paid a visit to what is estimated to be the largest and possibly oldest pohutukawa tree in the country. Named "Te Waho-o Rerekohu," meaning the mouth of Rerekohu, it is a magnificent monarch with twenty-two trunks and a girth of over twenty feet. Our reference book said the huge, twisted, wind-tortured tree was six hundred years old but the sign at the tree claimed only three hundred years.

Cutting inland again across the next tip of land, we paused briefly at Tikitiki which boasts the most eastern pub in New Zealand—it was closed—and is also the locale of a caravan camp—it was empty.

The Lady Navigator: "What are we doing out here?"

Answer: "We are exploring."

The Lady Navigator: "I'd rather be reading a book at Moose Lodge."

We were now heading south. We stopped at an open field where dismounted horsemen were tossing what looked like a soft ball among themselves and catching it with long sticks attached to netting cups, much like lacrosse rackets. The game obviously was a form of polo substituting the netted stick for a mallet.

But for the sheet of rain that came, we might have waited for the game to start. We noted here and in other Maori communities on the Cape the dominance of painted ponies.

The luxury of our Chilly Bin was demonstrated when we pulled off the road under a cluster of trees by the Mangaoporo River. The Lady Navigator made a fresh lobster salad, I pulled the cork on a Pinot Noir Blanc and then, after lunch, while the wind blew and the rains came, we stretched out on cushioned benches to zzzzzzz.

We continued south to Tolaga Bay and found an oceanside caravan park, plugged in our electricity, turned on the gas to make a pot of tea, turned on the television set and, there, sitting out in the middle of nowhere, we watched an informal interview with Prince Charles and Princess Di.

It was a biter wind that blew and a cold night outside but we were snug in our campervan between the automatic heater and our Woolrest which paid for itself those first two nights.

Tolaga Bay is historically significant because it was here that Captain Cook spent a week and Banks and Solander, the famous botanists, made their first significant collection of New Zealand flora.

Cook found a supply of water here and so did we. We needed to top up with diesel and fill our water tanks. In the village station as I was putting in water I suddenly saw a sign saying that the water was not potable.

"Naw, it should be all right," said the proprietor. "These last rains have lifted the water table and you shouldn't have any trouble."

I stopped filling the tanks immediately. But, he was right, we didn't have any trouble.

The Bay of Poverty, According To Captain Cook

The main route from Whakatane to Gisborne on Highway 2 turns upland at Opotiki, follows the Waioeka River to its head, crosses the divide then meanders downhill to Gisborne.

A highlight of the drive is the delightful forest of the Urewera National Park, the third largest of New Zealand's national parks and a place which we have always wanted to explore, a place nearing the top of our "to do" list. Friends of ours who conduct "wilderness" hikes in Hawaii took a five-day hike in the Urewera Forest, accompanied by Maori commercial hosts, and loved the experience. A better understanding of the Maori culture is one of the worthwhile results, they reported.

We approached Gisborne through fields of sheep and cattle and vast plantings of grapes, the largesse of a fertile land.

Ironically, Captain Cook labeled the area "Poverty Bay." He

left two days after landing, highly unimpressed. He wrote in his log:

"We weighed anchor and left this unfortunate, inhospitable place, on which we bestow the name of Poverty Bay, as it did not afford a single article which we wanted, except a little firewood."

This wealthy agricultural community calls itself the "City Of Bridges" (three rivers empty into the ocean at Gisborne) and the "First City In The World To See The Sun Every Day" (because of its juxtaposition to the international dateline). Nearby Napier uses as its slogan "The First *Principal* City In The World To See The Sun Every Day."

Gisborne is indisputely the locale of Cook's first landing in New Zealand.

A monument marks the spot above Kaiti Beach near the piers of Gisborne's extensive waterfront. Beneath a statue of the famous navigator a plaque bears this inscription: "This Memorial is erected to commemorate the first landing in New Zealand at Poverty Bay of Captain Cook on Monday, 9th October, 1769." (The original plaque dated the landing as 8th October, an error since corrected.)

You can walk or drive to the top of Kaiti Hill for sweeping vistas across Poverty Bay to Nick's Head, the land first sighted by an *Endeavour* cabin boy named Nick.

In driving up the hill you pass the Poho-O-Rawiri Meeting House, the largest Maori meeting house in New Zealand and heralded by some guide books as one of the best examples of Maori carving.

One of the tourist sights in Gisborne is the dwelling at the corner of Childers Road and Cobden Street which is made out of the bridge deck of the "Star of Canada," a wrecked vessel.

The Unusual City of Napier and the Hawkes Bay

It was a hard up-and-down twisty road to Napier.

The recent violent rains had created mudslides necessitating detours and one-way passages. Road conditions are constantly improving in New Zealand but there are still patches of difficult driving.

As a result of road maintenance, we didn't arrive in Napier until after four and then got lost looking for Kennedy Park, one of the new breed motel and motor parks springing up throughout New Zealand. You can rent sleeping arrangements your way: at a tent or caravan site, in a bare bones cabin (room only), a tourist flat with full kitchen and bath facilities (you rent linens) or in a first-rate motel unit.

In Kennedy Park's 17.5 acres, there were playgrounds and conference rooms, a television lounge and restaurant, a convenience store and, best of all, a rose garden.

Kennedy Park was the most pleasant, best run camper park we found in New Zealand. We liked it so well, we stay three nights.

On our first night, when it was pointed out that the dinner table was without decoration, the Lady Navigator disappeared into the rose garden—it literally was just over the hedge—and returned with a deep royal red Queen Elizabeth, an orangy Kentucky Derby and a variegated pink to red Bienvenutu.

There is a lot to enjoy in Napier and in next door Hastings, all part of an area called Hawkes Bay.

One of the most unusual attractions in a season which goes from October to April is the Cape Kidnappers sanctuary for 15,000 black-eyed gannets on a dramatic promontory at the south end of Hawkes Bay.

You can take a "Gannet Safari" by driving out to Summerlee Station, a high country farm carrying 7,500 ewes and 600 breeding cows, and joining an 18km safari to Cape Kidnappers. You will be only a few feet away from the swooping, diving for fish or the preening of the "dance of the gannets," the breeding ritual.

We didn't visit the colony on our first visit and it was high on our list to do on the new visit. We didn't make it on the second visit either. Lunch and dinner meetings cut across our schedule. It is back on our yet-to-do list.

The first place we go in any New Zealand town is the Public Relations Office. Napier's office is centrally located on the Marine Parade. They have always had an abundance of promotional literature. One delightful pamphlet devoted to "Art Deco Napier" is typical.

Napier awoke in the early 1980s to the fact that it had a rather unusual tourist attraction in its art deco architecture. Napier is the leading example in the world of a city built almost entirely in the style of the '20s and '30s.

The "Art Deco Napier" pamphlet takes the visitor on a short but fascinating walk of the city built—rather rebuilt—under somewhat tragic circumstances.

On February 3, 1931, shortly before eleven on a sunny morning, Napier exploded under a sledge hammer of the first of a series of heavy earthquakes that continued for ten days with many subsequent quakes as violent as the first. What the shaking earth did not destroy, devastating fires did.

The city disappeared. Over a hundred lives were lost.

But the spirit of the Napier citizenry was undamaged. They set about clearing and rebuilding with determination. All of the new buildings were created in the pseudo-Spanish, stripped classical Art Deco style.

The handful of buildings which had withstood the earthquake were rebuilt to reflect the same architectural theme.

Another hidden blessing of starting fresh was that all the streets were widened and the utilities went underground.

The result, then and now, is that Napier is a city of a singular design, an architect's dream come true, consistent in scale, materials and visual style.

Before taking the self-guided walk, spend 20 minutes watching the audio-visual backgrounder on the 1931 earthquake at the Hawkes Bay Art Gallery and Museum.

When we attended the slide show in the basement of the museum, we sat with a tour group led by a Napier citizen.

He related to his audience how, when the local banks lost their records as well as their buildings and asked depositors to report the amount of money they thought they had in their accounts, the reported estimates balanced with the banks' totals. Isn't that a marvelous story?

"You couldn't do it today but you could then," added the tour director.

We took the 45-minute self-guided city walking tour and enjoyed a Napier that had been there but that we had never seen before, a city decorated with stepped beams, etched glass designs, friezes, geometric patterns including lightning flashes and rising suns and leaping deer and dancing women—all motifs established by the International Exposition of Modern Decorative and Industrial Arts held in Paris in 1925.

A very unique experience.

The museum devoted a major space to William Colenso, the printer we first encountered in Paihia, in the Bay of Island. It was as if we have run into an old friend. We learned in Napier that Colenso was born in Cornwall, England in 1811 and was apprenticed to a printer, bookbinder and stationers at the age of fourteen. In 1834, he arrived in Paihia and printed the first Maori language book, including a translation of over 300 pages of the New Testament.

He moved to Hawkes Bay in 1843 where he established a missionary station at a time when there were no other white settlers in the area. He was married the same year and was ordained in 1844.

In 1853, Colenso was almost destroyed by scandal when a mission station assistant bore him a son. His wife, Elizabeth, left him and his missionary license was revoked.

Colenso moved to Bluff Hill in Napier and became active in politics representing the Maoris—he spoke their language fluently—and the small business people. He was active in education, was an inspector of schools, secretary of the philosophical society and a contributor to the botanical society. A remarkable man for all seasons, highly respected. He died in 1899.

Another pleasant Napier visual is the Marine Parade, a wide two-mile park along a waterfront lined with tall Norfolk pines. A segment near the city center includes various visitor oriented attractions: a marineland and aquarium, a Lilliput Village, a bandstand, gardens, fountains, swimming pool, children's rides, flower clock, etc.

There is the ever present Nocturnal Wildlife Centre, open from 9am to 4:30pm with artificial night lighting to view the national bird.

A brochure reads: "The Nocturnal Wildlife Centre exists to let visitors see the world as the sun dims. A secondary goal is to stimulate breeding by the creation of the most natural environment possible. So come and see where they do-it-the-dark." (!)

One landmark in the gardens is the statue of Pania of the Reef, a bare-busted bronze of a legendary maiden who belonged to the Sea People, fell in love and came to live with a mortal on land, but when she returned for a last visit to her home in the reef, the Sea People trapped her in underwater caverns so that she could never return to her human lover.

The earthquake helped create additional land for the Marine Drive which was already underway in 1931.

Much of the tidal land on the north of Napier was uplifted from six to eight feet. Where there used to be a yacht club, there is now the airport plus much rich agricultural land.

It would be in keeping with the *upgraded* theme of this book to report in Napier the usual swell of new, exciting restaurants found in most parts of New Zealand. We didn't find any—and we'll probably get a stinging letter from someone in Napier.

In a previous visit we had dined at the traditional Masonic Hotel on the Marine Parade in an old-fashioned turn-of-the-century dining room with potted plants, a bandstand, a high ceiling and a fixed menu that included soup, salad, fish, main dish, dessert. Coffee and liquors were served in the lounge after dinner.

Gone. The Masonic Hotel has become a Cobb & Co restaurant, a large chain found throughout New Zealand and Australia whose history is more interesting than the food.

Freeman Cobb was an enterprising young American who saw Australian miners pushing their wheelbarrows from Melbourne to Ballarat. He founded a successful coaching company using drivers from Wells Fargo and American Express.

He started a similar coach service in New Zealand when the gold rush started in the South Island's Otago. Coach service mushroomed into inns and inns into the present-day restaurants.

One restaurant which received a star from us was the Lord Tennyson Restaurant in the Tennyson Hotel because it had a note on the menu—a step forward in New Zealand—that said, "Our chef advises that the longer a steak is cooked the tougher and smaller it gets. There is no juice left in a well-done steak." Bravo!

The wine steward in the restaurant also told us that Mission Wineries' Tokay d'Alsace (Pinot Gris) was one of New Zealand's most popular wines. When he worked for a large company in Wellington, any staff member on a business trip to Hawkes Bay was instructed to bring back a case or two. The wine was so popular that local residents were restricted to a two-bottle purchase.

Which leads us to wine touring.

Another pamphlet we recommend is "Tread the Wine Trail"

with maps describing nine wineries in the region.

We hit only three: McWilliams Winery and Mission Vineyards in nearby Taradale where we sampled and bought a few bottles for the road and Vidals in Hastings where we sampled the grape over lunch.

The McWilliams Hospitality Cellars is large and first class in keeping with the reputation of one of New Zealand's largest wine makers.

The Taradale facility was built to cater to vineyard buyers. Special McWilliams limited editions are sometimes released exclusively from Taradale.

On the other hand, the Mission Winery is sort of old shoe in keeping with the secular nature of the establishment, one of the first formal wineries in New Zealand, where the Fathers and Brothers of the Society of Mary study learned writings—and make good wine—which they have been doing in Hawkes Bay since 1851.

Being traditionalists, they crushed grapes wearing wood sabots until 1898.

We toured the winery a long time ago when Brother John was the chief winemaker and we found him disgorging the top of champagne and putting in the sugar-brandy adder by hand, a one-man operation which he was performing in peace and quiet.

It was literally a 'bottled-on-Thursday-sold-on-Friday' operation.

Brother John had been transferred to Christchurch and the winery no longer produces champagne.

We picked up a bottle of Tokay d'Alsace and pushed on.

Hastings is less than twenty minutes from Napier, a farm city, laid back, but the scene of the important Hawkes Bay Agricultural and Pastoral Show. The Agricultural refers to farm produce and Pastoral refers to livestock. An A&P show in New Zealand is a combination of county and state fairs with races, all kinds of competitions involving manual skills, exhibits, beer gardens, fun rides, etc. A big social event of the area.

If you are interested in farming, Hawkes Bay is a good place for overnight farm stays or farm tours, easily arranged by the local public relations office.

Hastings is also the locale of Vidals Vineyard Bar where we

joined two members of the Daimler Club for lunch. The Lady Navigator, being the owner of a 1955 "drophead" (convertible) Daimler, belongs to Daimler Clubs in New Zealand and in England. She bought her car in London in 1976, shipped it to Honolulu, where it was repainted, refinished, reupholstered, rechromed, and re-topped—a jewel that stops traffic.

Our friends, the Tolleys, also had a 1955 convertible Daimler.

Vidals is most satisfactory. It is a large complex including a pottery and gift shop, a wine bar, a "Barrel Room" where the walls are made of giant barrels—a natural setting for good food—and it is good. A recommended place to go.

For desert, the Tolleys took us to a downtown local ice-cream parlor, Rush-Munro's Ice Cream Garden, which is famous in Hastings. Try the passion fruit. A ten-point find.

After lunch, we stopped by Fantasyland, a Disneyesque park created for children and supported by the City Council. It is charming.

So are the Hastings golf courses.

A quiet sensible productive corner of New Zealand.

You can continue down the east coast, actually inland on Highway 2, through Waipukurau and other small towns to the capital city of Wellington.

Or you can cut back to Lake Taupo, a magnet for fishermen, and stay in one of many motels.

The Lady Navigator: "I prefer Huka Lodge."

Or a public campground—.

The Lady Navigator: "Forget it. Huka Lodge."

Or the THC hotel at Wairakei.

The Lady Navigator: "Huka Lodge."

Or the most expensive accommodation in New Zealand, Huka Lodge.

The Lady Navigator: "You got it."

6. Lake Taupo And Surroundings

Huka Lodge . . . Famed Fishing . . .
Challenging Golf . . . Volcanic Skiing

Heavenly fish, heavenly golf, heavenly Huka Lodge.

The new international elegance to be found in upgraded New Zealand outside of Auckland is best exemplified by the Huka Lodge, a couple miles north of Lake Taupo.

A young (thirtyish) Dutch businessman, Alex van Heeren—steel and shipping—settled in Auckland and bought the old Huka Lodge as a hobby, removed the old lodge, constructed a new main building to house a library and fireplace, lounge and dining room, breakfast bar, kitchen and office, and, in a series of small chalets, created 17 suites, all overlooking the green flowing Waikato River as it leaves Lake Taupo. A heavenly setting.

The rooms in the guest units are large and quietly elegant in understated tones of grey and peach. Your giant bed is draped decorously with mosquito netting. Wicker lounge chairs and a sturdy desk and chair lend a country air. No radio or television, or even telephone unless requested. That's not what you need at Huka Lodge.

The two-room bath/dressing room facility is designed to make women squeal with pleasure. First there is generous skylight which not only floods the area with natural light, it fills the roof with greenry—redwood, fir and pine. Each bath has terry towel guest bathrobes, heated towel rails, electric hairdryer.

A wooden deck outside faces the river where wild ducks land and rainbow trout occasionally break the surface sending round ripples through the water.

Behind the guest cottages is an all-weather tennis court and a sauna pool.

The routine is for guests to gather around the fireplace for an hour of cocktails and hors d'oeuvres—part of the package—and sip and chomp and chat. Nice. Pick out your wine—not part of

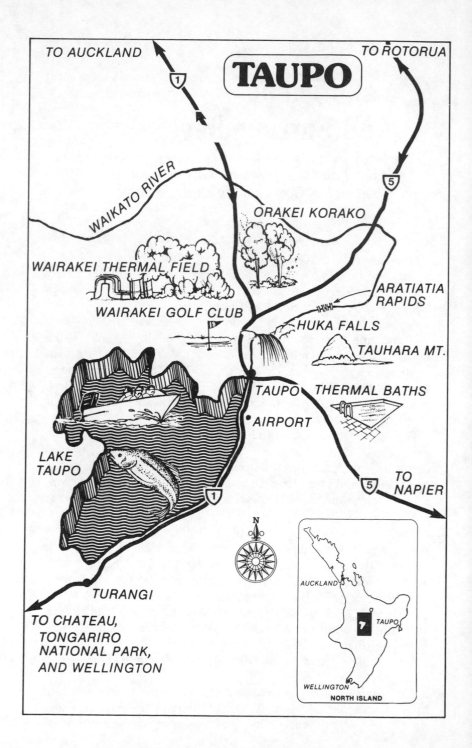

the package—from an excellent selection of New Zealand, Australian, French wines. Were there California wines? Not in my notebook.

Guests, now on a first name basis, are summoned to dinner either in the library (small groups, up to eight) or in the larger dining room. Each course is announced by a gracious hostess.

I asked Monique Engels, the hostess serving us, to send me a menu for a reminder. It was a superb dinner starting with a scallop and paw paw salad (We call it papaya). A rich pumpkin soup had been topped with a thin line of cream and laced with Madeira. Oysters Parmesan. Honey dew sorbet—to cleanse the palate. Venison St. Hubert, very tender, not gamey, very rich, graced with Marquis potatoes, asparagus mousseline, carrots a l'orange. The desert was a strawberry mousse followed by coffee, and petits fours, and liqueurs served in the lounge. Very civilized.

Our fellow guests were an opinionated California doctor and a likable sophisticated New York couple seeing New Zealand for the first time. The New Yorkers caught their first rainbow trout the next day.

Americans and Australians comprise the bulk of the guestlist but there has been surprising support from New Zealanders.

(The price is about NZ$500 a day per couple.)

Prices do not exclude characters. Monique described one New Zealander who wouldn't join the guests at dinner but ate alone standing up in the kitchen, reading the newspaper, and drinking a bottle of Chateau Margaux.

Breakfast is as delightful as dinner. There is a breakfast bar with high cane chairs padded in plaid fabric to match the breakfast china pattern. Men notice those things too.

You order whatever pleases your fancy. Try the wild boar sausage.

The snob appeal of Huka Lodge goes back to the '20s when it was founded by a young Irishman, Alan Pye. Although conditions were spartan—guests slept in canvas covered slatted-floor accommodations—the famous dry fly-fishing drew members of the English royal family, American celebrities such as Charles Lindbergh and James A. Michener, and government and business leaders from all over the world.

Fishing rods were named for Alan Pye as was an American angling club.

We knew Huka Lodge when it was still spartan but had progressed to frame cottages . . . before it all disappeared under the magic wand of van Heeren.

The only holdover from those days is a fat cat which we last saw purring contentedly on the lap of Monique in the lounge.

Save enough money for at least one night at Huka Lodge. Well worth the experience. It is the way you deserve to live.

Are There Still Rainbow Trout in Lake Taupo?

You'd better believe it.

We went out on one of Simon Dickie's launches, the *Awatea*, captained by Miles Johnstone, a most talented guide, from the boat harbor at Taupo and hooked five fish around three pounds each in less than two hours.

Two fat trout we kept for eating. Two we released, in keeping with the fishing industry's new emphasis on conservation. One got away without permission.

Simon Dickie is a former cox of an Olympic gold medal New Zealand eight and well-known throughout the country. He has been so successful in building the South Pacific Sporting Adventures fishing fleet on Lake Taupo and in packaging hunting and fishing options via launch, aircraft or foot that the government borrows money from him. (He hoots in protest whenever we say this.)

He is a delightful pixie of a man who gets clients what they want—fish and game.

His prices are relatively modest.

If you have the time and a small party of people and can get a reservation, we strongly recommend an overnight fishing expedition to Western Bays on the lake with Simon.

Our trip, many years ago, is still one of our favorite adventure memories of New Zealand.

South Pacific Sporting Adventures, P.O. Box 682, Taupo, New Zealand. Telephones: 89-680 or 88-115. Taupo's area code is 074.

Lake Taupo is the largest lake in New Zealand, an expanse of 239 square miles, and a thing of beauty as you approach it. You come over a crest of a hill and there it is, an ocean perfectly reflecting three giants of nature: Mt Ruapehu, its 9,000-foot peak perpetually wrapped in a snow shawl, Mt Ngauruhoe, frequently belching smoke from its volcanic top, and the manly but tranquil Mt Tongariro.

The beauty of Lake Taupo is also enhanced by the action that flutters on its surface: colorful sail boats and power boats and motor launches, water skis and windsurf boards. And by the float planes that take off from the pier near the boat harbor lifting sightseers to bird's eye heights.

Rainbow trout were introduced in the lake in 1897 and its high volume of plankton in the lake fed the smaller fish which in turn provided food for the larger fish. The rainbow grew to monstrous sizes and monstrous numbers. At one point the government had to seine tons of rainbow out of the lake to keep the fish population under control.

I must tell you two quick fish stories.

Everybody in the world had heard about the legendary New Zealand rainbow, even terrible fishermen like me. I was attending a boring travel conference in Australia and suddenly got the itch to tie into one of New Zealand's famous trout. I called a friend in Auckland telling him of my ambition, asking . . . if I sneaked out of the conference a couple of days early, could he?

This friend, Berney Bookman, is one of those people to whom a hint is a signal for immediate action: itineraries, costs, schedules, hotel reservations, plane reservations, guides. Ticket counters light up at the mention of his name.

One early morning I was in Sydney, the afternoon in Auckland, that evening in Taupo where I was met by Tony Jensen, a famous guide, driven to Turangi, his home base at the south end of the lake, ensconced in a motel, and the next morning driven to a nearby Maori-owned lake, Rotoaira.

As I have said, I am not even a fair fisherman. I can't pound a nail, fix an engine, or catch a trout. The talents go together.

In two and a half hours I had caught the limit, ten at that time, all over 14 inches long. It was stunning.

You know the greatest feeling in the world? Sitting in a boat, just bobbing there, not fishing but ego secure because the limit is already bagged. You are wearing slickers because there is a cold wind blowing and black rain clouds scudding overhead and you are drinking black coffee with one hand to get the hand warm and then shifting the cup to the other hand to warm it and nibbling on a thickly buttered scone, letting the crumbs melt in your mouth. You don't say anything and the guide doesn't say anything, and there you are with God and silence and the beauty of forest and water all around you and you have this deep contented feeling of the hunter-home-from-the-hills.

That's as good as life gets.

The next morning, on Lake Taupo, we again had the limit in the boat in half a day.

The first thing I did after setting up a base camp in Taupo the second time around was take the Lady Navigator fishing. She caught the first fish, the largest fish and the most fish.

It reminded Tony of one of his favorite fishing stories . . . an American client had come fishing every year for 25 years, sometimes with his wife who refused to fish despite his persistent pleadings. One glorious day she finally, if reluctantly, agreed. The beauty of the lake—pancake smooth—and the cloudless windless day may have persuaded her, Tony said.

She caught the first fish.

The husband was delighted.

She caught the second fish . . . the third fish . . . the fourth fish.

The husband, a skilled veteran of Taupo, had caught but one fish.

The wife, hooking into the eighth rainbow, exclaimed with joy, "Oh, look darling, I have another one."

Said the husband slowly and grimly: "Just-shut-up-and-pull-in-he-goddam-fish."

For years it has been one of our favorite family slogans.

Are there still fish in Lake Taupo?

In a 1985 study of Lake Taupo fishing, licenses totaled around 70,000 and grossed NZ$500,000.

The total number of fish caught in the lake and its feeding rivers exceeded 600,000.

The fishing rights to Lake Rotorua were bought by the government for a fixed price before the turn of the century.

But the chief of the tribe controlling Taupo, supposedly influenced by a Scot friend, said, "No, we want half of the revenue of the fishing licenses."

For years fishing produced no revenue for the tribe but today it benefits from an annual income of about NZ$250,000!

Does Taupo have anything other than fish? The question was

posed to Joseph Lane, the man in charge of the public relations office. "What is upgraded in Taupo?" we asked.

He bombarded us with material.

New buildings are everywhere including many time-sharing ventures.

New boats have been added to the lake.

New rafting companies are in business.

New activities, new attractions.

A leading sports event is the Mazda Taupo Cyclethon, a neat 100-mile race around the lake. It drew 100 riders in 1983 and over 700 riders in 1985. Circle the last Saturday in November if you are interested. You don't have to make the whole 100 miles; there are refreshment stations every 16km and vehicles to take you back to Taupo if you want to quit.

Contestants receive certifications, computer placements, substantial randomly awarded prizes, free T-shirts and a final night social.

An international fishing tournament on the lake for the biggest and best conditioned rainbow in April attracts over 800 eager fishermen.

Another annual April event, a privately organized competition, is the New Zealand Big Three Challenge. Contestants stalk a trophy sika deer in a four-day hunt, go for the prize game fish in a four-day fishing charter, and wind up with a two-day fishing expedition on Taupo's lake and rivers. Interested? Write Big Three Challenge, P.O. Box 761, Taupo.

Or, Wilderness Safaris can take outdoor buffs on one- to five-day horse treks, river rafting, tramping, hunting, or fishing adventures. Contact the same address as Big Three Challenge.

If all that sounds like more work than fun, pick up a pamphlet detailing 29 different walking trails around Taupo, go at your own speed and commune with nature.

Honey Village, just north of the lake, is a unique tourist shopping complex with multiple attractions. It is to Taupo what the Herb Garden is to Rotorua: refreshingly different. There is a "honey store" with live bees and hundreds of honey products, many of them unique, a Maori arts and crafts store, an active pottery kiln and showroom, a jade design center, a woolen products shop, of course . . . and even a helicopter concession.

On the other side of the highway is another new attraction:

Huka Village. Huka Village has twenty buildings, some of which house crafts stores and food concessions. Carriage rides behind Clydesdale horses is a feature.

Craters of the Moon is a spectacular thermal area between Taupo and Wairakei in an isolate setting—don't leave your valuables in the car—and, at Wairakei, there is an electrical power generating thermal field that looks as if it came out of a Star Trek movie.

The THC Wairakei Hotel is also there, perpetually engaged in its annual upgrading. We were told by other hotel operators that THC would like to level the whole property and start all over again, but the hotel enjoys a year-round occupancy of over 80 percent and they can't afford to close down for the two years required to build a new complex.

We stayed in one of the new villas, not unlike a one bedroom apartment, except the refrigerator is stocked with Continental breakfast makings and room service is provided.

Our Taupo fish caught with Miles Johnstone went to the kitchen, one for the hotel manager, the other for our dinner that night. Poached and covered with thin slices of lemon and bits of onion, ours was delicious.

The Lady Navigator wanted the recipe. The chef said, "No, I have to save a few for myself."

"Right," said the Lady Navigator, "And we don't tell you where we found the trout."

One reason that Wairakei has such a high occupancy rate is the popularity of the Wairakei Golf Course, considered one of the best championship courses in New Zealand.

Additionally, the hotel has a nine-hole family golf course.

Two eighteen-hole courses are available for guest play at the Taupo Country Club.

Another course is available at Turangi which even invites guests to play on club day—a rarity!

Thermal baths are popular. A modern facility replaced the AC Baths of our memory. "AC" stands for "Armed Constabulary." Presumably these baths once were reserved for the military. The DeBrett Hotel pools, also renovated, are available to non guests for a fee.

If you don't like to share your spa with strangers, Lanecove on Lake Taupo, features a private pool with every suite, a new upmarket concept.

Also at Taupo you shouldn't miss the botanical gardens about a mile off the highway south. Signs show you the way. The Waipahihi Botanical Reserve is a charming, hilltop garden created by professionally talented but amateur volunteers who spend many man-hours of loving care creating a delightful retreat with picnic tables and short walks. The spring azaleas and rhododendrons are especially beautiful.

South Taupo and More Fish Action

A few miles south of Taupo city you cross the mouth of the Waitahanui River where so many fisherman line up in early dusk to deepening evening to fly cast that is known as the Picket Fence.

A greatly improved highway takes you inland and around a bluff and back to where Hinemaiaia River empties into the lake. At the head of the river is Hinemaiaia Dam and a place where Brook trout have been raised successfully. The "brookies" couldn't survive the competition in Lake Taupo but do very well in the protected dam waters.

Vacation homes and campgrounds abound alongside the shore to Turangi, the little town that owes its existence to the construction of nearby hydroelectric works. After the dams and power stations were completed, the little town has won over some permanent residents and, today, continues to win recreational and fishing fans.

One continuing attraction is the Tongariro River which flows by the town and into the sea. Fished by the popular western writer Zane Grey in 1926 who declared it the best trout stream in the world, the Tongariro has tenaciously upheld its reputation ever since.

That 1985 fishing study indicated that almost one third of the license holders who fished Lake Taupo also tried their luck on the Tongariro which yielded just over 100,000 legitimate trout, a staggering figure. But another figure indicates that the average fisherman caught one fish per day.

There is no figure on poaching but it exists.

A popular place to fish is from a boat at the river mouth where it spreads like fingers on a hand into several outlets—Main Mouth, The Hook, First Mouth, Blind Mouth.

I've fished the mouth outlets and several of the river's famous pools. In Major Pool, I managed to catch a rainbow all by myself. The guide had gone into town to get lunch.

Another time, while fishing below the bridge, a gentleman angler hooked into a trout and—maybe because he heard my American accent—handed over his rod to me, the overseas visitor, insisting that I play and land the fish. Sportsmanship of the highest order.

The most popular lodge in the area among overseas visitors is the small, ten-unit Tongariro Lodge owned by Tony Hayes, a fishing guide, and Margaret Coutts, a superb chef. The cozy main lodge lounge features a noble hunting dog and a fat lazy cat curled up in front of a noble fireplace. Its dining room opens onto the kitchen, a place where Margaret Coutts makes magic. This blond gregarious lady is a champion angler as well.

We suspect that people come to fish and stay to eat.

The uncut gem of a dining room called The Freshwater Admiral Restaurant is open to outsiders with reservations. If you don't stay at the Lodge, be sure and go by for lunch or dinner. Excellent.

We stopped by for lunch and Margaret whipped up homemade biscuits with blackberry jam, an avocado salad and crepes filled with a light, creamy mixture of ham and fresh asparagus.

"I find that Americans prefer spicy foods such as my home-made sausage and venison sausage," Margaret said.

The lodge had been opened three years prior to our visit but landscaping was still sparse. The separate cabins which the promotional literature calls "luxurious" are rather simple but clean with everything that a fisherman would need or want.

Boats and guides are available for hire. Tony Hayes has a fine reputation as a guide. He freely admits to getting lots of clients from the his mistaken identity with the famous fishing guide, Tony Jensen, now retired to Hawkes Bay.

Tony Jensen told us, "I couldn't do it anymore. To catch a trout on the Tongariro meant getting up before dawn and crawling through the brush and muck to find a private place on the river, and when you got there, there were already half a dozen fishermen in place."

Among the several pictures on the lounge wall is one of an Englishman who set the one-day record in March, 1911 when he caught 78 rainbows weighing an average ten pounds on Lake Taupo's Western Bays. He is shown with his valet. Somebody had to take all of those fish off the hook.

Also on the wall is an 8-pound rainbow caught by former USA president Jimmy Carter in February, 1984.

Tongariro Lodge is not too expensive—less than Huka Lodge and Moose Lodge—and when you add all of the meals from Margaret Coutts' kitchen that are included in the package, it is good value.

When we were there in October, all accommodations had been booked out for February and March—75 percent of the guests being American.

Write Tongariro Lodge, P.O. Box 278, Turangi, New Zealand. For restaurant or guest reservations call 7790.

The Turangi Visitors Center—an indication of the new importance of tourism to the town of nearly 6,000 people—has models of the hydroelectric works in the area and graphics pertaining to activities in the area. Among the many pamphlets and fishing recommendations you'll find a list of ten licensed boat operators and five registered guides.

One guide we had hoped to meet is a character called "Louie, the Fish."

"Louie, the Fish," according to Andrew Thomson of the Regent Hotel in Auckland, can *smell* fish when no one else can get the slightest whiff.

He was in Auckland at the time but normally works out of the lodging facilities of Alpine Active Adventurers whose accommodations for 120 are to be expanded by another 80.

The tours packaged by Alpine are mainly for the young, trekking, hiking and climbing in the summer. In the winter, the lodge is booked solid for the skiing at nearby Ruapehu.

We rounded the southeastern corner of the lake to stay overnight at Tokaanu Hotel, another THC facility. Unlike Wairakei, the old Tokaanu Resort Hotel had been completely removed and a new facility built in its place.

The hotel dealt in creative marketing, offering a "trout guaranteed" package for NZ$300, double or single, which included two nights accommodation, guide, boat, fishing rods, licenses and a guaranteed fish, or the NZ$300 was refunded.

Funny hotel. In our bath was a sign reading: "Notice. Attention Anglers. Please do not wear waders in the bath."

Another sign by an outside locker: "Notice. Attention Anglers. No fish over 40 kg are to be stored in this locker."

Guests are offered a "Back Pack Lunch" of chicken, cold cuts, cheese, fruit, tomato, and a Steinlager beer or soft drink.

One of the wall decorations in our room was a framed dry fishing fly. When we checked out, we received its duplicate and a card from the manager: "We hope you are hooked."

Highway 1 leading south from Turangi follows the Tongariro River and convenient signs point to the famous pools: Admirals Pool, Cattle Rustlers Pool, Barlows Pool, Birch Pool, Duchess Pool, Red Hut Pool, the Bank, Breakaway Pool.

Near the Upper Birch Pool is a turnoff to the Tongariro Trout Hatchery which ships millions of eggs and small fish to the lakes and streams throughout New Zealand.

You can make a small side excursion and visit the hatchery—win ten points in the Non-Zip program—where there is an underwater station. Here you can watch the trout in their natural habitat swimming and feeding.

A detailed series of pictures above the viewing glass illustrates the breeding cycle of the fish.

Thank the Lions Club of Turangi.

The First National Park In The Country

The highway belts the west side of the snow-covered peaks of Tongariro National park which was the first national park in New Zealand, established by an act of Parliament in 1894.

The action was initiated by the gift to the government of sacred tribal lands by a local chief, Te Heuheu Tukino, who feared that the land-grabbing settlers would take possession of the mountains where dead chiefs were buried.

Originally encompassing some 5,000 acres, the park today has tripled in size and is a recreational ground for hikers and climbers in the summertime and is tremendously popular with skiers from Auckland and Wellington in the winter. Two ski fields occupy the slopes of Ruapehu.

The volcanoes in the park are still active, the most recent eruption being on June 11, 1969 when hot lava and ash melted tons of snow and created an avalanche, called a lahar, which boomed down a slope where it was estimated 2,000 skiers had been only twelve hours earlier. The lahar's only damage was to take out a refreshment stand.

In 1953 a similar lahar caused by the dropping out of the bottom of Mt Ruapehu's crater lake, created a torrent of water which rushed down the mountainside and into the Whangaehu River where it tore out a bridge minutes before a northbound express train arrived.

The train toppled into the raging river and 151 lives were lost.

Center of the activity in Tongariro is the Chateau, a gracious, Georgian-styled establishment. We have stayed there and skied on Ruapehu—keeping one nervous eye on the smoking mountain tops. At the bottom of a third lift a sign reads: "You are in a lahar area. In case of an eruption, seek higher ground." Oh, we'd do that.

We have also gone around the mountain to ski the south side at Turoa above the village of Ohakune.

Turoa is a privately capitalized skifield representing millions of dollars of investment capital with a beginners area, T-bars and two major chair lifts to intermediate and expert runs which take you up to 7,600 feet, a restaurant, a cafe, a service center.

During a space of four hours we skied every run, peeling off layers of clothing until we were in shirt sleeves. This was in September.

During our last October trip through the park they were just closing doen the spring skiing on Turoa. Snow conditions are not predictable in unpredictable New Zealand, but the snow can last a long time.

Our itinerary did not call for a revisit to the heart of Tongariro National Park. Instead, we left Turangi on Highway 1, bound for Waiouru.

Between Turangi and Waiouru, an army center, is the Desert Road and one of the few places in New Zealand where you are surrounded by tussock and scrub brush. Good country for military exercises and maneuvers which is exactly what the area is used for.

Waiouru, being a military center, was the natural location for an army museum. It was opened by Queen Elizabeth on October 15, 1978 and named the Queen Elizabeth II Army Memorial

Museum. It contains a collection of weapons from times past to the present—Maori, English, American, German, Japanese—spears, muzzle-loading guns, Springfields, automatic guns, cannons, tanks, armored car carriers.

One display shows 17 Victorian Cross awards given to New Zealanders—one with a bar signifying a second award.

There are pictures and war posters and recreated war scenes.

One heart tugger is a canteen truck, camouflaged in desert colors, which served in the North Africa desert fighting during World War II. "Presented to the Maori Battalion as a token of love from the Children of the Native Schools of New Zealand."

The Ford V8 served the Maori battalion from El Alamein to Takrouna and besides the usual cigarettes and candies, it was stocked with tinned toheroas, mussels and muttonbirds.

After the war, the truck was brought back to New Zealand and toured the contributing schools.

One showcase recreates mementos of World War II prisoner of war camps in Germany. A sign from a German stalag commander stated firmly: "Escaping from prison camps has ceased to be a sport." Ex-prisoners of war are invited to sign their names, prison camps and dates on the rough wood that makes up the sides of the exhibit.

A small cafe is part of the museum—tea and scones—and the modern building has excellent and popular restrooms. Plan to arrive before or after the tour buses.

A small charge is made for admission to the museum which was built entirely of donated funds.

We started an addition to the Chilly Bin Non-Zip system in Waiouru for museums only. The person who found the most unusual item received a twenty-five cent award.

The Lady Navigator won with the children's canteen truck.

I had to pay her cash before we left the building.

7. The Southern Half Of The North Island . . .

New Plymouth to Masterton:
Dairy & Sheep Farms . . . The Rarest Museum
A New National Park At Wanganui

If it seems awkward to travel south to Masterton from Taupo via New Plymouth, let me tell you how it happened.

One morning in Honolulu, the telephone rang and this voice said, "My name is John Murphy and I am from New Zealand. My wife and I have just come back from touring North America. We took along a copy of your book, *How To Get Lost and Found In California And Other Lovely Places*, and I wanted to tell you personally how many good suggestions and how many good tips we got out of the book. We estimate that you saved three weeks in time and a lot of money, and I just had to call and say thanks."

Well!

No writer can get enough complimentary gush . . . so we asked the Murphys out for a beverage, and they accepted.

John and wife, Marion, are a handsome fortyish couple who own a farm outside of Hawera in Taranaki on the east coast of the North Island. He is a strapping ski buff, over six feet with enviable thick brown hair. She is winsome, attractive, almost blond. After our visit we received a valuable picture book of New Zealand from them and we exchanged telephone calls and letters.

In planning our current trip, Taranaki, the district around New Plymouth and Mt Egmont, was not on our revisit list. What would be new and upgraded in Taranaki?

We called the Murphys from the Waitomo Hotel, however, to ask if they could come for dinner, not realizing that Hawera, their home town, was three hours away. John was out. Marion declined and regretted that Taranaki was not on our route plan.

John called back, "There is no way, no way, you can come back to New Zealand and not come to Taranaki. I can arrange a

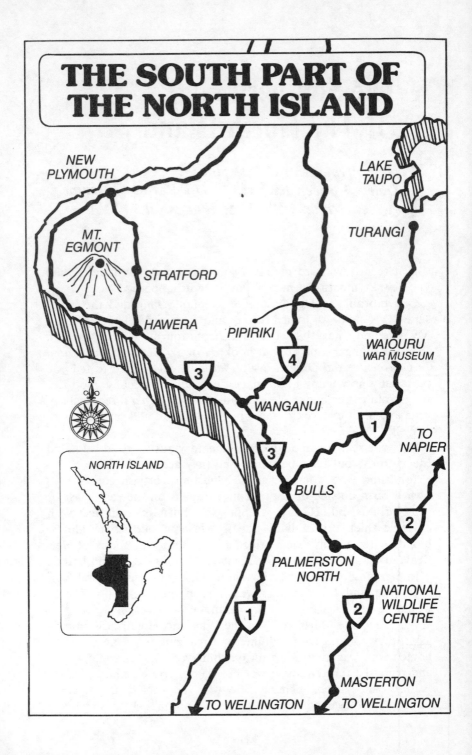

THE SOUTH PART OF THE NORTH ISLAND

NEW PLYMOUTH

LAKE TAUPO

MT. EGMONT

TURANGI

STRATFORD

HAWERA

PIPIRIKI

WAIOURU
WAR MUSEUM

3

4

N

WANGANUI

1

3

TO NAPIER

NORTH ISLAND

BULLS

2

PALMERSTON NORTH

NATIONAL WILDLIFE CENTRE

1

2

MASTERTON

TO WELLINGTON

TO WELLINGTON

flight around Mt Egmont that will be a bigger thrill than the helicopter ride on Kauai. I can take you to a farm like you have never seen. I can take you fishing on a lake that didn't exist the last time you were here. I can show you a one-man museum that you won't believe. No, no, it is unacceptable. Give me two days. Just two days."

That night at Waitomo I ordered a bottle from Mike, an outstanding wine steward, and he brought it back, opened it for tasting and when it was okayed, he leaned over and said, "The wine is with the compliments of a Mr. Murphy."

John Murphy carries everything in front of him with the power and delicacy of a Ruapehu lahar.

That's why we changed plans, already too tightly scheduled, to include Taranaki.

Now, departing the Army Memorial Museum, we would drive west to Wanganui, north to Hawera—a four-hour drive and a two day detour.

John met us in Hawera with a thumbs up sign, his basic greeting and parting signal, and we followed him out to the farmhouse, "Four Winds," a modern, two-storey building which had been completely rebuilt from an old farm house. (Remember, you always keep one old wall in New Zealand.)

Our updating about Taranaki started before we unpacked personal items from the Chilly Bin. The first thing we had to do was visit the milking shed because it was time for the evening milking session. It was different. The herd of 280 grass-fed Jersey cows lined up voluntarily to slip, one at a time, onto a revolving, circular platform and into one of the 36 slots, or bails.

A worker at an underground station attached the automatic milking machine to the cows' teats and the platform slowly turned. By the time a full circle was made, the milking was finished. A dash of water sprayed onto each cow's head was a physical signal for her to back out, again voluntarily.

"Mostly, it is to wake them up," John explained.

Around 4,500 liters of milk are pumped daily into adjacent stainless steel tanks from the herd. A milk truck with stainless steel tanks transfers the milk daily to a giant cooperative plant in Hawera where it is emptied into processing stainless steel tanks. The milk goes from cow to customer untouched by human hands, or even exposed to the open air.

The production of each cow is tabulated daily and when a cow's output fails to meet a production goal, she is replaced from a standby herd. The farm has a constantly growing calf and heifer population.

An average farm will maintain 130 cows and produce a total volume of milk worth perhaps NZ$80,000, with an additional income from the sale of calves and excess cows. Out of his income, he must pay a host of bills: utilities, veterinarian, equipment, interest on loans, etc.

One saving grace is that the dairy farmer gets a monthly check from his Co-Op where a sheep farmer might collect a check twice a year.

"It's not big biscuits," said John who has other property besides his "Four Winds" homestead. His new house and a new four-wheel-drive station wagon that had everything on it but wings indicated that his "biscuits" were slightly larger than the biscuits of other farmers.

A Different Sort of Museum

Before the advent of the giant cooperatives, the New Zealand countryside was sprinkled with small dairies designed to process the milk from surrounding farmers.

One of these old dairy plants has been converted into one of the rarest museums in New Zealand. John Murphy was absolutely right about the Tawhiti Museum.

It is a one-man operation, without telephone, and not open every day.

To see it—maybe—you must stop by the Hawera Public Relations Office. The Tawhiti Museum is located out in the middle of nowhere and you will need a map to find it. Or, the local PR person may call Nigel Ogle, the 32-year-old art teacher at the local high school who created the museum, to open the doors for you.

When we pulled up to the old dairy we were not impressed. John had to scramble around in back to find the "curator" who was creating life-sized human figures to use in his exhibits.

Once inside the museum itself our skepticism changed to open-mouthed wonder. That this one man could have structured a museum of such incredible scope, should have built such a variety of exhibits, many of them animated and functional, should have had the intensity and the intelligence and the perseverance to have completed so much in such a short period of time, was truly astonishing.

For example, in a room about the size of your average kitchen, Nigel has recreated a miniature working railway system of the 1920s. Protected from little hands behind glass panels, the model engine and freight cars go through typical countryside and a small village that existed around Mt Egmont at that time. There is a coal mine, a brick kiln works, a forest, a lumber operation . . . all faithfully reproduced from old photos down to the finest details.

The detail is perfect including the locomotive shed, the storing sheds, the station, the water tower.

Nigel's objective for his museum, according to his pamphlet, is to bring the history of South Taranaki alive.

One section of the museum is devoted to the Maori past.

There is a section of a Maori village, so dimly lighted that we thought we saw moving figures in the dark. Far off we heard the sound of night birds—recorded by Nigel. Spooky.

Another exhibit is a diorama of the flax-making process used for ropes in sailing ships. So important was flax as a barter item for muskets that flax making, we learned, dominated all other industry, including the growing of food crops.

Nigel has also built a full-sized replica Normanby redoubt (fort) and a blockhouse so real that standing inside it, alongside the uniformed soldiers on guard, looking at the slitted openings for rifle fire in the wooden, dirt reinforced walls that, suddenly, the tragedy of the times of the Land Wars come alive. It was not a time of fun and games but a time of fighting for survival, according to the beliefs of both sides.

Another section is devoted to the time of the settlers—their old farming, printing, and milking implements. New Zealand is filled with pioneer exhibits but, in Nigel's museum, the equipment exhibits function with the touch of a switch or are peopled with the life-sized lifelike "humans" he creates in his backyard work sheds.

One scene, I remember, is of a World War I doughboy in uniform, jacket and puttees, and campaign hat, wheeling an old bicycle and talking to a farmer.

"Oh, I know that scene," said one old-time visitor. "At the end of the war when we got de-mobbed, we went around the countryside begging the farmers for work. There weren't any jobs to be had and you were very lucky if you could get *any* job as a

farmhand." A poignant scene.
It's an amazing museum.
We asked Nigel how he got started.
"Well," he said, "I used to like to collect old firearms and it just grew from there—." Amazing.

The Tawhiti Museum, Ohangai Road, 50 meters from Tawhiti and Ohangi crossroads, P.O. Box 121, Hawera.
It really deserves to be picked up and put down in the middle of Wellington or Auckland where the world could see it.

(Dinner at home at Four Winds consisted of tender lamb and three helpings of gravy and delectable homemade ice cream. You get this kind of treatment at farm stays, commercial or non-commercial.)

The next morning was windy and wet and our scheduled flight around Mt Egmont was rain-checked.
We flew instead in the station wagon at velocities just below takeoff speeds towards New Plymouth, the capital of Taranaki, stopping off in Eltham to buy a hunk of the famous Blue Vein cheese and then barreled through the town of Stratford where many streets are named after Shakespearean characters and places.
"Look at the pretty courthouse and Country Hotel," said the Lady Navigator. By the time she finished her sentence the buildings were miles behind us.

One pastime we had while driving with John, besides grimly gripping safety straps, was to find an alternate word for "fat."
Fat, once a highly acceptable word as in "fat cat" has become a negative. It means obesity. Heart attacks. High cholesterol.
New Zealand prospers on the fat of the land. Fat calves. Fat lambs. Marbled (fat) steaks. Butterfat. Whole cream. Cream cheese. Fat as a pig. Suddenly, fat is a no-no and New Zealand needs a substitute word.
Finished? Mature? Top grade?
We never did find a satisfactory replacement.

Gardens You Will Love

One reason for diverting from the usual routes south to take in Taranaki is the gardens.

The most famous garden of the region, internationally famous, is Pukeiti.

Over 900 acres on the side of Mt Egmont are devoted to walks and tracks that take the visitor by almost every color and shape of the 800 types of rhododendrons in the world. The area's humus soil and its damp weather duplicate the Himalayas, home of the rhododendron, which is why the site was chosen.

The Pukeiti Rhododendron Trust started the garden in 1951 to promote the understanding and development of the rhododendron, to beautify the whole of the land acquired, and to provide sanctuary for all bird life.

The trust has succeeded beyond imagination.

The number of original 23 members has grown to over 3.000.

Fortunately, our fierce weather changed to God-loves-us sunshine as we wandered up and down grassy and gravel paths pointing out to each other the never-seen-before exotic colors, the violent and the subtle. It is a place, especially at the time of spring blossoming, to walk and marvel.

You have to visit the moss-covered water wheel built in 1957 which pumped water to the gardens and also generated electricity. A pretty picture.

After the acres of flowers and bushes, we also visited a small "hothouse" where frost sensitive plants from Malaysia, India and northern Australia are grown and protected.

Pukeiti is always expanding. The Lodge, built for members only, is to be augmented with a gatehouse, reception center, souvenir shop, restaurant facilities and staff accommodations.

It will take NZ$200,000 but Pukeiti will raise it.

(An understanding member took the Lady Navigator to the members-only restroom in the Lodge, without which the visit could have been either a disaster or extremely short.)

If gardens are your thing, put Taranaki on your itinerary. Go to the Public Relations Office in New Plymouth and get pamphlets on Holland Gardens and Tupare, two horticultural destinations under the ownership of the Queen Elizabeth II National Trust.

After Pukeiti, John took us to The Steps in New Plymouth for lunch.

The Steps is in an old home in the center of town. It is a vegetarian cafe with imaginative, tasty dishes including vegetable patties, Hunza Pie, silverbeet cheese pie, quiches and drinks like apple juice, boysenberry and raspberry juices.

If you had told us ten years ago that a local dairy farmer would take us to an upbeat vegetarian restaurant for lunch, we wouldn't have believed you.

But that is what is happening in New Zealand today.

Another new note in New Zealand cropped up during a radio interview in New Plymouth.

The Maoris had succeeded, at least temporarily, in getting Mt Egmont renamed Mt. Taranaki, its original Maori name.

Cook had named the mountain after the First Lord of the Admiralty and, historically, that is the way it should remain, said the Pakehas.

Why, asked the Maori. Historically, it was first Taranaki.

(Historically, the First Lord of the Admiralty was less than admirable. He was charged with playing fast and loose with chancellery funds and was later found mentally incompetent.)

Would the Maoris now try to get Mount Cook renamed Mt Aorangi?

Sacrilege.

There was a lot of ethnic muttering going on in New Zealand at the time.

In the middle of New Plymouth stands a new Clock Tower.

While we were in the vegetarian restaurant, we met an architect who, John Murphy said, submitted a design for a clock tower resembling the Leaning Tower of Pisa. The architect said it would make New Plymouth famous. It certainly would.

New Plymouth wasn't ready for the Leaning Tower of Pisa.

The new Clock Tower looks much like the old Clock Tower which didn't have much to recommend it to begin with.

We revisited our favorite place in New Plymouth, Pukekura Park, where you can find the only do-it-yourself waterfall in the world.

Insert a twenty-cent coin—it used to be ten—into a slot, turn the handle, and behind you a waterfall cascades down a high ladder of stones. Evenings, for the same price, colored lights backlight the shelves of water and the lights change from yellow to pink to green to orange.

In the middle of Pukekura Park is a large boating lake which is divided by *The Poet's Bridge*. Romantic, eh? It is until you find out that the name comes from a racehorse called "The Poet" and the money for the bridge came from a winning bet on the horse. The donor later committed suicide on the bridge. Probably placed a bet on a wrong horse.

Pukekura Park is back-to-back with Brooklands, another park, adding more luster to New Plymouth's reputation for outstanding gardens.

We remember another garden outside of New Plymouth, the New Plymouth Golf Club whose gracious greens are highlighted by a lovely, two-storey clubhouse—in truth, a relic. It smells and creaks but is filled with memories.

The secretary with whom we spoke said, "We bit the bullet several years ago. You'll find many golf clubs in New Zealand today facing the same problem. Keep the old, the dear, the inefficient. Or tear it all down and build a new clubhouse. We elected to stay with the old."

It is still there.

One of the industrial sights of New Plymouth is on the highway north toward Hamilton. It is Motunui, a giant conversion plant for changing natural gas taken from the offshore Maui gas fields to methanol to petrol. Another major petralgas chemical methanol plant is on the Waitara River, two reasons why Taranaki calls itself "the energy province."

The post-construction slump following the completion of these major construction projects is one reason Taranaki is vigorously pursuing its visitor market.

We returned to Hawera to change for dinner, stopping first at the village TAB office to place a bet on Fox Seal running the next day in the Melbourne Cup. The man in the TAB office was very patient despite the heavy sigh I heard as he tore up my ticket and showed me how to fill it out properly.

"This is the worst time of the year," he said. "Everybody who bets once a year comes in for the Melbourne Cup."

Dinner that evening was at Stratford Mountain Lodge in Mt Egmont (Taranaki) National Park, a sizable domain which offers skiing in winter and walking in summer. A lovely piece of bush country.

The local feat on New Year's Eve is to hike to the top and light a bonfire. Not an easy job. Overseas visitors are not advised to try to walk to the top without a guide.

The Lodge was taken over by Keith Arden and his Swiss wife, Berta, in 1985. A pleasant dinner with fireplace, wine, good people and good food.

The next morning the clouds were down among the cows' udders. The Mt Egmont airplane tour was scrubbed again.

We boarded the station wagon and headed for the hills, specifically Lake Rotorangi, a 25-mile long stretch of water behind a recently constructed earth-filled dam.

The new lake was filled by rainfall in only three months after its completion. John said it was built to help supply the country with electricity at that time of year when everybody turns on electric blankets.

At lakeside we were met by Gary Brown, a guide with boat, and Ross Mathews, a low-key, languid sheep station owner who had developed thousands of acres of land by the lake and had over 7,500 sheep running on the property, a sizable reduction in number from the 10,000 he and his brother normally ran. (Fat sheep, you see. The sheep farming business was terrible.)

So was the fishing. Of the party, Gary, the guide, got one fish.

"At least you know they are there," said John, the promoter, whose dominating personality had little effect over fish and weather.

When we were walking across the dam at the end of the lake, Ross told a story which I didn't believe. Grown eels in the area annually migrate *overland* to the sea from the river—and the lake created by the dam—to breed.

The baby eels then instinctively return home. They can't go overland. They can't go over the dam. So an eel ladder has been built from the stream bed below the dam up and over the top so that the baby eels have a highway home.

The ladder is a plastic tube, perhaps three inches in diameter, with corkscrew bristles inside which the tiny eels can climb, going up to the top and down to the water on the other side. Gary took the top off the tube so that we could look inside. I still don't believe it.

Ross led the party on an easy walk through the bush, one the many planned "Walkways" found throughout New Zealand. It was an educational pleasure because Ross conveyed the history of the flora and fauna so articulately.

When we returned to the Mathews homestead, Ross's wife, Anne, had a bountiful spread of lunch waiting.

They were considering going into a farm-stay venture. The farm is remote but gracious with swimming pool and a dining pavilion for barbecues. If overseas guests want the real thing including the peacefulness of a faraway location, they would probably take guests. Ross Mathews, Hawera, New Zealand should reach them.

From the farm in the mountains we went to a farm on the plains to watch the running of the Melbourne Cup on television.

The old two-storey homestead was the property of David and Hilary Brewer who do take paying guests. Wood paneling, stained glass, billiard table, pet sheep in the backyard and horses.

Refreshments were poured and cheese was passed and the race was run. Nobody in the room had the winning horse. Fox Seal was never seen. He might still be out there running.

In tiny Hawera we took our hosts to dinner at Barry's Restaurant, surprisingly good, huge portions, and a decent wine list where we toasted the fish, and Fox Seal and our good hosts.

"The point of the whole exercise," said John, the convincer, "is that Taranaki is a place where people like yourselves in a campervan or a rental car can get off the beaten path and see an unusual part of New Zealand."

We said we would write it just like that.

Wanganui: A River, A Church, A Museum

After leaving John and Marion at the door of Four Winds and receiving the thumbs up sign from John, we headed back down the highway to Wanganui.

The scenery going to or from Hawera, on Highway 3 reminds us of Surrey or Essex in England. The green hills roll off into the distance like waves on a vast sea becoming purple fringes in the distance.

Beautiful country.

One oddity on route is in the village of Patea where a concrete canoe is suspended over the entryway to city hall. The canoe represents the canoe *Aotea* which brought the Polynesians to the area in the 14th century from "Hawaiki." It was erected in 1933 by the tribal descendants of the voyagers. Represented in the canoe are Turi, the captain, his wife and infant son and six others.

The entry into Wanganui from the east is by a pretty park with lawns and water and ducks.

The focus of the city is on the water, being a port and the main city on the Wanganui River. Once, transportation to the interior was an important function of the river and was one of the reasons for Wanganui's development by the New Zealand Company when, in 1840, the company "bought" about 40,000 acres of land for a few hundred pound sterling worth of traders junk.

"No sale" said the Maoris. Trouble followed trouble until the issue was finally resolved in 1847 with a £1,000 payment for 80,000 acres of land.

Visitor traffic tends to center around the river. There is every sort of activity. Jet boat rides, paddle-wheeler tours, coal-fired steamer tours, flat boat river trips, canoe trips, walking tours.

How much of an adventure do you want? You can take a jet boat tour for an hour or a steamer for a half a day or a canoe, flat boat or hiking tour for from two to six days—tours that take you as far north on the river as Taumarunui.

(We are sorry we have never made a tour on the Wanganui River. Just following the highway alongside the stream bed from Tongariro National Park gives you snatches of forest beauty; teasers, we're told, for what it is like on the river.)

The best place to go for current information and tours on the river is to the Visitors Information Centre on Guyton Street. In Wanganui, or almost any other town in New Zealand, you follow the directional sign of the big "I" to the city's information office.

"What is new in Wanganui," we asked Annette Main, a vivacious blond, and she unloaded a packet of river trips on us among others items of interest.

"The big news is that the Wanganui River area might be

declared a national park—not the river bed, that belongs to the Maoris—but the land on each side of the river. It means that land can be protected and developed properly for visitor enjoyment and would become an even bigger attraction than it is now because the Wanganui River is relatively unknown, especially to the overseas visitor," she told us.

"Is St. Paul's still here?"

"Oh, yes. The only change is today the Maoris ask a NZ$2.50 donation for a guided tour."

Don't Miss St. Paul's Church

St. Paul's Anglican Memorial Church, a block off Highway 4, the highway coming down from Tongariro, is a white, simple steeply church from the exterior. Its interior is regarded as being as outstanding example of modern Maori design and carving. Each wall and panel has to be studied to be appreciated. The infinite precision in execution and the detail in color and line plus the abundance of it all makes the church, referred to as Putiki, a rare experience, even in New Zealand.

In the vestibule is a poem composed during World War I by the English poet Rupert Brooke which we have shared with many friends:

"They shall grow not old
As we that are left
Grow old.
Age shall not weary them,
Nor the years condemn,
At the going down of the sun
And in the morning
We shall remember them."

Two other attractions in Wanganui are the Wanganui Public Museum and the Sarjeant Gallery.

If you are one who tires of museums, save your energy for a visit to the Wanganui Public Museum because it not only has a wide variety of exhibits but the presentation is more professional than most and, therefore, more enjoyable.

Reproducing colonial cottages and recreating the colonial way of life is, seemingly, a patriotic duty of New Zealand museums and you will find the same at Wanganui.

Two musical instruments are worth noting. One is the first organ seen in New Zealand which was given to Henry and William Williams, the missionaries at Paihia in the Bay of Islands. Vintage 1829, it plays hymns from a rotating cylinder like a player piano. The other instrument is a polythron which rotates a flat, punctuated metal disc by means of a spring. You buy a token from the museum attendant, insert the token in the machine, and the room is filled with the remarkably clear sound of a Rossini melody.

The Maori Room in dominated by the war canoe, *Hoturou*, named after the captain of one of the original migration canoes, the *Tainui*. The elaborately carved canoe could carry seventy warriors. Bullet holes in its side are mementos of river battles in 1865.

Upstairs is a stunning, colorful collection of butterflies.

Not far away from the museum is the Sarjeant Art Gallery, one of the most important galleries in New Zealand.

The collection is mainly English—which is not very exciting—but what you'll find more absorbing are the works of New Zealand artists in the gallery: Charles Goldie, John Gully, Frances Hodgkins, J.C. Hoyte. The QEII Arts Council, which keeps abreast of such things, reported that a Goldie Maori youth brought $14,000 at auction in 1983, only to be surpassed a year later by his "Memories" at $22,000. (The record price of $50,000 for a New Zealand oil was paid in 1984 to contemporary artist, Colin McCahon.)

Also you will see designs for the brilliant post-World War II windows in the cathedral in Coventry, England by John Hutton who grew up in Wanganui.

A different place to stay in Wanganui is Bushy Park, an historic homestead and scenic reserve. The old wooden homestead was built in 1905 and is now operated as a lodge with six bedrooms. Facilities down the hall including a community kitchen where guests can cook their own food. NZ$25 double was the last price we saw.

Behind the manse 220 acres of virgin bush were deeded to the Royal Forest and Bird Protection Society by the original owner and, in 1962, he added the house and 23 acres of gardens to the gift.

Palmerston North, A Center Of Scientific Farming

From Wanganui we cut inland and were in Palmerston North in time for lunch.

On the way we passed through the village of Bulls—named after a well-known wood carver. The unusual name of the town must encourage other such names. My notebook records the name of a local barber: "Hair and There."

You go to Palmerston North to attend Massey University, which concentrates on farming or you go as a tourist to visit the internationally famous rose gardens or you go to attend a convention. Palmerston North is a big New Zealand convention town.

The Fitzherbert Motor Inn now boasts nearly 2,000 beds and a new convention center.

As capital of the Manawatu Region, Palmerston North moves in the right direction, we think, by promoting "agricultural tourism."

If you are in any aspect of farming, you will love Palmerston North.

Visits can be arranged, mostly through the Public Relations Office, to horse stud farms, deer farms, dairy and cattle stud farms—Friesian and Angus—sheep stud farms, historic farm homesteads, a Santa Gertrudis breeding farm, livestock sales yards, a milk processing plant or slaughterhouses.

A serious student of agriculture can go to a horticultural research center, an artificial dairy breeding center, a dairy research center, a seed testing station, farm training institute, a soil conservation center, or Massey University's school of agriculture.

If you want to vacation on a farm, that can be arranged too.

If outdoor action is more to your liking, the nearby Rangitikei River offers Grade 5 (dangerous) rapids for one- or two-hour trips, half- or full-day trips or a two-day outing where you fly in by helicopter ferrying your raft beneath you. Oh, yeah!

For calmer moods take in the Dugald McKenzie Rose Garden, symmetrically laid out with a fountain in the center and an elevated viewing stand—a splendid idea—the better to inspect the entire garden.

Palmerston North, incidentally, has the only Rose Trial Grounds in the Southern Hemisphere. Growers from throughout the world send their unnamed cuttings to be grown during all seasons then judged for color and general health at an annual Trial Grounds awards presentation.

What Palmerston North does not have is street signs.

We were parked in the middle of the city by a busy intersection and we could not find a single street sign.

"Go and find out where we are," I begged the Lady Navigator.

She came back ten minutes later and said, "From the only signs I could find we are between 'Police' on the left and 'Public Toilets' on the right."

When the railroad first came to town, the tracks were laid down the center of the city and the station built in the middle of the planned town square. Fitzherbert, an influential man whose name you'll find everywhere, was a director of the railroad.

Not until 1963 were the railway lines and station shifted to the north of town and the planned town square with clock tower built to its intended dignity and glory.

Palmerston North also has a museum, a modern art museum and even a rugby museum—and a host of new international restaurants including Indian, Italian, Chinese, French, Mexican—and a Jewish deli called the Posh Nosh.

Knowing that we were going to be only one more night on the road before arriving in Wellington and aware of Wellington's reputation for difficult-to-get accommodations, we asked the local AA to secure a hotel apartment for four nights. Service charge: $1.

Our stop by the local AA office was fortunate also because the lady said that the regular road to Masterton, our destination, was closed and we would have to take a secondary route.

Masterton And Our Favorite Farm

The secondary road, although it went through beautiful, rolling country, had one negative result. We arrived at the National Wildlife Centre at Mount Bruce at 4pm, just as the guardian was closing the gate.

I kicked myself later a hundred times for not talking our way in because we would not get back again and the National Wildlife Centre has become one of the leading attractions of the North Island.

Local people, not given to boasting, say it is superb.

"Whatever you do, don't miss the National Wildlife Centre at Mount Bruce. It is the most important, exciting new development in the area," the PR at the Masterton Public Relations Office said. Thanks.

What else shouldn't we miss?

"The Golden Shears, of course, but you know that. We have reduced it to three nights instead of four."

A good move. When we attended the Golden Shears, the stench of sheep by the fourth night could turn a city dweller cross-eyed.

"Oh, yes. We had a male strip show come to town. Drew a crowd of 1,000 women. Damnest thing I ever heard of. I understand the show is coming back."

We returned to the Chilly Bin and the grey-haired assistant in the public relations office came out, put on a white crash helmet, mounted a red motorized scooter and yelled, "Have a good 'un!" and roared away.

The whole world is changing . . . even in New Zealand.

Our first research trip to New Zealand brought us, by good luck, to the farm of Linden Downs, just north of Masterton, one of the first four farms in the country to pioneer the farm-stay for visitors.

We wanted to return to Fay and Phillip Evans and Linden Downs to find if it was as good as we thought it was—and wrote it was. We wanted to disprove the Thomas Wolfe "you-can't-go-home-again" syndrome.

Having traveled from Masterton to the farm twice a day for four days while attending the Golden Shears—although it was ten years ago—we were sure we could find it without trouble.

We got lost. Not once but three times, twice after asking travel directions. But we finally pulled through the old white wooden gate, eased the Chilly Bin up the narrow tree-shaded hill, looked across the pond at the two-storey white homestead and felt as if we were home.

Bouncing Fay, never a small women and now no smaller, was the same otherwise: cheerful, full of life, tireless.

Quiet, introspective Phillip was now almost gregarious.

We later agreed that hosting farm-stay visitors had done it for him.

Fellow farmers, Phillip said, who used to think it kind of demeaning to take strangers into their homes for money were now asking him how they could get in it.

Nothing like a little green envy to bolster one's confidence.

Also, the Evans had wisely exchanged raising bullocks for sheep before the market for sheep had softened. He still fattened 1,000 lambs each year for other farmers and raised his own grain, enough to sell on the outside as well as feed his own animals. He had built a new silo.

Over the dozen or so years, their farm-stay business had prospered.

That night, besides us, Linden Downs hosted two representatives from the Japanese agricultural department who, after official conferences in Wellington, had come to Linden Downs as the guests of the New Zealand government to experience a working farm, and to fish.

A New Zealand foreign service officer was with them and the local agricultural officer and his wife joined us for dinner.

"How difficult do you find the New Zealand accent," we asked the Japanese at the big family gathering dinner table while Phillip carved the roast beef.

"Very difficult," the leader of the two said. "Even the newspapers are hard to understand."

Pre-dinner cocktails and post-dinner coffee were served in the spacious living room where the pictures hung slightly askew on the wall, just as they always had. Part of the charm.

So is the entry foyer, a room of times past. Dark wood paneling matches the wood in the staircase leading to the second floor bedrooms. A spray of decorative peacock feathers adorn one wall accompanied by crossed bayonets and a saber. A broken tennis racquet rests in one corner.

Two tapestries grace the stairwell. One is an Arabian desert scene. A sheik lies in his oasis tent watching a dancing girl while a messenger waits holding a prancing Arabian horse.

The other is of an 18th century French salon. The richly gowned madamoiselle is playing the piano and singing coyly to the white periwigged, silk-ruffled gentleman leaning over her decolletage.

A bronze figure of Mercury decorates the pillar at the foot of the banister.

The ancient bathroom has been enlarged downstairs. Still no bathroom upstairs.

"We encourage people to stay two nights so that they get the flavor of the farm. If they are non-smokers, we tell them that we won't take anybody else and they can have the house to themselves. They like that," said Fay.

"Our only trouble is with the guest book. Some people want to go on and on. A party from Chicago took a whole page.

"No, we don't belong to any farm-stay association. They want too big a percentage. We are listed with the government tourist offices and in *How to Get Lost and Found in New Zealand*, and that's all we need!"

The only cloud on the farm was the recent lingering death of their oldest son to cancer. They had contributed the flagpole at the National Wildlife Centre in his name.

Linden Downs can be reached by writing Rangitumau, Masterton, New Zealand. It is just as good as it ever was.

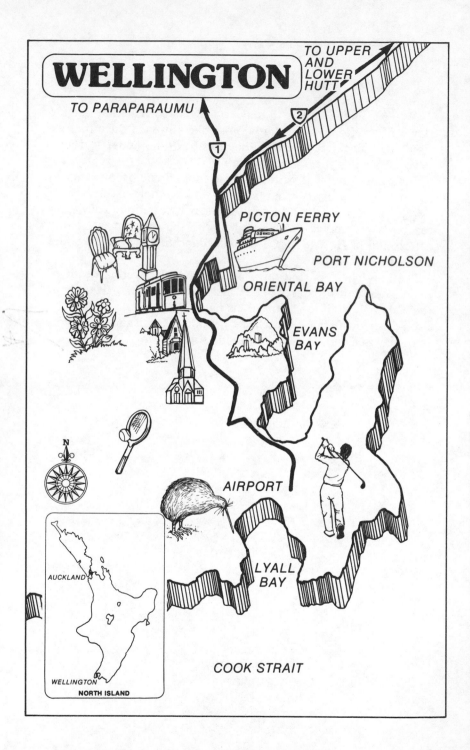

8. Wellington—Wow!

Sparkle Comes To The Capital . . . New Walks
The Wakefield Scheme . . . Historic Buildings

Wellington, the capital city of New Zealand, is wearing a new set of clothes.

When I think about Wellington a decade ago compared to Wellington today—and what Wellington is obviously going to be tomorrow—I shake my head in disbelief.

Wellington, in fact, was just yesterday a grown-up country town with turn-of-the-century buildings and terrible blatant street signage, one decent hotel, mediocre shopping facilities and, with a couple of exceptions, very few innovative restaurants.

The dowdiness of the city was particularly surprisingly in light of the fact that an international corps of diplomats resided in the nation's capital.

Now it is verging on the sophisticated.

Bright new buildings have sprung up everywhere.

Shopping arcades are downstairs and upstairs at every corner.

Restaurants abound—even fish specialty restaurants where there was not one before.

Hotels and motels have increased in number and improved in quality, and more are on the way. Despite the increased number of accommodations, space is still tight. Make sure you have a reservation before going to Wellington.

Thanks to forethought and AA in Palmerston North, we held confirmed reservations for four nights at Iona Towers, a 14-storey fully-serviced apartment/motel, where we had two bedrooms, living room, an airy bath, and kitchen. The location was a short walk from the center of town. We parked the Chilly Bin in one corner of the parking area and didn't move it for four days. The 1986 price was NZ$60 a day (US$35).

The same management group owns the nearby luxurious Terrace Regency Hotel and another full-service apartment/motel called the Melksham Towers in the center of the city.

On the waterfront the Parkroyal, another upgraded, upmarket

hotel has been added to the list of needed first-class places to stay. Facing the waterfront on the Oriental Parade, the porte cochere is in back of the hotel. We were told that the Arabian sheiks like to stay at the Parkroyal because the hidden entry protects them from being seen going in and out.

Of the two major things to appreciate about Wellington, the first is its location which is probably as attractive as any city in the Southern Hemisphere.

Perched in the hills surrounding a wind-swept bay, it has the crisp feeling of San Francisco. It even has a cable car.

The easiest way to see the beauty of the city is from the mountain terminus of the famous Kelburn Cable Car which yields views in every direction.

White sails commingle with cargo ships on the deep blue bay and the daily ferries departing for, or arriving from, Picton on the South Island.

It is easy to accept the city's motto, *"Suprema a Situ"* from this vantage point, looking down over the lovely Botanic Gardens.

You say "thank you" to the city fathers for building the cable car as a visitor amenity, and then you learn it was built in 1902 to help sell house lots in the upper hills. Reserve your thanks for the Swiss company who rebuilt the system in 1979.

Catch the cable car at the foot of Lambton Quay.

While you are at top, have lunch at the new Skyline Restaurant, a delightful place designed by one of New Zealand's leading architects. Big full windows and a decent menu make it a huge improvement over the dilapidated structure and fast-food atrocity that used to be there.

Smartly dressed local matrons, socialites, business and artistic types meet at the Skyline for lunch. You know it has to be good.

Wear comfortable shoes so you can comfortably walk back down to the city center via the Botanical Gardens, Anderson Park and the Parliament buildings. Or take the opposite direction, the "Town and Gown Walk" route, through Victoria University. But, first, pick up the self-guided walk pamphlet from the big "I" on Mercer street.

The Wakefield Scheme

The other aspect of Wellington to appreciate is its intriguing history. It began in a jail cell in England.

Edward Gibbon Wakefield (1796-1862) was doing time in an British prison for having eloped with a teenage heiress to Gretna Green in Scotland where only one witness to the wedding vows was needed—usually the blacksmith.

This criminal act gave Wakefield three years to think and write and talk to prisoners who had been in Australia. He wrote a book on future Australian colonization out of which grew his "Wakefield Scheme."

In essence, the plan called for a cross-section of the English society—leaders, tradesmen, farmers, laborers, the gentry—to unplug itself from the home country and plug itself into the new country of Australia. When Australia failed to develop, New Zealand was chosen.

A basic tenet of the plan was the assumption that everybody would promise to keep his same station in life—not try to change—thereby avoiding the danger, as Wakefield saw it, "of becoming rotten before they are ripe."

The Wakefield theory was endorsed by the Duke of Wellington. In two years the New Zealand Company established colonies in Wellington, New Plymouth, Wanganui and, across the Cook Strait, in Nelson on the South Island.

The Wakefield Scheme also served as a fundamental recruitment policy for the founding of Christchurch and Dunedin in which Wakefield was involved but with different companies.

In the end, the companies which were in reality get-rich-quick land development schemes failed for many reasons, not the least of which was that the settlers really *wanted* to rot before they ripened, or, more simply put, improve their station in life.

The by-product of Wakefield's dreaming and scheming was an influx of 19,000 immigrants into New Zealand between May, 1839 and January, 1843. It constituted the backbone population of the new country.

A few years later, a 1865 Commission ruled that the capital of the country should be moved from the thinly populated desert of Auckland to the superior port and more substantially populated Wellington, thus completing the founders' first hopes.

Aucklanders are quick to point out that the Commission was made up of Australians and that today, Auckland, with a population approaching 1,000,000 is being ruled by a city of bureaucrats whose residential numbers are under 200,000.

There exists the same affection between Auckland and Wellington as that of Los Angeles and San Francisco or Sydney and Melbourne.

Poking Around the City

Good information abounds in Wellington.

The national offices of the New Zealand Tourist and Publicity Office are on Lambton Quay.

On one floor is a sign reading: "Everyone brings joy to this office. Some by entering. Some by leaving."

A Wellington regional office of NZTPO is on Mercer Street just off of Willis where you can find the latest news about the region.

A block farther down Mercer is the Wellington Public Relations Office (the big "I") where you can pick up the newest materials. They have some exceptional pamphlets, for example, on city walks: Town and Gown Walk, Wharves Walk, Thorndon Walk.

Historically, the Thorndon Walk is the most absorbing because it encompasses an area at first called "little Italy" because of its land-and-sea beauty. The area was occupied after the original settlement was flooded out of Hutt Valley.

Go to Tinakori Street, known for restaurants and antiques, and just above the Territorial Tavern you'll find Ascot Terrace, the oldest street in Auckland with its 19th century houses. Tiny boxy wooden cottages shaped at the base to the contour of the hill on which they stand because, when they were planned in London, they were not designed for hills. The roofs are of corrugated metal because this is an earthquake zone and tiles in the times of a quake would constitute an overhead danger.

This area is full of architectural goodies. Take the house at 25 Tinakori Road where New Zealand's most famous authoress, Katherine Mansfield, was born.

In a small wooden building on Tinakori Road, you'll find a restaurant called Pierre's, awarded top honors in the Listener-Montana readership contest as the best BYO restaurant in the nation. You'll be lucky to get in.

Our favorite building in all of New Zealand is Old St Paul's Cathedral, circa 1866, a classical white church with steeple and an outstanding interior of warm stained woods—rimu, totara, mati, kauri—complemented by shined-daily brass dedication plates and stained glass windows.

Incredibly, a move was made to tear down this original church to make way for what some locals refer to as "The Elephant House," the *new* Anglican Cathedral ultimately built across the street. The giant concrete monstrosity is tasteless.

The move to demolish the gracious old church divided the city. The Friends of Old St. Paul's was formed, £35,000 was raised and the church was saved. Subsequently, NZ$1,000,000 was spent in restoring the structure to its present perfection.

It is a favorite place for weddings. A sign outside says "No confetti in the church or on the grounds." Impossible to pick up, we were told.

Just around the corner is the Vogel House, home of the Ministry of Works. If you'd like to do something few tourists know about, go to the top of the building—it's permitted—where the views of downtown and the harbor are special.

You are in the center of the principal federal buildings. A block away is the Parliament Building. Find out the latest tour hours and go on a short tour of the Parliament; it represents the architecture and the spirit at the turn-of-the-century. Marble floors and columns, dark woods, ornate cast-iron decorations. Somber. Serious.

Peek inside the Library next door and admire the carved woodwork and the stained glass.

On the other hand, the Beehive, across the street, is a distinctive new building which we thought would become the architectural symbol for New Zealand as the Syndey Opera House has become for Australia. The Beehive, so named because that is what it looks like, is an administration building holding the offices of the Prime Minister, his cabinet and other functionaries, and is light, modern, almost gay. But you wouldn't think anything is lighthearted the way its occupants talk about one another.

Segments of the Parliamentary debates are on radio and it makes amusing listening, even for an overseas tourist.

What is obvious is the New Zealanders' instinctive talent for oration. The loquacious phrases. The dramatic pauses. The lovingly, delicately placed verbal stilettos just above the heart. Listen one time.

The restaurant for parliamentarians is known as Bellamy's after its

English counterpart. Not open to voters.

While you are collecting buildings in the area, add two more. One is the old Government Building, completed in 1877 of wood made to look like concrete. It is the second largest wooden structure in the world; the Japanese temple of Todaiji in Nara is larger.

The other is the railway station. It is a grand, domed, high-ceilinged building that recalls the days when railways were so important. If you are driving, here is where you buy tickets for the Picton ferry, it being a part of the government rail-bus-ferry transportation system.

You can pick up a bundle of Non-Zip points in five blocks, depending upon your focus.

While the dominance of railroads has passed a good deal of Wellington's lifeblood is still tied into the ship traffic flowing in and out of its harbor.

The wharves were the heart controlling the flow.

Take the "Wharves Walk" tour suggested by the pamphlet.

Not too long ago the city fathers awoke to the fact that the wharves had become unsightly and they set cleaners and painters to work facelifting the architectural veterans.

The "Wharves Walk" is a shed-by-shed tour of the entire cleaned up waterfront.

Read the pamphlet as you drive—or walk, if you have the time—along the piers.

A poignant memorial is outside the Queen's Wharf gates. It is a small marble dog watering trough with a metal plaque embossed with the head of an Irish setter.

The setter was Paddy, the Wanderer, who used to accompany his tiny mistress on her daily visits to her father, a seaman who worked on the wharf. The girl died prematurely, but Paddy continued the daily visits for thirteen years. Everybody knew Paddy, the Wanderer. When he died, his coffin was escorted by a fleet of twelve taxis carrying his waterfront friends to the funeral.

Go and give yourself ten point on the Non-Zip score card.

A Visit With An Old Friend

We never go to Wellington without making a pilgrimage to the

National Museum and Art Gallery. It continuously improves. Galleries are added, re-designed. Besides, we have old friends there we feel compelled to visit.

The large entry gallery, Maori Hall, is dominated by another historically important war canoe, *Teremoe*. It, like the *Hoturou* in the Wanganui Museum, was involved in the Wanganui River Campaign.

Maori Hall provides the interested visitor a thorough overview of the Maori's origin and early settlement, his house and fort designs, tools and weapons, clothing and ornaments, and of his carving, weaving and other decorative arts, along with explanations of Maori mythology and insights into the Maori religion, death and burial.

Following along chronologically is the Colonial History Gallery tracking the first explorers, Tasman, Cook, de Surville, and the first Western-introduced industries, whaling and sealing. The history of the New Zealand Company is presented, as is a bust of that captivating man, Edward Gibbon Wakefield, and a model of the *True Briton*, one of the immigrant ships.

(The names of ships that brought the first settlers to the land were names of honor to be preserved forever. The Maori tribes today root their history in the names of the canoes that brought their ancestors to New Zealand. The Europeans do the same thing.)

Early Wellington is recalled in exhibits. There is the inevitable Colonial Cottage containing of-the-era furniture.

A preserved poster reads: "New Zealand Company Emigration are prepared to assist in emigrating to their Settlement in New Zealand: Agricultural Mechanics, Farm Labourers, Domestic Servants."

A footnote could have been added: "Providing you remember your station and stay in place."

My personal favorite exhibit centers around Captain James Cook. Cook dressed in his lieutenant's uniform sits in a replica of the captain's cabin aboard the H.M. Bark *Endeavour* in conversation with the moneyed gentleman botanist, Joseph Banks.

One of six cannons jettisoned when the *Endeavour* went aground off the Great Barrier reef is displayed in the gallery. The ship had to be lightened to lift it off the reef. Four cannons were recovered. Two are in Australia—at the War Memorial Museum in Canberra and at a small museum in Cooktown (Queensland). The other two are in New Zealand, here in the Wellington museum and in Gisborne.

An equally important relic is the figurehead from the *H.M.B. Resolution* which overlooked the beach at Kealakekua Bay that morning in February, 1779 when Cook was murdered. The figurehead is of an open-mouthed animal known in heraldic terms as a "Talbot" and represents a hunting hound in full cry.

Adjacent is the Pacific Gallery where, among the Hawaiian exhibits, is the magnificent red and gold cape made of rare bird feathers which had been presented to Cook on January 26, 1779—just nineteen days before his death—by Hawaiian chiefs who had feted him as a distinguished visitor.

The cloak went to the Leverian Museum in England then, in 1806, to the Bullock Museum. In 1819, the cloak was purchased at auction by Lord St. Oswald whose family presented it to New Zealand in 1912.

A new gallery, very well done, is the fish gallery called "Life on the Rocks" with three-dimensional fish floating about in space.

Points North

During our first six-month-long research visit we had a penchant for collecting antique shops and golf courses.

Expensive and time consuming.

Antique shops are everywhere, providing delightful browsing.

Golf courses are everywhere, too. The Wellington Club in Lower Hutt is the most social club in the country, probably, and has a most pleasant golf course.

North of Wellington is the town of Paraparaumu which, typically, New Zealanders have bastardized to "Paraparam." Its antique stores and brute of a golf course, as tough a links in a high wind as you are apt to play anywhere, are reasons enough to recommend the 50km drive up the west coast.

But Paraparam's Southward Museum of vintage cars is another. It has undergone dramatic upgrading since our last visit. The collection of over 250 cars now is housed in a new great hall with natural lighting for indoor photography. You can look and shoot an 1895 Benz, a 1904 Wolseley, or 1915 Stuz racer from Indianapolis, and 247 others. The museum claims to have the largest and most comprehensive collection of veteran and vintage cars in the Southern Hemisphere.

On the North side of Paraparaumu and visible from Highway 1, you will see Lindale, still another addition to New Zealand's long list of visitor-oriented attractions.

Lindale labels itself "a growing experience." Having begun with separate sheep and cattle shows in its animal center, its ambitious program of development includes a cheese factory, a winery, a crafts center, a horticultural exhibit and, of course, the ubiquitous tea room.

Back in Wellington, we continued our prowl of an ever changing city.

The gracious old, two-toned Town Hall where we once enjoyed a "box-lunch" symphonic concert now has a glittering new next door neighbor, the Michael Fowler Centre, a huge entertainment and convention facility. It is a pearl in the crown of upgraded Wellington.

Named after Sir Michael Fowler, mayor of Wellington for nine years, the needed facility is an attractive modernistic building of molded shiny metal, concrete and glass.

The building was opened on September 16, 1983 by His Grace, the Duke of Wellington.

Tours are usually conducted around the Centre seven days a week throughout the day but we arrived the day they were rehearsing for the entertainment industry's annual awards night. Huge production. No tours. Damn.

Remembering our failure to get in the National Wildlife Centre at Mount Bruce, we sought out the security officer, explained our predicament—we were leaving the next day—and asked for a quick peek.

The security officer, Robert Burton, couldn't have been nicer.

He personally escorted us on a run through.

"The building cost NZ$19,000,000—that's a lot of sheep. You can rent it for $3,000 a night.

"The main theater holds 2,500 and there are side rooms for small conferences. It is 80 percent occupied during the year.

"The Town Hall next door is now used for less cultured shows. Rock shows and the like.

"See the two giant totems? They were carved by prisoners. Took three years from the day the trees were topped until they were placed in the lobby."

We remarked on the twelve modern appliqued flags hanging in the upstairs lobby. Rather eye-popping.

"Supposed to represent the twelve seasons and the way Wellingtonians feel and all that rubbish," said Robert, a proud native. "I've lived here all my life and I've never felt anything like *that!*" he finished waving at the flags as if to make them go away.

A coffee/tea shop downstairs offers scones and "Sammies"—sandwiches.

City Tours

Several tours have been packaged to introduce visitors to old parts of the city and to new parts of the city and include shopping, in some cases, or tramps in the bush in others.

The City Transport Scenic Bus offers an afternoon tour of two-and-a-half hours, an inexpensive way to tour the city.

We opted instead for a morning tour with Joyceln Norris of "Out and About," a boutique tour company that designs personal tours in your car or one of theirs, to meet your desires: historic, horticultural, homes, lunches, commercial, scenic. Our tour included the original cottages on Ascot Terrace, Old St. Paul's and a wool shop removed from the usual tourist gathering places, among other points of interest.

Had we sufficient time, we would have taken an Elite Tours four-wheel-drive outdoor adventure trip. Many half- and full-day itineraries are offered in a wide spectrum from city tours to old gold mines, seal colonies and bird sanctuaries, sheep stations, or ecological trips to coastline and hill country.

Would you like something a little more exciting? How about a multiple day tour which would include diving for abalone, windsurfing, abselling down a cliff and whitewater rafting on a spine-chilling river? The company has lots of this sort of thing.

Elite Tours came to us highly recommended.

I remember two things about my first visit to "Windy Wellington." That day there were 85-miles-an-hour winds. It wasn't even noted in the daily newspaper the next day. Ho-hum. A bit of a breeze, eh?

The other: Wellington, surrounded by water, must have outstanding fishing, I thought.

"Where is the best fish restaurant?" I asked the taxi driver on the way in from the airport.

"Fish restaurants?" he sounded offended. "We don't have any fish restaurants."

I felt as if I had asked for a pair of pink panties in a men's store.

It is all different in upgraded Wellington.

Fresh fish, like lamb, is no longer a stranger in restaurants.

Nicholson on Oriental Parade is one outstanding fish restaurant in an appropriate setting overlooking the bay for which the restaurant was named, Port Nicholson.

We asked our hotel manager for his recommendations.

"Lavelle," he said, "the best restaurant in Wellington. Just around the block on Willis Street."

Across the street from Lavelle's, in a tiny house, is a five-table restaurant aptly named Petite Lyon which books parties at the rate of one per hour. Reservations are therefore essential. Supposed to be excellent. We couldn't get in.

Four blocks toward the center of the city, also on Willis Street, is Upstage, a restaurant high on the list of one tourist authority. Patronized by the entertainment crowd.

We know from experience that Plimmer House is a joy both visually and gastronomically. The fashionable, and expensive, restaurant is in a spired, white, curlicued century-old cottage wedged between skyscrapers. It is like a little white-haired grandmother surrounded by rock and rollers.

The Plimmer House is known for its mussel soup. Excellent wine list. Excellent service. Elegant ambience.

On previous trips we had tried and enjoyed Orsini's, the Coachman, Bacchus and others.

Today there are many, so many, new restaurants. Pick up a pamphlet "Dining Out in Wellington" from the city information center.

We severely reduced our dining-out research in Wellington. Our "pavloitis," by now into its sixth week, had reached serious pants-stretching limits.

"The reason," the Lady Navigator said to me in the tone she uses with small children, "for our problem in gaining weight in New Zealand stems from the fact that as we roll through the country we are surrounded by munch."

"Munch?"

"Precisely. Munch. Seventy million sheep everywhere you look are going *munch, munch, munch.*

"Ten million cows going *munch, munch munch.*

"Three million people in teashops morning and afternoon going *munch, munch, munch.*

"So here we are, surrounded by chocolate-covered Toffee Pops with all that luscious caramel that tastes so good with rich New Zealand milk which is half cream, lamb chops grilled in their halos of fat, ridiculously cheap steaks, a bottle of New Zealand wine a day, a Steinlager now and again, scones, pies and ice cream cones. And there we are, two starving travel writers following the example of the country and going *munch, munch, munch.*

"No wonder *you* are overweight," she concluded.

On a sunny Sunday you can do worse that cruise along the wharves and the Oriental Parade, the waterfront boulevard that fronts the bay. You pass girls walking dogs, runners, wind surfing schools, yacht harbors, the Nicholson, the very private Parkroyal, and beyond, you pass the Shorebird and Greta Point Tavern where you can drink hot butter rum—but not on Sunday—and watch the sailors freezing while racing on the bay. You can go as far out as the airport on a windy isthmus of land where only limited-passenger jets can land because the runway is too short for craft the size of a 747. The controversy surrounding the lengthening of the runway is one of Wellington's favorite sports, following rugby and cricket by a hair.

Or head for the Wellington Zoo, one of the oldest in the country. It is worth a visit. We awarded an "A" to the brown bear and a "B" to the elephant. The tiger is beautiful.

Or drive east on the Motorway, leaving it for a two-way, curving road that follows the coastline to Eastborne, a quiet homey suburb with sports fields and family picnic grounds, happy dogs splashing in the ocean chasing sticks their loyal friends have thrown. A big place for fish and chips and hamburgers.

And you wonder as you leave Wellington, what will it look like in another ten years?

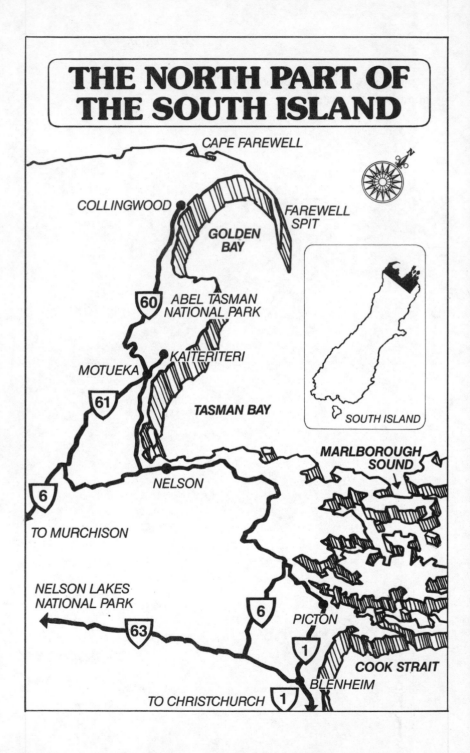

THE NORTH PART OF THE SOUTH ISLAND

CAPE FAREWELL

COLLINGWOOD

FAREWELL SPIT

GOLDEN BAY

60 ABEL TASMAN NATIONAL PARK

KAITERITERI

MOTUEKA

61

TASMAN BAY

MARLBOROUGH SOUND

6

NELSON

TO MURCHISON

NELSON LAKES NATIONAL PARK

63

6

PICTON

1

COOK STRAIT

BLENHEIM

TO CHRISTCHURCH **1**

SOUTH ISLAND

9. The North Part of The South Island

The Marvelous Marlborough Sounds . . . Nelson Wine Country . . . Able Tasman National Park

In Wellington, we rolled the Chilly Bin into the embarkation area for the ferry to Picton.

We turned over our tickets and were checked off the list and waited.

Looking around I saw nearby rental car agencies and I found out something I didn't know. You can leave your rental car on one side of the Cook Strait, buy a passenger ticket, and pick up another rental car at dockside when you arrive. You save a good piece of vacation money in doing so. Smart.

The government-run ferries run several times a day and carry railroad cars, campervans such as ours, trailers, large trucks and automobiles. It is a big operation.

Our ferry was a new ship, the *Ararua*. Impressive. The *Ararua* was designed for the winds and high swells that roll through the Strait. The price tag was NZ$45,000,000.

The flagship of the Railways Corporation fleet has airplane-type reclining seats for easy sleeping in the forward lounge, a senior citizens lounge where grandmothers and grandfathers go to get away from screaming moppets, a video games room where moppets go to get away from silence, a music lounge, a TV lounge, snack bar, sundeck, bar, shop—everything to pass the time in the three-hour trip.

On previous ferry crossings, we had noted that the experienced Kiwis took their own nibblies. Today, signs forbid you to eat outside of the snack-bar area, but in old fashioned New Zealand tradition, you can still take your own picnic but eat in the snack bar.

The mid-November crossing, which can be very rough, was calm. Rainy, but calm.

155

Entering into the protected Queen Charlotte Sound is the glory road. A long, winding stretch of water snakes between tree-covered hills occasionally marked with summer cottages. Passengers lined the deck looking at the vacation homes thinking envious thoughts.

The ferry arrived in Picton, a summer colony town living off of the ferry trade. We were swiftly unloaded. Having pre-selected a nearby campgrounds from an AA accommodations directory, we followed the map to the grounds, paid NZ$10 and hooked up for the night.

The Marlborough Sounds is one of the New Zealanders' private secrets. A great place to explore for wine, for water adventures, for arts and crafts. A great place to fish, walk, hunt, swim, camp and relax. A great place to be by yourself.

We went back into Picton the next morning to explore. It is a village of 3,000-plus inhabitants, a population figure that swells by thousands in the summer when the Kiwis head for the bays and inlets of their private corner of the South Island to play.

Facing the Queen Charlotte Sound with a patch of lawn and flower gardens bordering the waterfront, the commercial buildings of Picton offer a visual feast for sensitive photographers.

At one corner of the waterfront is the Hotel Oxley's Hotel—that's how the sign reads—a cream colored building with brown trim and balconies of lacy iron. Victorian-Australian-pub architecture.

At the other corner, a block away, is the Terminal Hotel—the sign is in neon—its windows protected by little red and white awnings.

In between the two hotels the photographer will find the Seaspray Cafe, Rosa's Boutique, Hotel Federal and Ballinis for "soft drinks, hot pies, cakes, Coca Cola and tearoom dining."

While the Lady Navigator went shopping I nosed around the piers. There I found Southern Marine Charters, an operation with twelve rental sailboats and launches.

You have to look at a map of Marlborough Sounds to appreciate geographically what a splendid idea it would be to have a boat of any kind and, on your own, go sailing and bumming around the thousand little protected islands and inlets and islets that comprise the Sounds.

The present fleet of Southern Marine Charters consists of 34-foot launches powered with 80 HP diesels and 30-foot Y.88 yachts with supplementary 18 HP diesels.

The young lady in the office said her company had just bought the operation and was in process of upgrading the fleet.

From the first week of December to the last week of January, every yacht was booked but some of the best sailing is during February and March when the weather is very settled and boats are more readily available.

Contact Southern Marine Charters at P.O. Box 246, Picton, New Zealand.

You don't have to charter a boat to enjoy the waters of Queen Charlotte Sound or the Marlborough Sounds.

Another of the favorite water activities at Picton is cruising on the *M.V. Rawene* Royal Mail boat as it makes calls at the homesteads and farms around Queen Charlotte Sound. It is a full day bring-your-own-lunch cruise, part of Friendship Cruises with offices on the waterfront.

Other cruises consist of daily scenic tours to various bays around the principal inlet, luncheon and evening cruises to the Portage Hotel plus a Saturday evening dining special at the hotel.

The Portage Hotel is a famous inn of the Sound which we tried, but failed, to visit. It stays on our "futures" list.

The historic resort occupies the site where ancient Maori seamen dragged their canoes from one side of a narrow peninsula to the other to save a lot of long hard paddling out into the Cook Strait and down the Sounds again to reach the other side.

Once, the quiet, remote lodge and its self-contained chalets were accessible only by boat. Today, you reach the Portage by car (difficult) or by boat (easy) then a short bus trip over the saddle. The most romantic way (and easiest) is by floatplane that takes you to the dock at the front door.

Float Air operates from an office in the Ferry Terminal Buildings on the waterfront. Besides the Portage excursion, the floatplane flies scenic tours and luncheon trips to Castaway Resort on Tory Channel and Tira Ora Lodge on Pelorus Sound.

One of the future projects in Picton is to restore the old Edwin Fox, now a broken up hull resting in Shakespeare Bay near Picton.

The old sailing ship was built of East Indian teak in Calcutta in 1853 and was, at various times, a troop ship in the Crimea War, a convict ship to Australia, an immigrant ship to New Zealand, a refrigeration ship, a coal hulk and finally a breakwater. It is estimated that it will cost NZ$2,000,000 to restore the vessel as a national attraction docked at the Picton wharves.

Blenheim: Land Of Cheese And Wine

The Chilly Bin rolled south towards Blenheim stopping en route at Koromiko for a pound of Marlborough cheese from the local Co-Op—thereby earning ten points. We stopped again at a nearby historical site—ten points—which was where the "Wairau Affray" took place in June 17, 1843. A disputed land claim led to the death of 22 Europeans including Arthur Wakefield, leader of the Nelson colony and Edmund's brother. The titoki tree on the bank of the steam where the white party crossed to talk to the Maoris still survives.

Blenheim prides itself as the sunniest place in New Zealand. At one time it was known as "Beavertown" because the first settlers had to live like beavers above the swamplands which eventually became the middle of the village.

The swamps have long since been drained and Blenheim is now a prosperous farming community named after the battle place where the Duke of Marlborough defeated the French in 1704.

The first pamphlet we saw at the Public Relations office was a map of a local wine tour.

Hunter's Wines, not that far away, had a restaurant, and it was lunch time. Map in hand, we took off. A fifteen-minute backtrack on the highway to Picton brought us to Spring Creek. Turned left on Rapaura Road and there was Hunter's.

It was a beautiful morning as we drove through the vineyards to a tidy complex with separate rustic buildings for a tasting room, the restaurant and, behind them, the winery. There was only one other couple in the restaurant.

Your option was to pick out your own steak or breast of chicken and barbecue it to your taste on outside grills or have the staff cook it for you. You could dine inside or outside.

We ordered a bottle of Hunter's fume blanc, piled a plate full of fresh salad, grilled a steak and a half of chicken and sat under an umbrella and wondered why every lunch wasn't this perfect.

The restaurant operation was very new and run by a young couple under concession from the winery owner.

We pray they prosper.

We asked questions about the winery they couldn't answer which brought forth Ernest Christopher Hunter, a handsome Irishman still blessed with the brogue of his homeland. His smiling eyes, happy countenance and curly, grey flecked hair endeared him to the Lady Navigator.

The Lady Navigator: "I think I have found a new souvenir from New Zealand to take home. All right?"

Answer: "You stick to handknit sweaters."

Hunter had abandoned a successful discount liquor business—and was wondering why—seduced by the glamor of making the world's best wines. That's the single ambition of every winemaker. Only poets are less commercial.

"It was marvelous to begin with. Our wines won awards all over the place. Whatever we did was right. Then word began to get back to me that the new vintages were off. And they were. We had to go back to square one and start all over again. Now I think we are back on the track again."

Hunter's winemaker is a rarity. Almuth Lorenz is a young blond lady, 27, born in Mainz, Germany who graduated after five years of wine-making studies at Greisenheim University.

Hunter has 65 acres in grapes specializing in sauvignon blanc, chardonnay, cabernet, gerwitztraminer.

Part of the property is Commodore, a Great Dane big enough to lift up the Chilly Bin in his teeth. He watered a tire rim after lifting his left leg, thereby claiming it "Mine" and I didn't argue with him. If we wanted it, he could have it.

"You could call in at Mac's Real Ale Brewery outside of Nelson before you leave the area," Hunter suggested. "It is a new small independent brewery, one of only two independent breweries in New Zealand and makes as excellent, successful dark ale."

A postscript to the story: Hunter stopped off in Honolulu after being at the *London Times* Wine Show where he entered three wines and won three gold medals. Yes, he was back on track.

Our next call down the road and around the corner diagonal opposite the Marlborough Zoological Park (a 35-acre spread wi lions, tigers, water buffalo, otters, monkeys, and birds) and ne the intersection of Highway 5 and Highway 6, was the Cellier

Brun. Monsieur Daniel Le Brun, a French immigrant had opened his first bottles of champagne from the new venture just the week before.

Built against the side of a cliff, the neat new boutique winery was quite petite. Its slim, dark-haired owner spoke English with an intriguing French-flavored New Zealand accent.

"My family has been making champagne in Epernay for twelve generations.

"I could see in New Zealand, specifically this part of New Zealand, a chance to create new horizons.

"The weather is ideal for growing chardonnay, pinot noir and meunier grapes which I combine on a 40-40-20 ratio to make a blanc de blanc champagne in the traditions and methods of my forefathers. One of those methods, the replacement of wine after the *degorgement*, is a secret family formula.

"I started planting in 1980 and presently have 35 acres in grapes. My first production yielded 1,300 cases. Next year I'll have 4,000 cases. By the third year, 10,000 cases."

His first tastings received laudatory praise from the press. After a personal tasting, we concurred.

The problem facing Le Brun, we feel, is economic. His wine, at NZ$18, is competing against well-known French labels at about the same price. By some strange quirk in the tax laws, French champagne in New Zealand is about 50 percent cheaper than it is in Paris.

Daniel Le Brun should be congratulated for his courage and his product. Stop by, have a sip and buy a bottle.

Five miles south of Blenheim on Highway 1 is the largest winery in New Zealand, the Riverlands Winery of Montana.

Montana was brought to the Marlborough District in the early '70s under the direction of its boss, Frank Yukich, after a confirmation study by the University of California Davis that the weather, soil, lie of land, rainfall were suitable for grape cultivation, particularly for the early maturing varieties.

The first commercial vintage in 1976 was packed in apple boxes and filled three trucks. Production now is over 20,000 tons.

Visitors to the winery can view an audio-visual presentation of the vineyard, tour the barrel hall where over 800 casks, each holding 300 to 500 liters, are stored.

Interestingly, the oak barrels arrive in kits and cost from $450 to $900 each, depending on size. The kits come from the USA,

France and Yugoslavia and are assembled by Montana's cooper, one of only three full-time coopers in New Zealand.

The cooper is also charged with maintaining the barrels which means scraping them down to new wood every five years then reassembling them. The staves are thick enough to hold up under four such strippings.

The new winery's technology, equal to any in the world, is also matched in the field. Vines are irrigated by an automatic, clock-controlled trickle system. Harvesting is mechanized and testing is underway for mechanized pruning, thereby reducing the cost factor of the labor-intensive production.

The complex extends complimentary wine tasting at its retail outlet. Put a case of Montana's prize winning sauvignon blanc in your Chilly Bin and go sipping around the country.

The only wines packaged at the Riverlands property are cask wines. All bottling is done in Auckland, the center of wine sales.

It was a good day. One cheese factory, one historical monument, three wineries. Fifty points chalked up in the Non-Zip Enjoy It More Drive System . . . and several bottles of wine for the road.

By late afternoon we had pulled into the A-1 Holiday Park just outside of Blenheim and found a power point at the back of the property in a wide green field, close to the tree-lined river. Our only companions were one lady duck and a gaggle of drakes. The ducks would waddle up to the Chilly Bin, obviously expecting handouts. They received copious crusts of bread and we were rewarded with a constant chorus of soft quacks.

The sun sank in the west leaving a peaceful spot in shadows.

Marvelous Marlborough Sounds

We had looked forward to the next day's adventure with puppy-dog anticipation.

A full day on a Royal Mail boat calling on vacation homes and farms in the Marlborough Sounds.

Our trip was part of Glenmore Cruises leaving from Havelock, a small waterfront village located between Blenheim and Nelson. The two-boat cruise line provides transportation for scenic cruises, fishing trips, picks up and retrieves isolated trampers, and provides diving charters for groups.

The divers, mostly New Zealanders, are after scallops and lobsters and paua, a shellfish similar to abalone.

Glenmore is owned by Ken Gullery and his sparkling blond wife, Dianne. They won the Royal Mail route on bid. Homesteaders pay the government a modest amount to belong to the aquatic rural mail delivery and they pay Glenmore equally modest amounts to deliver beer or milk or groceries or needed pieces of equipment.

After buying bits and pieces for lunch supplemented by refrigerator items from the Chilly Bin—tea would be provided—we embarked about ten ayem. Half a dozen other passengers came along for the ride. A good cast of characters.

One couple—I thought at first he was part of the crew because he was always up front wherever we docked, handing out newspapers and mail and taking aboard empty mail sacks—lived on a farm on the Sounds. It was their first trip to the "Mainland" in over a year. He made noises as if he would never leave again.

Another young couple was on their honeymoon headed for a friend's cottage on the water for a week. They were taking a week's supply of groceries with them. What a great way to spend a honeymoon.

An attractive young man named Kevin, originally from Los Angeles, now a chef in St. Thomas in the Caribbean, was on an extended holiday bicycling from Auckland to Invercargill, almost the entire length of the country. Kevin had budgeted US$20 a day for expenses and intended to spend two months roaming the country, camping out and staying in youth hostels. He would manage on a total US$700.

Another loner, a New Zealander, sat quietly apart from the rest of us. It took most of the eight hours of the cruise to break through his reserve.

He worked in a freezing plant near Oamaru. The season for processing lambs for export hadn't started yet. The season usually began in December and went to May.

How big were the freezing works?

"Oh, we kill about 13,000 lambs a day."

A day! And this is a modest sized plant. It takes 32 freezing works in New Zealand to process 60,000,000 lambs a season.

What an industry. No wonder it provides the largest source of income for New Zealand.

Another passenger whom everybody wanted to talk to was an attractive young university student and part-time waitress who had been invited to spend a week with a family on their homestead.

The Lady Navigator: "Don't forget the Halls."

The Halls, Dennis and Joy, were typical laid-back New Zealanders . . . at first reserved but old shoes by the end of the eight-hour cruise. On a small boat you tend to become family very quickly. The Halls had a deep knowledge and pride in the flora and fauna of the country which they shared under an eight-hour bombardment of questioning by the Lady Navigator.

She learned, for example, that the rimu tree *matures* at 300 years, the rata at 600 years and the toara grows to a ripe old age of 2,000 years.

Our captain was Noel Parsons who worked mainly as a commercial fisherman doing private charters on the side.

Our first call was at a vacation home to deliver a crate of milk where two men in swimming shorts awaited on the pier. One of them had just come out of the water from a morning swim.

How was it?

"Not bad. Fifteen degrees, I'd say." (That's Celsius, you understand.)

The second stop was to drop off mail, newspaper and milk.

Our third stop, a rendezvous with a speedboat in the middle of the Pelorus Sound, was to pick up passengers from a nearby lodge who wanted to join the Royal Mail Run.

Beyond the vacation houses are the homesteads, probably an hour and a half from dockside. There are livestock farms running sheep, cattle or deer some of which operate fish farms in protected bays for mussels and salmon.

Each stop was a different experience. At one, the boat pulled alongside the end of a long pier where a man collected his groceries in a wheelbarrow; at another pier-less stop, the boat nudged gently up to a pile of rocks where mail sacks were exchanged with two older men dressed in torn sweaters and baggy trousers. Not your mind's eye picture of gentlemen farmers, these.

"How do they build houses way out here?" we asked Noel.

"They don't," he said. "A prefabricated house mounted on a truck is shipped on a roll-on, roll-off barge and trucked to a site."

"Even in such isolated areas, you always find power lines," we noted to Noel.

"Oh, yes. It's part of the government policy. These sheep stations, for example, need power for shearing. Some of the stations bring in teams of contract shearers but, for the most part, the shearing is done by cooperative neighbors, farmers throughout the Sounds."

We reached the top end of our run, Beatrix Bay, a little past noon. Schofield Station is at the end of nowhere.

We had lunched on "sammies" and hot tea and cookies (they are known as "bickies").

The green forests of the Sound had slowly dissolved into barren, scrubby land that appeared impossible to farm for profit.

A young boy about ten years old stood with his mother on the end of a pier and picked up the locked mailbag tossed to him. He returned an outgoing bag stenciled "Schofield."

I called up to the mother, "Where does your son go to school?"

She answered down, "Correspondence School."

"Does he do well?"

"Oh, yes," she said proudly.

"Does he take correspondence lessons in cricket?"

She laughed and waved us away.

(In Auckland I talked at length with a farm-stay organizer who said he had a cooperating property located "away from everything at the end of Marlborough Sounds." To reach it, you had to take the mail boat or a floatplane. He has never gotten anybody to try it. It smelled like Schofield. I'd love to try it.)

On the return trip to Havelock we stopped at a sea farm where a contract harvesting machine pulled huge ropes encrusted with green-lipped mussels onto a floating barge, stripping the shellfish off the ropes mechanically.

"Last year they harvested 15,000 tons of green-lipped mussels out of Marlborough Sounds," said Noel.

We stopped in front of a long beach and a man and his dog rowed out in his aluminum rowboat to get the mail and rowed back again to his station, not another house in view. Was it a lonely life?

"I think there are about 150 families living around the Sounds. See that bay in there and the white building on the shore? That is a community meeting house for the get-togethers of the local families. They'll have a party at an excuse. Yes, they come by boat. They know their boats as well as I know this one.''

We passed a quinnat salmon farm consisting of a dozen sea-cages where tiny salmon—smolts they are called—are fattened on special food for harvest. They thrive in the cold water. The Sounds people are hoping that salmon farming will succeed as a new, profitable aquacultural industry for the area. Eight farms are experimenting with it.

Closer to Havelock we passed another mussel harvester on the way to home port, loaded with huge bags holding mussels.

"I count about twenty bags," said Noel. "That load will be worth about $14,000."

And, occasionally, we saw the tiny bobbing heads of blue penguins who, at maturity, are only a foot tall.

It was a great day. Relaxing, involving, enlightening about another way of life.

Glenmore Cruises makes the run Monday through Friday. Or, at least they did on the last schedule we saw. The cost for joining the all-day cruise is a great vacation bargain. Write P.O. Box 34, Havelock or call—in the country—(057) 42-276.

With another two hours of daylight left, we drove over hill and dale to Nelson.

Nelson: Captial Of The "Sunshine State"

Nelson is a sweet city. Capital of the province with the same name, it prospers from government payrolls, from agriculture and aquaculture—Nelson scallops are famous—from the growing of hops and tobacco, from sheep and cattle and apples and, increasingly, from the arts. An influx of arts and crafts people are finding the ambience and the gentle weather of the area conducive to their creative juices. The clay around Nelson also has a well-known reputation which draws hordes of potters. There are more potters in New Zealand than sheep.

We had called the Nelson Public Relations Office to arrange an appointment for the next day. They, in turn, made reservations for us at Tahuna Beach Holiday Park, a major municipally owned, non-profit holiday park on the fringe of town with a mix of campervan sites, tent sites, tourist cabins, lodges and flats. Its adjacency to the beach and proximity to a sportsground, tennis courts and the Nelson Golf Club make it popular indeed with Kiwis.

Perhaps it was for our education that we were assigned a two-bedroom "paraplegic" flat. In addition to its spaciousness, it contained—luxury of luxuries for long-haul travelers—a clothes washer and dryer. It would have been too much to expect good reading lights.

Later we found that accommodations for the disabled are requisites of any new major accommodation project. It is another facet of upgraded New Zealand.

On our first trip to Nelson, we arrived on a Sunday night. Dining out was difficult because there were no restaurants open on Sunday night in Nelson, a fact of life about which we commented in the earlier book.

"The first thing I want you to know," said Peter Heath, Nelson's PR officer, the next morning, "is that Nelson has four restaurants open on Sunday night." (He had read the book.)

"Also," he said, referring again to the first book, "one, hops are grown *only* in Nelson, two, you can't take a private car on Farewell Spit and, three, the Cawthron Museum is closed."

"What's new in Nelson," we asked meekly.

"We have come up with a new title for our province. We call ourselves the 'Sunshine State'—of course, we are not a state, we are a province so, right off, it draws a lot of attention.

"And it's true. Even during two-thirds of the winter, we will have frosty mornings and then fine sunny days.

"We have a stable tobacco industry and our Nelson School of Music is one of only three in the country," continued Peter.

"Grapes are now growing in the area and we are starting our own wine tour. Here is a wine tour map."

He did an excellent job in pointing us in right directions.

New buildings have been added to the capital of the "Sunshine State." Take, as example, the new post office opposite the main intersection of Trafalgar and Halifax. (Most streets and parks are named after places and associates of the famous British admiral.) It is called the "drain pipe" locally because of a giant cylinder rising to its rooftop on one side with the clock from the old post office at its apex. It looks like a Vulcan missile with a timer.

We walked the city so the Lady Navigator could sleuth for treasures and we found an absolutely marvelous building on

Bridge Street—an apt address it turned out—housing a clutch of different "works"—the Cane Works, the Clay Works, The Sound Works and the Food Works. The weathered rough wood used to construct both the massive entry doors and a trestled second level interior once was the Hokitika Bridge. It had been dismantled and reassembled under a glass skylight. Architectural imagination is loose in Nelson.

You can't miss the Cathedral. It dominates the hill in the middle of town and reminds the visitor of the history of Nelson, the second colony started by the New Zealand Company under the direction of Captain Arthur Wakefield.

Immigrant ships brought 4,000 settlers to the area and the tough job of clearing the bush for the initial village proved disheartening in itself. Then there was neither enough money or land.

The aristocracy class which was supposed to be transplanted with their banks accounts and credit never came. Why should they leave the comforts of London? Besides, they were never encouraged to, because the New Zealand Company would have had to return 75 percent of their investment, under the sales agreement.

Buying land from the Maoris was equally difficult. Misunderstandings leading to conflicts with the Maoris were inevitable and an almost fatal blow to the entire Nelson enterprise came when Arthur Wakefield was fatally struck down at Wairau.

Tested by adversity, Nelson came through.

Military barracks occupied the top of the hill initially, until the Cathedral could be built. The present Cathedral is the third constructed on the site.

On the north side of the Cathedral are the old frame cottages of military non-coms, later to become brothel row and now charming boutiques and unique living quarters for lucky residents.

Part of the sweet city comes from its plethora of gardens and parks. You shouldn't miss Isel Park where a gardener and son spent a lifetime planting the grounds with trees from all parts of the world. Two rooms have been refurnished in the decor of the period and are open to the public on weekends.

The Provincial Museum, behind the Isel House, is of interest because of a most unusual man, Baron Rutherford (1871-1937), the first man to split the atom earning him the title of "the father of nuclear physics." He was born in the area and educated at

Nelson College, won the Nobel Prize in 1908, was elevated to the peerage in 1931 and is now buried in Westminster Abbey.

Broadgreen, another manor house and public garden, was our first favorite historic building in Nelson, particularly with its expanse of green lawns and rambling rose gardens.

The Lady Navigator talked to a lady gardener whose only job was to snip off the wilted roses.

"How long do you do this each season?"

"From October through June," was the reply. Nine months.

We went away with a handful of "wilted " roses that would have cost a fortune at any Honolulu florist.

On the way out of Nelson we remembered Ernie Hunter's suggestion and stopped at McCashin's Brewery, a small, independent brewery, only five years old, which is based on the real ale concept of creating its own malt, no rice or sugar or corn syrup additives, and has carved out a successful niche in the New Zealand beer market.

We were in England several years ago when a consumer rebellion started to fight the dominance of giant breweries. The rebels believed the ale formerly produced by the country's small breweries was becoming an homogenized, characterless brew.

A campaign was initiated called CAMRA—Campaign for Real Ale. It gained national media attention and public sympathy. As a result, several small independent breweries sprung up.

McCashin's is of this mold, a boutique brewery with a special concern for discriminating quaffers. The brewery produces a robust, black stout, porter, ale and lager.

Lady Navigator: "A porter? A porter carries luggage."

Response: "Among beverages, a porter is a weak stout."

Just down the road is Robinson Brothers, an orchard and a major producer of fruit wines.

We stopped by and talked to Colin Robinson, a grandson of the founder, an affable young man who was supervising the change from a small drop-in, buy-a-bottle operation to an major tourist stop with restaurant, gift shop, tastings and all.

The newsworthy hook at Robinson's is the founder, Thomas Kennedy Robinson, a government surveyor who retired at 65, bought an existing orchard in 1910, married—for the first time—at age 70 and sired three children. What a great advertisement for his product.

Robinson's bottles 700,000 liters of apple wine, boysenberry wine, and natural fruit juices a year. We took along a jug of apple wine—not cider—and found it most refreshing. It became a favorite nip.

We stopped at only one of the wineries on the wine tour en route to Abel Tasman National Park. Siegfried Winery's new tasting room was closed. The owners were in Nelson, according to the sign. The small winery had a popular rhine riesling and had won a gold medal for its 1985 sauvignon blanc.

Then we cut northwest across country backroads via the "three bridge" route to Motueka, passing many signs directing travelers to local potters' studios.

The South Island's Northwest

The wild country between Nelson and Farewell Spit is seen by too few overseas tourists. It is way, way off the usual visitor route but it is one of the most attractive playgrounds in New Zealand.

Its remoteness is one attraction. There is a rare variety of soils and rocks—marble, limestone, granite, volcanic remains. There is a profusion of greenery. Rugged mountains rise behind the sparsely scattered farms. You have it to yourself.

The farthest point west is Cape Farewell, so named by Captain Cook when he left New Zealand to sail for the uncharted land of Australia.

Curling back to the east is Farewell Spit, a long claw-shaped peninsula that is home six months of the year to some ninety species of birds, predominately waders from Siberia, who arrive in the Spring to breed in the summer. You can experience the remote, carefully guarded bird sanctuary on a four-wheel-drive Safari Tour. Know that you must travel over twenty miles of sand and that you must have reservations. Times of tours are dictated by the tides. Call TAK 48-257 (Collingwood) for details.

The bay protected by the spit is now called Golden Bay and was the first anchorage of Abel Tasman in 1642, the first European to see New Zealand. He anchored on Christmas Day but his landing party was attacked by two canoes and he lost four men. Eleven other war canoes came from shore to give battle but were turned away by cannon. Tasman pulled anchor and sailed north, naming the area Murderer's Bay.

Captain Cook sailed across the mouth of Murderer's Bay in 1770 and D'Urville followed 58 years later. D'Urville surveyed parts of the same coastal line adding further detail to Cook's surprisingly accurate charts.

In 1857, gold was discovered at Collingwood prompting the decision to name the bay Golden Bay.

Today Collingwood lives on dairy farming and is known as the take-off point for the Heaphy Track, a particularly popular but non-guided 70km hiking track with huts provided along the way. The trail ends on the West Coast.

The Collingwood area is also known, you learn, as "Cannabis County."

Golden Bay and Tasman Bay are separated by a thumb of granite hills covered with "native bush" which in 1942 became Abel Tasman National Park, a 50,000-acre playground. Few roads penetrate the park making it an idyllic camping and hiking area, particularly along the leeward east coast.

Within the park is Harwoods Hole, a 1,000-foot deep sinkhole, the deepest in New Zealand.

Entry to the playgrounds of Tasman is the little town of Motueka, population 4,600, the center of the rich hop and tobacco growing country, and also a growing community of artists and craftsmen.

A recommended stop is at the Post Office Hotel which advertises "3 bars to choose from—all our prices are subject to inflation as from 1870."

A more elegant refreshment stand is the Manor Restaurant. It enjoys a reputation as the best dining in the area.

In order to experience at least part of the Abel Tasman National Park even on a time-limited schedule, we called John Wilson from Motueka. He holds the concession from the Park Board to conduct all of the boat tours up the east coast of the park and guided walks in the park.

Our rendezvous was set for 9am on the beach at Kaiteriteri the following morning.

From Motueka, we drove the few miles around the coast to Kaiteriteri, one of the prettiest coastal stretches we found in New Zealand. A long golden beach connected two prominent outcroppings of rock. Back of the beach we found our motor camp, snug harbor for the night.

A loud American voice from a nearby campervan prompted me to wander over and introduce myself to Gena Sanders, the exuberant blond caravan coordinator for a tour out of Louisiana.

Seventy-four people in thirty-five caravans from twenty-eight U.S. states had come to New Zealand, not all of them to Kaiteriteri, an optional stop, on the tour. Organized group caravaning from America, we discovered, was big business.

Her group had finished a flying tour of Australia and, after their 17-day caravaning tour of New Zealand, would go to Fiji for a four-day rest before returning home.

As we waited on the beach the next morning, a middle-aged couple with large backpacks joined us. They carried bedrolls, tents, cooking utensils and all their food for a three-day 15-mile coastal hike. Captain Wilson's boat would take them to the north end of the Park at Totaranui and then they would hike back to the south end at Marahau.

Hikers plan to finish their trek at Marahau to coincide with the mailman's run who gives them a ride back to Motueka or else they pre-arrange to be met by a taxi at the end of the road.

John Wilson backed his 70-passenger ship, the *Waingaro*, up to the beach and extended its long gangplank to the sand, and we clambered aboard along with a variety of young people on holiday, some of them with backpacks. There was great interest in the ship's bulletin board where tidal warnings were posted. "High tide Awaroa 14 Nov. 11:30am. Cross inlet 3:30-7:30pm today."

Tides reach sixteen feet and hikers must time inlet crossings perfectly.

The first bay we pulled into was a rare stop. We picked up a bundle of young school kids, a never-stop-moving-or-talking group. "We don't come in here very often," said John. "This bay is dry a mile out to sea at low tide."

We passed Honeymoon Bay, Ngaio Bay, Tower Bay, Split Apple Rock—which looked like a giant split apple. Tobacco and hops farms and vacation homes dotted the shoreline.

As we crossed the official boundary of the park, signs of civilization disappeared except for an occasional walker in the tree line or tents camouflaged in the forest.

Many of the landmarks still bear names given them by

D'Urville: Adele Island named after his wife and Astrolabe Roadstead, Astrolabe being the name of his ship.

Other bays and inlets are named after early settlers.

We pulled into Fairy Cove and, because the tide was high, we were able to cruise up to the mouth of Falls River. There, a spider suspension bridge gives trampers a scenic view of this beauty spot, probably the most postcard-familiar picture in the park.

Fairy Cove at high tide is wilderness at its best.

We were surrounded by groves of manuka, stands of beech and lacy native ferns reflected on the mirror smooth water. Water so clean you could see the grains of sand on the bottom.

You can hardly believe it when Captain Wilson says that this deep water cove behind its protective sandbar reverts to a trickle of water at low tide.

Waingaro, the larger boat in the Wilson fleet, was continuing on to Totaranui, near the top of the peninsula, but at this midpoint site of the cruise, we transferred to *Ponui* to return to Kaiteriteri, giving us at least a taste of the park.

The 70-year-old launch, *Ponui*, licensed to carry nineteen passengers, was the original Wilson tour boat. Just out of the family dry-dock where it had been lovingly scraped down to the tiniest corner and repainted, she glowed.

We motored south to Torrent Bay which is the base camp for the Wilson's four-day, three-night guided walks which are limited to parties of fourteen, all the lodge will accommodate.

Hiking the first day starts from Tonga Bay, after tea, of course. Large packs are left on board. Hikers walk down the coast, have lunch at Bark Bay, cross the suspension bridge and walk down the coast to the base camp at Torrent Bay, an easy day's hike.

The base camp is a comfortable rustic cabin with bunks, flush toilets and other amenities including hearty food. (Bring your own spirits.)

The two following days are spent exploring the pleasant surroundings around Torrent Bay in make-your-own pace walks. The fourth day the hikers walk out.

Darryl Wilson, John's son who commanded the *Ponui*, spoke of the advantages of the format. "A couple can elect to do different things because they have options. He can hike. She can stay on the boat and then join the party for lunch. Or hike until lunch and then get back on the boat. Or, instead of hiking out, either—or both—can take the boat out.

"Guests like the fact they don't have to carry their own backpack; the accompanying boat does that."

The popular tour increases its number of hiking patrons by ten percent every year.

The quoted NZ$300 includes boat transportation, meals, bunks, bedding and towels for four days.

For more information write John Wilson, Green Tree Road, Motueka RD #3, New Zealand.

Note: the summer period at Abel Tasman is busy. In late February and March, during the Indian summer when the leaves begin to turn autumnal colors, is a prime time for beauty, weather and uncrowded conditions.

The gorgeous weather that morning on the boat was a prelude to the glory road south.

We returned to Motueka, battened down the hatches of Chilly Bin and headed south on Highway 61 to join Highway 6 en route to Nelson Lakes National Park.

A fine, sunny, no-wind day, we passed old farm houses, drying tobacco sheds and hop kilns, singular in design, tiny communities, neat orchards and well-kept farms.

We kept pointing out different montages of beauty. "Look at that. Look over there. What a picture."

Although we have traveled ninety percent of New Zealand, we are amazed at how frequently we encounter new corners of the country with different dimensions of rare beauty.

We left Highway 6 and cut across country on a secondary road to reach Birchlea Farm, a side destination we had in mind.

In Nelson we had expressed our desire to visit a goat farm, a new industry in New Zealand. Goats' wool was attracting ever increasing prices for use in both industrial and consumer products (mohair sweaters being one), and the price for the purebred stock had skyrocketed.

"You need to talk to Hazel Nichols of Birchlea Farms," Peter Heath told us and gave us a directional map to the homestead.

On a bluff high above the dirt road, we found a modest, one-storey house surrounded by green pastures.

A large lady with a large smile came out to meet us. She was

Hazel Nichols, a lady with soft curling grey hair and happy eyes.

After introducing ourselves—Peter's office in Nelson had told her we were coming—she took us over to the nearby pasture populated with white goats and leaned on a fence post.

"In the beginning we had two brown kids. We borrowed one good buck and bred them. Their kids were beautiful. That was the start.

"When we really began to get serioius about it, we bought one Australian doe for NZ$6,000. Our neighbors thought we were mad. I wondered myself. I used to go into the paddock every hour to look at her.

"We got $4 for her first fleece. That same fleece today would bring $45.

"I sold one of her sons for $15,000."

"$15,000! Do you have any more like that?" we asked.

"Oh, there are three out there in the paddock that are better. I sold a doe for $2,500 in 1983. The following year it would have brought $20,000.

"We've been into goats for ten years—purebreds for six."

"What makes a purebred?"

"You have to prove the goat's lineage through registration papers and it takes five crossings or breedings to be eligible for registration.

"Eight out of ten farmers in our district are into goats. You know one reason why? We don't have to worry about weeds anymore. Weeds are good goat tucker. We also have 1,700 ewes. The ewes eat the clover and the goats—they hate clover—eat everything else. There are no thistles in our paddocks anymore.

"Goats are almost human. We've had only two ewes who had any trouble kidding, (birthing) and they came to the fence to get our help. A ewe in trouble would have run away if a person approached her."

We followed Hazel into the house to see samples of goat fleece.

"Feel this," she offered a small rope made of white fleece. "They call this 'cashgora' as opposed to cashmere or angora. Cashmere is measured as being up to 19 microns in diameter. Mohair, from angora goat wool, is up to 24 microns. Fiber in between is called cashgora." She lovingly fingered the fleece. "We can sell all we can produce.

"In the season of 1981-82, total export sales were $20,000. This last season the sales were worth $3.5 million.

"In 1978 we had sixteen members in our association. Today we have 2,000 members.

"How far is it going to go? Who knows. All I know is that one fifth of New Zealand is covered with fabulous goat tucker."

It's a smelly business—but it also smells of money.

Lake Rotoiti And Nelson Lakes National Park

The secondary road south joined Highway 63 from Blenheim near Lake Rotoiti, a favorite fishing spot. At lake's edge, the Alpine Lodge has lifted the outings of many a fisherman to a new level of luxury.

Success has come from having 20 first-class hotel units (more were planned) that are easy to get to yet removed from the crowds and surrounded with sporting activities: fishing on Lake Rotoiti or surrounding lakes and rivers of the park, hunting for red deer and chamois, white water rafting, hiking and mountain climbing and, in the winter, nearby skiing.

Situated at the edge of Lake Rotoiti, part of Nelson Lakes National Park, the lodge was typical of upgraded New Zealand.

Our destination, however, was Lake Rotoroa Lodge, recommended by several friends and professional contacts.

Highway 63 blends into Highway 6 following the Buller River on its descent to the Tasman Sea. We left it at the Gowan River turn-off. The Gowan River is a fast-flowing stream, "gin-clear" is the expression used by fishing writers.

We followed the river upstream seven miles to Lake Rotoroa.

We were now in the Nelson Lakes National Park. We crossed a bridge, turned left and stopped in front of a brown, two-storey lodge built by stagehands for the film adaptation of a Victorian novel—or so it seemed. This was Lake Rotoroa Lodge.

I love the world of yesterday and all of the lodge smacked of yesterday.

Wading gaiters and fishing rods and a wall decorated with antlers cluttered the entryway. Inside, the lobby had lamps with fringed shades, a chamois head, a hand-cranked telephone.

Down a hallway to the left two doors with frosted glass panels etched with the words "Dining Room" in a 1920s full flowing script.

The walls of the corridors and dining room were paneled in dark wood on the lower half and the upper half was of off-white pressed metal, the kind you find in Irish bars, and divided into rectangles with slats of stained wood.

A giant fireplace was the central attraction of the lounge, winning out over mounted trophy fish and animal heads on the walls. Tiffany lamps and overstuffed chintz-covered furniture welcome the jet traveler back to the turn of his century. A pour-your-own-drink bar is to one side of the fireplace.

Upstairs in the bedrooms, brass bedsteads and chenille bedspreads and antique furniture are contrasts to the private bathrooms that have been modernized. Charming and warming is the small flask of sherry and wine glasses on the dressing table.

All in all, a charming inn.

"You should have seen it when I took it over," said Bob Haswell. The handsome young ex-banker left a 27th floor office in Auckland to become the proprietor of a remote fishing lodge.

"The roof had caved in, the interior was a shambles. It had to be rebuilt. New plumbing. New wiring throughout. Finding the right antique furnishings took time.

"The original building was put up in 1924 by a Scottish family who sold their farm and built the lodge as an investment. It could just as well have been a one-storey building but, probably for prestige, they wanted that European look and made it two stories."

"How did you get involved?" we asked.

He gave a deep sigh. "I got trapped. Bewitched. I arranged the financing for a friend who wanted to buy the lodge and redo it and open it as a commercial, upmarket fishing lodge. He was stricken with cancer. Well, by that time I was deeply enmeshed in the potential of the place, the setting, the mountains, the country charm, and I took it over.

"We are doing well. We cater to the accomplished fisherman who knows what it is to stalk a giant trout, land it and release it. It is challenging and rewarding.

"The river is open from the first of October to April 30. The lake is open year around except in September.

"We can arrange boat fishing, river fishing with guides, helicopter fishing and hunting.

Two other guests included an airline pilot for an American national carrier and an oilman from Texas, old friends who got together once a year, somewhere in the world, for fishing.

After a wild boar dinner, we all went down the few yards to the bridge across the Gowan and listened to the splashing of trout in the evening rise as the fish came out of the water to feed on tiny moths. It was enough to send you after your waders.

The lodge is also surrounded by excellent walks through the bush and after breakfast the next morning, we went for a constitutional along the lake shore on a short loop track that took us through forests of beech and fern.

In the distance were snow-covered peaks of the Traverse Range. A place of peaceful mountain beauty.

Lake Rotoroa Lodge is expensive but not unreasonable. It attracts the kind of clients who don't mind renting a helicopter from the Picton or Nelson airport to save the two-and-a-half hour drive.

If a budget is on your mind you can stay at the nearby YMCA camp for $5 a night. You share the same lake. Bring your own bed linen.

A park ranger station located just across the bridge from the lodge dispenses local information.

For more about the lodge, write Lake Rotoroa Lodge, Owen River RD Nelson, New Zealand.

Mrs. Collins' Scones

We pointed Chilly south on Highway 6 to Murchinson where we stopped—ten points—at Collins Tearoom, greatly enlarged since we last stopped by, for scones and tea and coffee. We asked if Mrs. Collins was still there, and could we see her. She was, and we did. Was she still adding an egg to her scone batter (they are delicious)? Indeed she was.

We told her that we had written a book about New Zealand and had recommended stopping off in her tearoom for the scones.

"Oh, you're the ones." she exclaimed.

She offered to pick up the check, too.

The Lady Navigator, "Are you going to let her pick up the check?"

Answer: "People like to do things like that for other people. It makes them feel good."

The Lady Navigator: "It doesn't make me feel good. Pay the check."
Women.

Murchinson, population half a thousand on crowded days, is at the junction of the fish-filled Buller and Matakitaki Rivers.

Originally a gold rush town, it literally exploded in a violent earthquake in 1929.

Murchinson is also famous as the stage setting for Captain George Fairweather Moonlight, the perfect comic opera character. An American gold prospector in California and Australia, he made successful finds in the goldfields of New Zealand but left the claims for others to mine. In Murchinson he became a hotelkeeper and a self-appointed keeper of the law. He was handy with his fists and was called "Yank" with respect.

His standard dress was Wellington boots and jodhpurs, crimson shirt tied with a maroon sash. When he traveled, legend said, he traveled only at night.

His end was tragic. His wife died. His business failed. Returning to prospecting, Captain George Fairweather Moonlight died alone in the bush.

10. Westland

Funny Rocks And Seaside Glaciers . . .
Jade Carvers And Whitebait

The Buller River, flowing from Lake Rotoiti, is joined by the turbulent white water of the Gowan River coming from Lake Rotoroa and falls rapidly to the flats at Murchinson where it flows through quiet green meadows. Gathering strength from half a dozen contributing rivers, it starts a wild slashing romp fifty miles down to the sea at Westport.

The drive from Murchinson to Westport is a romantic, remote drive because of the beauty of the gorges. It is also awesome. You are ever aware of the power of the rushing waters of the Buller River as it tumbles and falls, gouging at dirt-stripped cliffs through the Upper Buller Gorge, then surging past the silver and red beech trees of the spectacular Lower Buller Gorge beyond Inangahua Junction.

Craggy hills overlook the raging river. At one point, at Hawks Crag, the highway had to be carved into the stone cliffs.

Stop below Murchinson at the sign indicating a rift caused by the 1929 earthquake. You can see where the earth parted and one side of the river bank was lifted to a higher elevation.

If you'd like to have a closer encounter with the Buller, make contact with Back Trax, a river rafting company that operates on most of the rivers in the area. Their Lower Buller Gorge trip takes only two and a half hours. But before you sign on, preview some of the names of the Grade 4 rapids you will encounter: Whopper Stopper, Waterslide, Gunslinger, and Wringer.

Arrival in Westport brings you to the West Coast of the South Island.

The narrow strip of usable land from Westport 440km south to the Haast Pass in called Westland. They should call it Skinny Westland. It is one of the few places in New Zealand where you are not surrounded by sheep.

This strangely beautiful country shadowed by the towering peaks of dozens of different ranges is imprisoned by the Southern

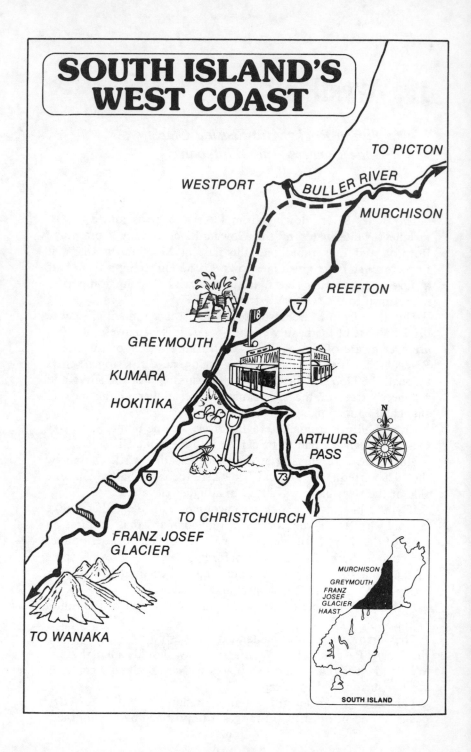

SOUTH ISLAND'S WEST COAST

TO PICTON

WESTPORT

BULLER RIVER

MURCHISON

REEFTON

18

7

GREYMOUTH

SHANTY TOWN HOTEL

KUMARA

HOKITIKA

ARTHURS PASS

N

6

73

TO CHRISTCHURCH

FRANZ JOSEF GLACIER

TO WANAKA

MURCHISON

GREYMOUTH
FRANZ
JOSEF
GLACIER
HAAST

SOUTH ISLAND

Alps. Tasman, the first European to see the coast, called it a "land uplifted high."

An English naval survey ship first saw a "stupendous mountain" in the distance and named it Mount Cook. The year was 1851 which jolts you back to the realization of how new New Zealand is to the Western world.

What the modern visitor sees on his journey from Westport to the Haast Pass is a country of virgin forests, scenic beaches— many of them excellent for swimming in mid-summer—quiet lakes and spectacular glaciers whose long white tendrils stretch from mother lodes atop towering 12,000-feet peaks and flange out into river beds at sea level.

Where else in the world can you see glaciers stopped just short of the ocean and fringed with palm trees?

It is a land, too, blessed with mineral riches.

Explorers found valuables.

The Maoris found greenstone, a hard, distinctively colored jade rock which was fashioned into family heirlooms, adzes, hand weapons. Expeditions from the other side of the mountainous divide made tortuous trips over Lewis Pass to trade or mine for greenstone. (Their slaves, used as pack animals, sometimes were eaten on the way back home to the East Coast.)

The first European explorers found coal. Later gold was discovered which created an invasion of gold miners from Australia.

Native timber was also a valuable commodity.

The drifters of the gold rush eventually disappeared but the coal and the timber remained and the West Coast ports, Westport and Greymouth, are still shipping terminals for the raw materials.

Westport, at the mouth of the river, is the largest coal exporting town in New Zealand, an industry augmented by timber milling and fishing.

One of the catches in season along the Westland tidal river basins is whitebait, a product that makes normally sane New Zealanders drool at the corners of their mouths and behave as children do when offered a hot fudge sundae. Whitebait is *the* delicacy of New Zealand, a country overflowing with a cornucopia of goodies.

The fish is no longer than your wife's little finger, translucent except for its tiny mouth and popping dark eyes. Gourmets make patties of batter and whitebait, fry the patties, and sigh to heaven as they devour the fritters.

My problem is that every time a fritter is put before me, the host of little black eyes staring up at me affects my ability to lift a fork.

The dominant species is Inanga, the most prolific of the six species in New Zealand. About 250,000 pounds a year is harvested in shoals of rivers in the three-month spring season.

Once, the village of Okuru in South Westland held an annual Whitebaiters' Ball. Beer was served from 18-gallon kegs even though in those days the country was "dry." Brawls between rival riverbank fishermen helped make the event one of the more memorable social highlights of the year. (They were hard up for highlights.)

Between Westport and nearby Cape Foulwind, is Carter's Beach, one of the better swimming beaches on the coast. Camping grounds and tourist flats are also available.

Highway 6 south cuts inland briefly then returns to the coast at Charleston, a town which once held 80 hotels plus dancehalls, brothels and barbershops following the discovery of gold in 1866.

Gone are the giant hammers and batteries used to pulverize the gold found in quartz-bearing reefs. How these major pieces of equipment were hauled to such remote areas under such primitive conditions, I cannot imagine. It had to have been a lesson in hardship and perseverance.

Today, the gold star attraction mid-way between Westport and Greymouth is the work of Mother Nature. Fleets of tour buses disgorge their passengers at Dolomite Point to see the pancake rocks and blowholes of Punakaiki.

You should begin your visit across the street at the information kiosk for a greater appreciation of the natural sculpture. Or in their clean restrooms for a more comfortable tour.

Next door is a forgettable "No-Points" souvenir snack shop.

The trip to the rocks and blowholes is a ten-minute walk—unless the blowholes are performing. Then, for some reason, audiences become mesmerized.

We have a blowhole on the island of Oahu where we live, and, when we're taking visitors on a scenic ride around the island, stopping at the blowhole is a must. What is particularly unreal is the amount of time visitors—and especially photographers—will spend waiting for a jet of water to spurt into the air . . . and how many useless pictures they will snap.

Snap, snap, snap. Kodak, we think, invented blowholes. The several blowholes at Punakaiki—Sea Spray, Chimney Pot and Sudden Sound among them—were off duty during our visit but that didn't discourage an optimistic German photographer. He had crawled over a protective fence and stood dangerously perched on a pile of rocks awaiting the fountain squirt that never came. How to Get Lost Permanently in New Zealand.

Vegetation resistant to salt spray covers the point. The nikau palm with its long trunk and branches rising from a bulbous top is the most spectacular. Tree ferns and rata vines add a semitropical air to the point. Watch for, or listen for, the bellbird, tui, fantail, tomtit and wood pigeon.

Black-backed gulls and shags fly off the point and white-fronted terns nest in the rocks.

The pancake rocks are almost funny looking—like giant plops of mud pies thrown there by children. Actually, they are alternate bands of limestone and mudstone and siltstone lifted off the ocean floor by an early cataclysm and, as the softer mudstone eroded, the other layers endured.

Back from the edge of the cliffs is a big open hole caused by the collapse of the roof of a sea cavern. Now you look down into the surging waters of a sea roaring in and raging to get out. Entrapped in this cauldron of churning water are giant arms of kelp kept constantly in motion by the wave action. It took very little imagination to see denizens of the deep, huge and hungry octopi, waiting for a human sacrifice.

The coast run down to Greymouth is quite scenic and we were happy to have made the drive.

In a previous trip heading north to keep a hard-to-get ferry reservation at Picton, we had deleted the Pancakes Rocks, Westport and Buller Gorge corner from the itinerary, turning inland from Greymouth to Reefton to the Inangahua Junction.

This short cut took us through Reefton which, like the sea coast town of Charleston, also was a gold-boom town. Its original glorious name was Quartzopolis. Speculative companies were formed and, aided by the then instant communications afforded by the telegraph, Quartzopolis was a boom town. On paper. The boom went bust destroying many paper fortunes although millions of dollars were pulled from its mines before the end of the century.

A unique historical fact is that tiny Reefton had its first electric light only six years after the first streets of New York were electrified. An English engineer installed a demonstrational one-kilowatt lamp in Dawson's Hotel, now the Masonic, and Reefton gained an early appreciation for electricity. By 1888, this little town out in the middle of nowhere was enjoying the benefits of hydroelectric power.

Just Call It "Grey"

Greymouth, the largest city in Westland, population 11,000, commonly referred to as "Grey," was named after Sir George Grey, the first governor of New Zealand. The storm wind that whistles occasionally through the area is known as *The Barber*.

We had two memories of our first trip to Greymouth. After being washed off the Greymouth Golf Club—par 72, flat, tree-lined—we stopped at a fruit stand and asked the Irish proprietor "Have you had much of this weather."

He answered quickly. "Since last Christmas." It was then early December and we laughed.

"You don't believe me? They've had seven *yards* down the road!"

We had stayed the night in Grey, during that same trip, at a motel. In those pre-Chilly Bin day, we had purchased a plastic ice tray because the pathetic little things in New Zealand motel refrigerators hardly iced one drink. We would make ice overnight, dump it into our styrofoam ice chest the next morning to chill foodstuff and give us enough ice for drinks that night.

However, we had not had a refrigerator the night before and there was nothing in our motel refrigerator in Grey, not even an empty ice tray.

I went to Mrs. O'Donnell, the proprietress, and asked for ice and a tray.

"You're an American, aren't you," she asked in a gentle way.

"Yes. How did you know?"

"Americans never ask first 'How are the beds?' They ask 'Where's the ice?' "

On our return trip we made our usual first stop at the Public Relations Office.

"We have a new attraction in Paroa Wild Life Park, one of the best in the country. You can see everything from Himalayan Thar to elk—at least eleven animals and many different birds," the young lady in charge told us.

"Shantytown has been constantly expanding since you were last here.

"Lots of new shopping including Beck's Emporium and we have one of the outstanding greenstone carvers in New Zealand living in Greymouth—Ian Boustridge. I'll give you his address and telephone number. You should go and see him. He works out of his home and is a first-rate craftsman.

"You can also hire a bike and go pedaling around and take walks. Tramping is good for you."

After shopping for groceries we checked into a seaside camping ground called the Seaside Motor Camp and hooked up. It was here that I learned why we had been drawing strange looks in previous camps. The function of the plastic bucket furnished with the van was not for soaking dirty clothes or washing feet but was to be placed under the sink's outlet pipe. Until then we had just let the water spill out onto the ground. Bad form.

A string of Newmans vans pulled into camp and hooked up. It was another tour group from America. All were owners of recreational vehicle at home. They were relaxing over Jim Beam and water.

"Never drive eight hours a day," said one tired driver, taking a sip. "On these roads it's murder."

A good reminder. The roads in New Zealand, especially in Westland, are not super highways.

I went to the office to buy milk and talk with Rhonda Levien, the proprietress, about what one did in the area. Visit Shantytown, fish, play golf, swim, walk, she said. "And go see Ian Boustridge," she said. "I'll call him for you."

We unhooked the lifelines, piled back into Chilly Bin and drove the few blocks to the greenstone carver's home.

Ian Boustridge alone is worth a trip to Greymouth if you are seriously interested in buying one-of-a-kind expensive jade jewelry. Ian is a handsome, articulate, knowledgeable artist. The Lady Navigator includes him in her shopping chapter.

The major tourist attraction of Grey is Shantytown, a heritage theme park, located five miles south of town.

A recreated West Coast gold-mining town, its retail shops, jail, newspaper, pub, stables are in the architectural style of its day.

Shantytown even has its own sluicing claim where, for a fee, you are guaranteed you will find "color."

Rides are available on a steam train or a four wheel buggy or a Cobb & Co state coach through the native bush.

The attraction was created after a member of the local public relations staff made a trip to Knoxberry Farm in Los Angeles.

Today, there are several authentic elements at Shantytown. The church is over one hundred years old, moved from the little village of No Town. The print shop has a genuine 1837 Columbian printing press. The favorite photographic spot is the authentic gallows—although hanging was not a large habit in New Zealand. There's a fire station, blacksmith shop, engine sheds and livery stables and—of course—a tearoom.

The 1900 railway station serves as a ticket dispenser for the Infants' Creek Bush Tramway, a ten-minute ride through the bush, almost daily. The specially built carriage is pulled by the Kaitangata, a genuine steam engine employing a certificated engine driver.

We thought the Coronet Hotel, self proclaimed "a better than average pub," was a beauty.

Continuing south from Paroa which is the turnoff to Shantytown, you come to the Kumara Junction which is the turn-off to Arthur's Pass, our next destination.

However, if you continue south on Highway 6 another 23 kilometers, you arrive in Hokitika.

Hokitika is known locally, as you would suspect in New Zealand, as "Hoki."

When it flourished during its goldmining days, it had a population of 50,000. There were as many as 60 ships anchored at one time in its small and dangerous harbor guarded by a sandbar. The favorite pastime was to go down to the cliff and watch the ships negotiating the passage over or around the sandbar and place bets on which ones would make it and which ones wouldn't. Many ships didn't make it. The average was one loss every ten days.

During the twelve years after gold was discovered in 1864, more than $27 million of gold was taken from the area.

Hoki remains today a timber center with a strong streak of leftover Irish stock from the goldrush period.

The area just north of the town is still a source for the nephrite jade or greenstone prized by the Maoris and today a local industry consists of grinding and carving souvenirs for tourists—earrings, pendants including copies of the traditional *hei-tiki*, the tribal neck pendant seen in museums.

Look for the tour buses to find the greenstone factories. You can see the boulders being sawn by diamond blades into workable sizes and then reduced to jewelry or souvenirs. You can buy junk and you can art. The art pieces are expensive.

We visited the West Coast Historical Museum, a small but informative museum recalling the history of the gold-digging past. A large collection of photographs and clippings from old newspaper stories was on display. Among the stories was one of Guy Menzies who filed a flight plan from Sydney to Perth and then took off in the opposite direction across the Tasman Sea. The year was 1931 and no one had ever flown solo between Australia and New Zealand.

Menzies made the South Island coastline but ran into bad weather and diverted to Westland where he turned turtle while making an emergency landing in a swamp. Having no other recourse, the adventurous pilot undid his seat belt and fell out on his head. A cut lip and probably a headache was the extent of the damage. But he set a record.

Seaside Glaciers

The stars of Westland's tourism are two very accessible glaciers, the Franz Josef and the Fox Glaciers.

In 1860 a James Mackay, acting for the Queen, bought more than 6,000,000 acres from the local Maori tribe for £300. Out of these government lands almost 200,000 acres were eventually set aside as Westland National Park which encompasses rivers, mountains, waterfalls, forests—and more than 60 glaciers.

Pack a raincoat.

The topography of the land is responsible for the heaviest rainfall and snowfall in New Zealand. Moisture laden winds rushing across the Tasman Sea are slammed against the towering wall of the Westland mountains and condensed into rain. The resultant showers make the seacoast heavy with greenery—and sandflies.

Pack insect repellent.

At higher elevations the snow falls in the crevasses of the

mountains in such volume that it cannot melt, packing the snow underneath so heavily that it turns to solid ice. The resultant glacier creeps slowly down the crevasse, crushing boulders and stones beneath to powder as it moves ponderously toward the sea, advancing in periods of severe winters and retreating in winters of mild weather.

During our last trip, the Franz Josef glacier, in an advancing period, was moving forward at a rate of more than a 100 feet a month.

You can't miss the National Park headquarters after entering the park. The displays and pamphlets give you more information about glaciers than you can absorb.

You learn that of the park's 60 glaciers only the Franz Josef and the Fox are accessible, although a scenic flight from the area will take you over a wonderland of snowmass. A nearby airstrip offers scenic rides.

Also available is a heli-hike tour where you are landed on the glacier and guided over this frozen river of ice.

The faces of the two glaciers are short distances away from fern groves and subtropical plants. Nowhere else in the world does this strange mixture of nature exist.

The Franz Josef glacier was named by the explorer van Haast after his Austrian emperor.

Park headquarters have map pamphlets detailing drives and walks that take from two minutes to all day.

Yes, there is fishing in the park.

Within walking distance of park headquarters is the St. James Church, a photographic stop for its Tudor architecture and the view from the sanctuary rail towards the glacier. At one time the wall of ice could be seen through the window—and if the snows keeps advancing at 100 feet a month, it may happen again.

If the church is closed, walk around to the window where you get the same view from the outside.

Visiting the glacier is an enjoyable experience.

Sign-posted sidewalks taking only minutes lead you to Peter's Pool, a "kettle" lake on top of a knoll. The pool—a kettle—is the result of melted ice. Clear and placid, it mirrors the surroundings, a favorite shot among photographers.

Sentinel Rock is a commanding viewpoint from which to see the glacier's path. At the time of its discovery in 1857, the rock fronted the face of the glacier.

The carpark abuts a mountain of rock worn smooth by the advancing and retreating glaciers. Wear your tennis shoes and climb the glacier. It is a great place to work out your muscle-tight driving kinks.

If you want to hike on the glacier, arrangements can be made through the Franz Josef Hotel for the proper equipment including boots, socks, alpen stocks.

Besides having a raincoat, you should make sure you have a reservation because parking space for bodies is limited. Coming from the north you will pass, in order, the Motel Franz Josef, the Franz Josef View Hotel and the Franz Josef Hotel, a THC operation.

Between Franz Josef Glacier and Fox Glacier the road is tortuous. An information sheet available at the park headquarters details interesting facts about the country you are driving through and, if you have a good Lady Navigator to read to you, you may not be able to see the country because your eyes are glued to the road but you will be able to hear about it.

If you overnight in the area, the Westland National Park Visitor Centre sponsors a ranger-narrated slide show nightly.

To the west of the Visitor Centre is a hotel, souvenir shop, tearoom, post office and an air strip. A road leads to Lake Matheson which has the reputation of being one of the most photographed lakes in New Zealand because of its reflections of distant mountains. Not when it is raining. And it usually is raining. A rowboat can be hired at the hotel to take you to the far side of the lake where the setting is even more photogenic.

You reach the face of Fox Glacier by driving back to Highway 6 and going a short distance south to the entrance.

Actually, the face of a retreating glacier is not very pretty. To satisfactorily experience a glacier you have to walk on it or ski on it or fly over it.

The face of a glacier is not an ice-cream parlor, snow-white wall but is part grey, part blue, part white, filled with dirty sand and rocks. The surrounding moraine is composed of the gravel left by the crushing weight of the glacier.

However, if you are game for an hour-and-a-half walk, round trip, up and down a steep and winding trail, follow the signs to the top of Cone Rock where you will be rewarded with spectacular views. "Now, that is a glacier!" you will say.

Or, if you are mountain oriented, Alpine Guides has several mountaineering adventures from one day trips on the glacier to mountaineering instruction courses on all levels. P.O. Box 38, Fox Glacier, Westland National Park, New Zealand.

Highway 6 continues south from Westland National Park to the Haast Pass and over the mountain to Wanaka. Negotiating the Haast Pass is best driven in the afternoon with the sun at your back. If you are driving north from Wanaka, you want to make the trip in the morning.

The Haast Pass is the newest road across the Southern Alps although it is the lowest and was long known to the Maoris as a trail to the greenstone country.

In 1863 a gold prospector by the name of Charles Cameron said he was the first white man to cross over the pass but his statement was doubted. In 1881 his powder flask was found at the summit and a nearby mountain is now named Mt Cameron.

Coming in second was Julius von Haast, the Austrian who had been brought to Christchurch as the Canterbury Provincial Geologist.

In 1929 a make-work project was started to build a road over the pass but it was not completed until 1965.

It is not the best highway in New Zealand but there are several interesting places to stop—ten points, remember—and short walks to take and photos that will make your stay-at-home friends hate you—and aren't those really the best photos of all?

11. Down The Middle Of The South Island

A Hairy Ride Into Arthur's Pass . . .
The Mount Cook Playground . . .
Pretty Wanaka . . .
Bustling Queenstown . . .
The Scenic Routeburn Walk

We had been down the east coast and crossed the Lewis Pass.
We had been down the west coast and crossed the Haast Pass.
But we had never been through the middle of the South Island
or crossed Arthur's Pass.

From Greymouth we pointed the Chilly Bin to Kumara Junction
and left Highway 6 for Highway 73 leading to Arthur's Pass.

Almost from the beginning of our adventure, whenever we
found a trustworthy travel authority, we asked, "Can we get our
four-berth campervan up Arthur's Pass from the west coast?"

The answer was never an unqualified, "Oh, sure it will be a
breeze." Rather it was always a modified affirmative.

"Ah, yes, you know, ah, I wouldn't do it in the dark or in a
heavy rain or windstorm but I think you can make it."

Uh-huh.

The citizens of Canterbury wanted a road to the goldfields
hoping that the gold would flow back through the capital city of
Christchurch instead of being sent overseas by ship. The citizens
on the west coast, however, didn't need the road or want the
road, and, forced to pay for part of it, seceded from Canterbury
Province and organized Westland as a political entity.

The route was found by Arthur Dudley Dobson in 1864 when he
was 23 years old, aided, it is said, with information given to him
by a Maori chief.

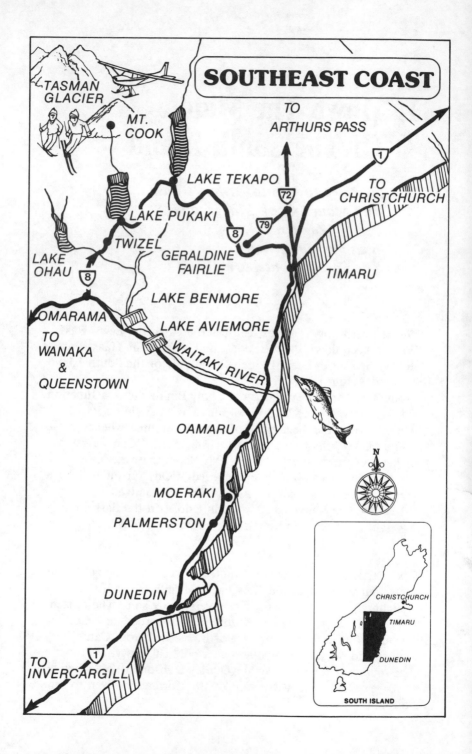

When the mountains were being surveyed by George Dobson, Arthur's brother, he was asked the best route through the mountains, and he replied, "Oh, Arthur's pass is the best."

George Dobson, who completed the road to Canterbury, was killed by road robbers in 1866. Arthur became a famous engineer in New Zealand and was knighted in 1931 at the age of 90.

We passed through small villages before starting to climb. The Lady Navigator read from a regional strip map: "Warning. Due to the steep and winding nature of the road and the strong winds blowing up the Otira Gorge, caravans, trailers and any vehicle over 12 meters is prohibited from driving on the Arthur's Pass Otira Road."

Silence smothered the air space in the Chilly Bin.

The morning was beautiful enough to dispel lingering fears.

We passed Jacksons where there is a turnoff to Lake Brunner, another of those closely guarded secret hideouts the Kiwis keep for themselves. Another route to Lake Brunner is Highway 7 north of Greymouth to a secondary road and the village of Moana on the northern edge of the lake. The route via Jacksons takes you to Mitchells on the south end of the lake. Shhh. Don't tell. Tuck it away.

A railway line paralleled most of the highway to Arthur's Pass. The railway was completed in 1922 with the punching through of a five-mile tunnel. It is the only rail traffic between the east and the west coasts.

As the grade steepened, valiant Chilly Bin, never overpowered, barely crept upward in the next to lowest gear.

We came to one heart stopping section where the road had been hacked out of stone. It was one way. A sheer cliff was overhead. A sheer fall was under the right tire.

My heart went on vacation. God and good luck were with us. The one-way traffic direction was in our favor. If we had had to halt and then start from a dead stop, I don't know if we could have made it. I do know I would have been more petrified than I was.

Once past that section, the worst was over. The summit is only about 3,000 feet.

We passed a turnoff to a parking area near Mt Temple where a skifield draws people from Grey and Christchurch.

In non-winter months, Arthur's Pass National Park is hiking country, and the sight of heavy-booted, wool-shirted, knapsack-carrying walkers is the most familiar sight.

We stopped at the Arthur's Pass township, the typical "convenience" village you find in national parks, with its general store, a tiny railroad station, a petrol pump.

The village store evidently is the communications center of the community where the newspaper is picked up and gossip exchanged. We bought an ice cream cone. A store across the highway sells hiking equipment, hand knitted sweaters and postcards.

You can't miss the Visitors Centre which has excellent graphic displays showing the construction of the highway and the railroad. A fine slide presentation reviews the history of Arthur's Pass and adds a dimension you seldom associate with tough engineering and construction feats. Vacationers made the arduous trip to Arthur's Pass on horse-drawn carriages. It was considered high adventure.

There is an 1888 Cobb Company coach on display from which you get an idea of the degree of comfort its fourteen passengers experienced.

An excellent brochure describes day walks in the area, on the back of which is a map of six good camping and picnic spots with cold running streams nearby and pit toilets.

"Be careful of Kelly Shelter," a young blond ranger advised in reference to overnight camping. "Lots of sandflies."

Sandflies are nasty tiny creatures whose nips produce swollen bumps. You wouldn't think anything so small could create such big problems.

We rolled down the road and over a bridge into a small parking area ten feet above the Waimakariri River under a canopy of podocarp trees. In the distance were the snow covered Southern Alps. An ideal spot where a constant diversion was spotting different species of birds.

After the emotional strain of driving Arthur's Pass—greater in anticipation than actuality—we took the rest of the day off and prepared a leisurely lunch preceded by the proper aperitifs and accompanied by wine.

Too many aperitifs and too much wine. Enthused by the beauty and nature of the place, I said after lunch, "Hey, let's go for a swim."

The Lady Navigator, more temperate in all departments and therefore not falsely encouraged by beverages, demurred while I slipped into swimming trunks and climbed down the bank to the river. She followed more as a lady banker protecting her investment than a spectator.

The river flat was filled with grey rocks and the river, well beyond its peak seasonal snow run-off stage, was narrow but swift. Too swift for swimming. Near the bridge I found a quiet hole apart from the rushing water. I stepped in and down.

Good heavens! It was shocking! The Waimakariri River flows off the Klondike Glacier and the water was colder than my vodka tonic.

"How is it?" asked the Lady Navigator holding her sides.

"Very invigorating," I replied, climbing out as fast as I had dunked in, only to be swarmed over by hungry sandflies.

Between being frozen to death and being eaten alive proved a sobering exercise.

The rest of the afternoon was spent reading and napping, mostly napping, inside the protective walls of our trusty home-on-wheels.

The evening was spent star gazing. The corner by the river was all ours. No traffic on the nearby bridge disturbed the quiet. The tiny twinkling Christmas tree lights of the overhead galaxies could be reached by stretching out an arm, they were so close.

The physical improvements in New Zealand, the upgrading in every area, are all marvelous. But the true heart of the country is felt when you get as far away from civilization as you can get. That's when you become a Kiwi.

The Route South

Our flight plan skirted Christchurch on the route south, leaving it as a grand finale of the South Island adventure. We would return up the east coast, turn in Chilly Bin and fly home. Sticking to the mid-rib of the South Island would also take us into unexplored country.

The next morning we coasted down Highway 73, up another grade to ski fields, and then down onto the Canterbury Plain.

At Sheffield, we turned south on Highway 72 in the foothills on the Southern Alps to pass Mt Hutt, one of the major international ski fields of New Zealand.

It was pretty sheep country. Unfortunately, we encountered high winds that rocked our solid Chilly Bin, made driving uncomfortable, and greatly distracted from the sightseeing. We were grateful to get the four-wheeled home to the gentle town of Geraldine, and our feet on firm turf.

In the domain, the public park, a plaque by a large tree proclaimed "This oak was planted to commemorate the coronation of His Most Gracious Majesty, King Edward VII. Mrs. W.S. Mastin, first Mayoress of Geraldine, August 1902."

And now a secret. There is in Geraldine a wool products factory called Lynn River Products that makes black wool mules, the most comfortable slippers in the world. I don't think they make them as a steady line product anymore but we have sniffled and whined and persuaded them to make us new pairs. I am on my third set. I put them on while flying in jumbo jets on long flights and they draw "ohs" and "ahs" from flight attendants.

At Fairlie, we joined Highway 8 and at Burke Pass we stopped to read the inscription on the monument to Burke.

"Oh, ye who enter the portals of the Mackenzie to found homes, take the word of a child of the misty gorges and plant trees for your lives, so shall your mountain facings and river flats be preserved to your children's children and ever more."

(Ten extra points in the Non-Zip System when you write down a quote.)

The country beyond the pass is known as Mackenzie Country named after a famous sheep thief who would hold his stolen livestock in the basin until he thought it was safe to herd them down to the east coast market. He was caught with a stolen herd in the same area.

By now you are facing the magnificent Southern Alps, a panorama of snow topped peaks and slow sliding blankets of white glaciers.

The first settler in the area, John McHutcheson, left these words: "All around me rose the grand everlasting hills whose clear-cut peaks stood out in bold relief against a cloudless sky, whilst above all loomed up the great white throne of the snowy crests beyond."

The fierce winds resumed at Lake Tekapo.

Lake Tekapo village has a milk bar which is the unofficial tour bus depot; most stop and passengers go in and buy ice cream cones. There is also a bakery, a post office and two hotels. Ours, the Alpine Inn, was dreadful but better than the campground which faced into the high winds coming off the lake.

Almost better. A graceless place with personnel to match.

One bath used up all of the hot water. "You have to wait two hours for more hot water," said the operator tersely when I complained. I took a shower in the spa bathroom.

It was a hotel fit for sheep shearers, goat milkers and English rugby players.

Perhaps the best reason to stop in Tekapo is to book a flight over the glaciers in an Air Safari airplane.

The Air Safaris' office, with six notices posted in different places asking visitors not to eat ice cream on the premises, was unmanned. It seemed logical; who would fly in such weather?

It was disappointing because the Air Safaris tour had been highly recommended. The 50-minute flight gives you a chance to appreciate the towering Mount Cook from several angles and to track the descent of the major glaciers, Fox, Tasman and Franz Josef.

The peaks of the Southern Alps, their 60 glacial floes, and the waters of rivers and lakes that dot the area make a majestic mosaic even from commercial air flights.

Tekapo is a relatively new ski area with a strong emphasis on heli-skiing. This was the first time I heard the name Tim Wallis, a dominant name whenever helicopters were mentioned. "If you want to know anything about deer farming or commercial helicopters on the South Island, you should talk to Tim," we were told repeatedly. We began thinking of this man, Tim Wallis, as a combination of Mr. Bambi and Mr. Whirlybird of New Zealand.

We subsequently learned from Ron Small of Whirl-Wide Helicopters that his Mount Cook heli-ski and helicopter scenic flights is the oldest heli-skiing operation in New Zealand having started in 1975.

Ron cited the height of the Mount Cook ranges as the advantage of heli-skiing in the area, giving the skier more vertical feet per run than can any place else in New Zealand.

"On average, three runs per day will give clients at least 10,000 vertical feet of skiing."

That is a lot of skiing.

North of Tekapo, on the banks of the Macauley River, sits Lillybank Safari Lodge, the only hunting guide service in New Zealand licensed under an act of Parliament. Simon Dickie had told us about the very upmarket commercial hunting property.

Lilybank has been in operation for over twenty years and operates for the hunter to whom the trophy is the only consideration and the expenses are incidental.

Here the hunter makes a choice between hunting for a standard trophy or a "Record Book" trophy or a "Supreme" trophy. Also, he hunts on a no-trophy, no-pay principle.

Animals are red stag, tahr, fallow buck and chamois.

Standard hunt rates are red stage and tahr respectively NZ$4,500, fallow buck NZ$3,000 and chamois NZ$3,750.

Record Book animals cost about 50 percent more and Supreme Trophy animals fees are available on request.

No charge is made for a hunter who doesn't get an animal. A non-hunting guest is charged NZ$200 a day for accommodations and all meals.

For more input write Gary Joll, Lilybank Safari Lodge, P.O. Box 60, Lake Tekapo, New Zealand.

The Mount Cook Playgrounds

Lake Pukaki lies just west of Tekapo and leads up to Mount Cook National Park and the famous Hermitage Hotel. The hostelry's latest upgrading enlarged the public area of the lobby and added 40 rooms, and extended the ski area.

The Heritage is a THC hotel and an excellent example of a far-sighted governmental policy set many years ago establishing inns in remote areas of rare beauty to be enjoyed by the public with more than a drive-in, drive-out experience.

There is much great walking, great photographic opportunities, great enjoyment of every alpine nature in the Mount Cook

National Park, but the biggest thrill is to ski the Tasman Glacier.
The first time we went to Mount Cook we took a sightseeing ski
plane to the top. But that wasn't enough. We talked to a skier
who had skied on the glacier.

"How was it?" we asked.

"Unbelievable," he said.

We are bad skiers, but enthusiastic. Gung ho. We have splat-
tered ourselves around the Alps in Austria, Italy, Switzerland and
France. We have fallen all over Aspen and Vail and Purgatory in
Colorado, crashed landed at Park City and Deer Valley in Utah
and disgraced ourselves at the major ski runs around Lake Tahoe
in California, Nevada and Vermont.

Our penchant for perfecting spread eagles on ski trails or
wrapping ourselves around trees didn't deter us from the magnetic
attraction of glacier skiing. We could hardly wait to take a ski
plane from Mount Cook to the top of Tasman Glacier and ski its
slopes.

The first time we tried to go it rained for three days. No skiing.
We were told "It's a mountain situation."

Five years later—still determined—we were back at the
Hermitage Hotel to try again. It snowed all night.

At 8:30am, the snow glinted off the whipped cream peaks as we
departed the Alpine Guides shop next to the hotel to board a van,
descend to the airport and load into an airplane with retractable
skis.

Hey, hey, hey. Tingly feeling.

There were two airplanes taking aloft five skiers, two guides and
two park rangers who would stay on the glacier as long as there
were skiers on the glacier.

Our pilot watched carefully as the first plane circled a designated spot, made an approach and swooshed into a landing. We
followed to land on packed snow at the 7,500-foot elevation of
the Tasman Saddle.

Deplaning, we climbed carrying our skis up another 100 feet to
the crest of the saddle. The view was over to another glacier, the
Murchison Glacier.

At the saddle we put on our skis. They had safety brakes but we
still had to attach safety bindings as a precaution. A loose ski
could disappear into the deep powder snow and take hours to
find. We then traversed almost a mile to gain another ridge and

from there it was all downhill . . . six miles downhill.

It *was* unbelievable.

Our guide laid down the rules before we took off on the six-mile run.

"Don't ever ski in front of me. I know where there are crevasses and you don't. Stay in my tracks when I tell you. At other times I will give you limits in which to ski on either side of my tracks. Don't go beyond those limits. If you go out of control, sit down quickly."

Attentive silence spoke loudly for the emotions of all of us were feeling.

We had a good guide who took it slowly for which we were grateful. Skiing in fresh powder that comes well above your ankles and gliding on a three-foot pack of barely crusted snow is quite an experience.

The truth is we followed form and flunked the Tasman Glacier. We fell sidewise, we fell backwards, the Lady Navigator almost made a complete forward somersault over her skis for the most spectacular crash. Excuse one: it was our first time on skis in a year. Excuse two: we had new skis, new poles, untested, untried.

Still. It was so damn beautiful.

The air was scrubbed crisp and squeaked it was so clean. Snow banks that resembled cream puffs and crevasses that really are pale blue rivaled the grandeur of the noble ice cream peaks. It was the silence that was unforgettable. Silence broken only by the swoosh of skis. Stand still, and you could hear nothing except pure, motionless, soundless silence.

And when we were finally running right, running clean, running fast with the nippy sunny air whistling by our ears and skis faithfully following the long continual tracks made by our guide, we wanted to yell with pleasure . . . to explode streams of joy. Thank you, God, for such a great world!

We made one right decision.

We signed up for only one run. The ski planes rendezvoused with us half way down the glacier. One plane took the other three skiers back for a second run down the other side of the glacier; we returned to home base slightly battered and ego-bruised but elated with the morning. It was a four-star experience and a five-star conversation dropper.

Mount Cook, a brilliant sight on a sunny day, is the highest peak in the park reaching almost 13,000 feet. It was first climbed in 1894. The more formidable Caroline Face was not conquered until 1970. Naturally, the whole park with the highest peaks in the Southern Alps is a favorite for alpine climbers and a training ground for Himalayan expeditions.

Twizel: Now A Permanent Township

Twizel, just south of Mount Cook, was built as a construction camp for a major hydroelectric project, and once held the dubious honor of having more hobby clubs per capita than any other town in New Zealand—some 90 clubs for a population of 6,000.

Twizel also had the reputation for drinking more beer per capita on a Saturday night than any town in New Zealand. Fighting words in some places but not subject to audit.

Once we had stayed the night at the Twizel Hotel because we couldn't get reservations at the Hermitage. We has to stop in to see what had happened to Twizel since the finish of the hydroelectric project. Was Twizel finished, too?

"Ah, it is better than ever," said the blond lass at the Information Office. "We are no longer a government town. We've been a permanent township since 1984. I moved away after the dam was finished but now I have come back . . . and glad to be here.

"The hotel is also privately owned now.

"We have 2,000 permanent residents, mostly retired trades people. We even have our own weekly newspaper, the High County Herald. Oh, if it misses an edition, people get very upset.

"No, we don't have as many clubs as we used to. The gun club, and the car club, the ice skating club have gone but the golf club is being expanded."

A bus tour pulled up to the information/souvenir stand. "What do you sell the tourists?" we asked.

"Well, they will have just come from the hydroelectric dam and they buy the book about the project."

We strolled around town center, bought brand muffins in the bakery shop, and—would you believe it—got lost trying to get back to the main highway.

The grey sky started to drip and then to cascade on the highway.

At the junction town of Omarama, we stopped to fill the Chilly Bin with diesel. "This rain has been following me all over New Zealand," I groused at the operator.

The countryside around had been going through a severe drought effecting the economy of everyone including service station operators.

"Give me your telephone number," he said. "We might pay you to come back."

After climbing and descending the low rising Lindis Pass we approached one of the most famous of the New Zealand sheep stations, Morven Hills.

In 1858 a Canterbury farmer, acting on a tip from a passing Maori, went to investigate an open country in the interior and was led by a Maori chief to a land of unending tussock, meaning unlimited grazing to a sheep rancher.

McLean succeeded in obtaining the grazing rights to about 350,000 acres of land. Sixteen years after his initial exploration the McLeans sold out with over 135,000 sheep on the property.

A jog off Highway 8 to the west after Morven Hills Station on Highway 8A returned us to familiar territory. Across the head of the mighty Clutha River and around Iron Mountain lies Wanaka, one of our favorite corners of New Zealand.

Our Wanaka. Please Do Not Trespass

We do not want to write about Wanaka.

We do not want people to go to Wanaka.

We do not want Wanaka changed.

We do not want Wanaka upgraded. (It already is.)

One look at the bustle and hustle of Queenstown and the skyrocketing land prices, and you know that one day the developers will say, "Why are we fighting for space in Queenstown when just over the pass there is all that beautiful open space at Lake Wanaka?"

And they will push a paved road over the Cardrona Pass and there will go our dream town.

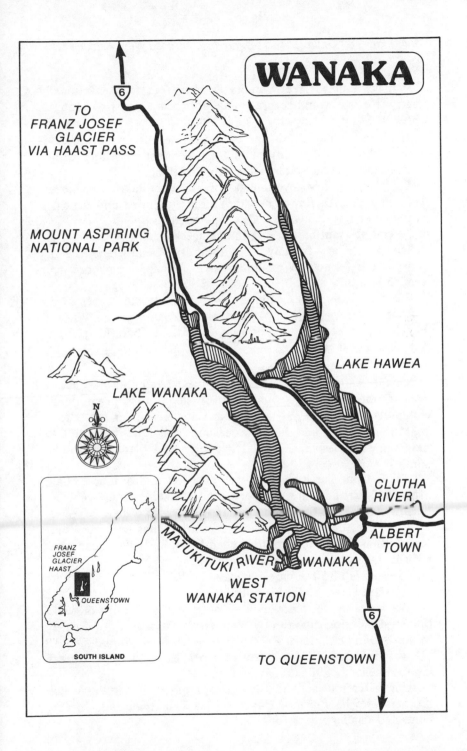

Wanaka facing Lake Wanaka is pretty but not sensationally pretty. No one would accuse Wanaka of being a nest of sophisticates. It is not an arty-crafty-cutsy village or area.

Small in population, it has two streets of basic, no-nonsense shops although a few souvenir shops have crept in, selling leather and sheepskins and pottery—that kind of thing.

There's the pretty government hotel near the lake whose green lawn and English flower beds are caringly tended and which is annually upgraded, remodeled, redecorated.

Several pleasant motels ring the village.

The people are friendly, the trout are friendly and the atmosphere is friendly. Wanaka is—*nice*. Perhaps even more than that, it is real.

We moved our nightly plumbing from a remote corner of an Arthur's Pass outhouse in the forest to a suite in the Wanaka Hotel with a step-up-then-down-again marble bathtub/jacuzzi. Yes, Wanaka is *nice*.

"Oh, it has changed dramatically," said Lyall Daly, the manager of the hotel and a member of the tourist promotional committee. "Wanaka has gone from being a summer resort to a year around resort and the basic reason is that it lies between two new skifields, Triple Cone to the north and Cardrona in the south.

"Triple Cone has a car park at 4,000 feet and a double chair lift, two T-bars and three learners' lifts. The ski trails are generally considered to be for those with above average skills.

"Cardrona, between here and Queenstown, has been very successful. In addition to the double chair lift, it has a new quadruple chairlift that's increased its popularity.

"Wanaka is also the base for excellent heli-skiing. You should talk to Paul Scaife about his operation.

"We are also the place to stay overnight before making the preferred morning-time run over the Haast Pass. And, of course, Mount Aspiring National Park is part of our recreational area.

"Wanaka has a fine golf course which has undergone several improvements including a new clubhouse.

"Our waterfront activities are now organized under the Miller brothers who have a new Hovercraft, a sightseeing launch, and boats and fishing guides for hire."

"And deer farming? Is that the next major industry around here," we asked.

"Oh, you have to see Tim Wallis."

There was that name again.

"He has a house in Wanaka, you know. I think he is here now."

We put on our rain gear and went sniffing around the village, bought stamps at the post office, sherry at the wine shop, Kleenex at the grocery store.

Looking around a new shopping compound, we were making a note of a new restaurant, Ripples, when a car slowed to halt and we heard "McDermotts!" It was Phyllis and Tom Cole, good friends and incredible hosts.

"When do we get together? What do you need? What can we do for you?"

We made a date and then I asked, "Do you know Tim Wallis? I'd like to talk to him."

"His wife just drove out," said Phyllis. "I'll call and make a date."

That night we had other friends over for dinner in the hotel restaurant made more pleasant by Loma, the room's hostess, an attractive gracious Maori lady.

Our guests were Hilda and Gordon Turner, a retired food executive who is a leprechaun of a man and a keen fisherman.

"I've seen too many of my friends die at their desks," he once told me while fishing just above the dam at next door Lake Hawea. "It is not a very smart way to go."

The conversation that morning years ago of two friends talking between fishing casts was greatly responsible for my leaving my advertising agency, a decision never regretted.

The next day I went down to the lakefront to talk to Wanaka Lake Services while Hilda took the Lady Navigator shopping. I introduced myself to Bruce Miller.

"Oh, I know you," he said and reminded me of copy from our first book about a lakeshore cabin sign that advertised "Marine Rentals, Power Boats, Mini Golf, Trampolines, Gold Mining Equipment."

"The cabin was unattended. That's Wanaka," we wrote.

The present operation is well attended and from the people buzzing in and out, busily supported.

The company's Hovercraft is scheduled for short and long trips around the lake. The launch *Ena* is used for afternoon trips to Pigeon Island and for charter trips. Jet boats run down the Clutha.

Bruce called over his brother, Paul. For some reason I expect fishing guides to be retired military types, grizzled, gnarled veterans but Paul Miller turned out to be a lithe young man, deadly serious, but attractively so. He is, also, a regular member of the New Zealand Professional Fishing Guides Association.

"Here in Wanaka, you have Lakes Wanaka and Hawea and the Clutha River at your doorstep," said Paul. "It is a great place to start fly fishing, spinning or trolling. For something more exotic, we can take you to the back country via jet boat, light plane or helicopter, or four wheel drive vehicle.

"Our cabin cruiser, *Goldie*, with ship-to-shore radio and all equipment, is a luxurious way to go out on the lake."

In addition, Bruce said, ticking the items off on his fingers "We have two-seater speed boats, aqua bikes for kids, row boats and canoes. We also rent bikes. And we are ALWAYS IN ATTEND-ANCE," he added meaningfully, "all year long."

That afternoon we racked up another we've-always-wanted-to ambition. We played a round of golf at the Wanaka Golf Club.

The clubhouse was closed, but play was permitted, said a sign. Fill out a card, put NZ$5 per golfer greens fee in an envelope, attach the stub to your bag or cart. The honor system lives on. But the problem was, I couldn't rent a pull cart or, as they say, a trundler.

For traveling, we stick the Lady Navigator's clubs and a canvas bag into my professional bag—a bag meant to be strapped onto an electric cart or carried by a seven-foot tall caddy.

Even with only half a set of clubs, carrying that monster around eighteen holes of golf was exhausting. Don't ask me what I shot. I finished alive. And slept like a child that night. Fatigued.

The first nine holes are hilly, the fairways surrounded by tall trees. It is a challenging nine with stances that usually have one foot up and one foot down. Par 36. One 5-par hole.

The back nine is flat and long with three par-3 and one par-5 holes. Par for the nine: 34.

After golf we stopped by the public pub of the hotel, a major after-work gathering place for people who use muscle in their jobs.

If you want local color, go into the public bar. But not if you are allergic to cigarette smoke. People in public bars puff a lot.

You drink draft beer by the pitcher or Lion Brown by the quart. If you are standing, you put the quart between your feet.

It is a masculine, muscular society in bars. If a woman is present, she listens and smokes but rarely talks. You could be in an Australian country pub.

Next to the public bar is the Stonehouse Restaurant and Family Bar, part of the hotel, where you can drink and eat without the crowd and the smoke. Quite nicely decorated and softly lighted. Order your meal and pay at a counter and take a numbered stub. Buy your beverage at the bar and join your lady at a table. A buzzer sounds, your number flashes, signals for you to pick up your order. Not fancy, but the meal is hot. It is a swept-up fast-food operation.

The wine selection at the THC hotels has always been well rounded—they make a practice of it—and reasonably priced.

An Interview With Mr. Bambi/Mr. Whirly-Bird

The next morning I cornered Tim Wallis. He had been having day and night meetings with his accountants but said, sure, he could spare the time. A busy man. He was the king of helicopters in New Zealand and a kingpin for much of the booming deer farming industry in New Zealand. Mr. Bambi and Mr. Whirly-Bird.

His office was just across the street from the hotel in an old one-storey white cottage which he shared with a major international accounting firm.

Deer farming had become a new economic factor in New Zealand. It had started with the discovery that the Germans would pay almost any price for venison.

What had been an amateur sport became a professional job employing hired guns, first using fixed planes and then helicopters.

Killing deer in the wild soon gave way to capturing feral deer to stock burgeoning deer farms as the new industry began to take hold.

Tim Wallis' secretary led me into a small back room filled with cardboard packing boxes that were brimming over with papers, a filing system as chaotic as mine.

A large, dominant man whose brown hair was touched with grey flecks waved me to a chair. His grey cashmere sweater torn out at both elbows made him look as if he needed a dime for a cup of coffee but he moved and talked in the quiet, controlled manner of a man of authority.

I studied his walls—walls always provide clues to their occupant's interest, often character. A poster of an American WWII fighter plane and a bumper strip advertised the fighter museum in Mesa, Arizona. A map of Fiordland National Park had been divided into twelve blocks. Hunting blocks, I wondered?

Tim Wallis got off the phone, introduced himself, and apologized for being so busy.

Tell me about deer farming in New Zealand, I said.

"Deer are treated like any other farm product in a farming nation," he said. "The progress has been slow but, as traditional farmers have become more competent, there are fewer problems.

"For today's farmer faced with a diminishing sheep market, deer farming provides diversification. A lot of farm land is being converted into deer farms."

What's the future going to bring?

"Because the first farmers were successful, more and more farmers are getting into it. The industry will continue to grow and will be very big. Venison today sells for four to five times that of lamb and the deer are relatively easy to farm.

"New Zealand has well over 300,000 deer on farms today. The growth of the domestic deer population will come from two sources, the annual birth rate on farms and the capture of feral deer in the wilds. About 18,000 female animals are being captured each year, mainly by helicopters."

Ah, the king of the helicopters. Tell us about helicopters.

"Helicopters have been the key to the success of the deer

industry. The techniques for capturing the deer live today are incredibly improved over what we did fifteen years ago. Here . . .," he rose from his desk and stiff-legged his way over to a book case. He handed me two pamphlets, saying "read these. They'll give you the background."

"Have you had a crash?" I asked.

Offhand: "Oh, yeah."

More than one? A nod. More than two? Another nod. It was embarrassing to continue to ask.

"How many helicopters do you control?"

"Oh, about 45. You wouldn't think it looking at all this," he waved his arms at the packing carton filing system, "but we run a multi-million-dollar operation."

I believed him. Tim Wallis comes across as a strong, likable, energized guy, full of creative ideas with courage to match action to the ideas. No airs, no pretensions, just a typical successful New Zealand businessman.

The brochure described the holding company, Alpine Helicopters, Limited of which Wallis is the group managing director. The group owns Criffel Deer Farm, Mararoa Station, Luggate Game Packers, Game Export Consolidations; and a percentage of Whirl-Wide Helicopters, Wishart Helicopters and Southern Lakes Venison Packers.

Included in the operation, besides 45 helicopters, are three deer recovery ships and seven deer recovery bases scattered around the South Islands, plus a maintenance base in Queenstown.

Some weeks later, we met a farmer who retired to the city to operate a motel. By this time we knew that any mention of helicopters or deer farming evoked the name of Tim Wallis.

"Oh, I flew with him once," our host volunteered.

"We had two live deer up in the mountains and Tim Wallis flew in to take them out. They put the deer into a sack but they were too heavy to let the helicopter lift off in that light air. Tim said to clear the bush on the side of the mountain and he would get a downhill start and thought he could get off the ground. I was going with him.

"Then when he got in the helicopter and wrapped a rag around his bum foot and the foot control to tie them together, I thought of getting out. But we made it.

"Tim Wallis always makes it. Well, almost always."

After my catch-him-on-the-run interview that morning we drove to the west side of the lake, about three miles out, to visit friends Margaret and Gerald Scaife, who retired from their high country sheep station to buy and operate the Bay View Motel, formerly the Hawthenden Motel.

They have a peaceful location set on a hillside above the lake, and a front lawn the size of a pasture, which it is for a few munching sheep.

"How does it feel to be a motel operator instead of a sheep farmer," we asked Gerald.

"It's trading carrying stones for breaking bricks," he said.

The half dozen concrete units are airy and spacious, have fireplaces, full kitchens and a full bedroom plus a sitting room with television. A small house. I think the price was about NZ$50 a night.

Most of their guests are drop-ins or returnees and, not infrequently, they check in for one night and stay a week.

One son, Paul, runs Harris Mountain Heli-Ski which has exclusive flight rights to three major mountain areas and a couple of glaciers. It is the largest area under license for heli-skiing in the country.

"Skiing in the back country can be anything from fresh powder to crud to spring corn," he told us. "We are weather-dependent but we average four heli-ski days a week. Nearby Cardrona and Triple Crown keep visiting skiers occupied during non-flying weather.

"Last year we had 1,200 paying customers. We are busy.

"Fifty percent of our skiers are returning clients. Our first priority is on safety but our second emphasis is fun—and we have a lot of that.

"We have day tours of varying lengths and costs and a week-long package.

"The week gives you 28 helicopter rides and about 50,000 feet of vertical skiing. There's nothing like it in the world. Our promotional theme is 'Ski a Dream'."

"By U.S. standards, it is cheap."

Write Paul Scaife, Ski Guides, N.Z. Ltd., Box 177, Wanaka,

New Zealand. The same address will get you a reservation or information about the Bay View Motel.

That afternoon we went out to Albert Town—not to be confused with Arrowtown in the opposite direction—to the Turners' cottage. Hilda served her Golden Trout for lunch—so good—and Gordon and I went fishing.

The established ritual is first we go to the rocks above the dam at Lake Hawea. The setting on the rocks is beautiful but we never, never catch a trout there. It is a good place to chat, however, about colleagues who drop dead at their desks.

After our usual settling-in time, we went below the dam to the start of the Clutha River.

As I was opening a gate, a fellow fisherman came over to the car and said, "There are no fish in there."

He was a Pom. An Englishman. It is not an appellation in New Zealand overburdened with affection.

"No, I've already tried," he said. "Waste of time. Better to go above the dam." (Where we had just been.) "Lots of fish there," he said with confidence.

Now Gordon Turner, I have to tell you, is a Scotsman from Dunedin. You don't find a more independent breed of Scots outside of Glasgow.

"Humph," was the only word Gordon muttered to the Pom. His always bright prankish eyes sparked fire.

And we drove through the gates which, incidentally, were marked 'no trespassing.'

In a corner by the river he parked the car and rigged a pole for fly casting. Fly casting compared to spin casting or trolling is ballet dancing to ballroom dancing to soft rock. It takes a great deal more skill, more experience, a more sensitive touch.

I am a mug fisherman but with Gordon as my coach I can cast. I think he mesmerizes me.

He reviewed quickly the essential techniques and we found a quiet pool at the edge of the rushing river. He put me at the head of the pool gently instructing my every cast.

Each cast improved under his watchful eye.

"That's champion," he finally said and no sooner were the words out of his mouth than the reel gave out a loud whine and a fish jumped clear of the water downstream.

The fish jumped and jumped again. "Tip up. Tip up." cautioned the coach. "When he makes a run, let him run but keep your line firm. That's it. Now bring him in a bit. Let him go. Let him go!" The fish jumped and twisted out of the water.

Adrenalin poured out of my ears. It was a beaut of a rainbow and I was almost sorry when we finally beached him. He was a keeper. "Must be three pounds," said the coach proudly. "All of three pounds."

We packed up and left. There was a party that night at the Coles and we were already going to be late. Fishing when you are going to be tardy somewhere else adds to the enjoyment.

As we pulled out of the gate, Gordon said to the air, "No fish. Hah. Bloody Pom."

At the Cole's party, where the tables overflowed with food—five deserts—and glasses were never permitted to be emptied, we met a man who was leaving for Nepal the next day. He was a director of the Himalayan Trust, an organization started by Sir Edmund Hillary to aid the Sherpas. Since 1961 the trust had established two hospitals, two airfields, numerous bridges and 24 schools, all at altitudes above 10,000 feet.

Climbing is a heritage of the area, we found out, when we stopped the next morning at the Mount Aspiring National Park headquarters in Wanaka and talked to the chief ranger.

"The mecca of climbing is Mount Cook," he said. "It is the most challenging and offers a variety of climbing experiences in snow and alpine conditions.

"Darrin Mountain in Fiordland is favored by those into rock climbing. Christchurch is a headquarters for those who want the strong climbing required in Arthur's Pass.

"Mount Aspiring is appealing because it has the classic triangular silhouette look and appeal of the Matterhorn. And the climbers like the long, forested valley walk to get to the mountain."

The headquarters is a classroom for the geological history of the area. And a travel agency for information about hiking trails and gentle walks, and the current weather.

At the time of this swing, all park personnel was in a slight state of shock because the departments of land and surveys, internal affairs, forest services and wildlife services were to be combined into one single service, the Department of Conservation.

Two Routes To Queenstown From Wanaka

One route from Wanaka to Queenstown is an almost straight drive over the Crown Range. It is a dirt washboard, tough-driving road through the former gold settlement of Cardrona, now the site of the popular ski fields. You can still see the diggings left by a former colony of Chinese miners.

We once drove this route with Gordon Turner. As we went on for mile after bumpy mile through clouds of dust that clogged the throat, he began to describe the Cardrona Hotel where we would find a bar with cool, dust-slaking, belly-satisfying beer. I could taste that beer.

When we finally approached the Cardrona Hotel, just before expiring from thirst, we found an abandoned shack whose roof had caved in, whose doors were missing, but whose legible sign still proclaimed "Cardrona Hotel." Our little leprechaun laughed and laughed.

Now, we hear, the Cardrona Hotel has been restored as a fine restaurant. Gordon Turner told us so.

Prove it, we cannot.

The Crown Range road was no place for our Chilly Bin. Instead, we took Highway 6, a circuitous route, leaving the highway only to drive through the new town of Cromwell which replaces the old Cromwell, doomed to flood by the waters of the new hydroelectric dam on the Clutha.

Cromwell's contemporary design gives it the opportunity of becoming an architectural statement of the 1980s the same way Napier has become New Zealand's 1920s Art Deco township.

Highway 6 follows the Kawarau River and passes the Roaring Meg waterfall which marks the 45th parallel. Roaring Meg was a well-known lady of pleasure during the goldrush days and is the name of a local river.

Another jaunt off the highway, a must, is to the little town of Arrowtown, a relic of the past whose small miners' cottages still stand under tall—very photogenic—sycamore trees, a five-star four-color scenic found on many New Zealand calendars.

Arrowtown started its rich history when an American prospector, William Fox, a veteran of the California goldfields, found gold in the Arrow River. He kept his find a secret but the rumor spread that he had been seen cashing in large amounts of gold dust.

Other prospectors tried to follow him. A local sport became Hunting the Fox. Eventually his secret was discovered and the gold rush was on.

Another American appeared on the scene, the terrible "Bully" Hayes, who later became a notorious blackbirder in the Pacific. In Arrowtown he ran a pub but was chased out of town when it was confirmed, as had been gossiped, that his ear had been snipped, a common brand inflicted in California for cheating at cards.

Arrowtown, famous for years as an ice cream stop for tour buses, has been vastly upgraded.

Importantly, there is an off-street parking area for tour buses which used to line the street opposite the miners' cabins, destroying most tourists' photographs.

The tiny museum has been expanded and redone with a highly professional touch.

Originally it was the Bank of New Zealand. "It was so small," the curator told us, "that if there were more than two people in the bank, they had to stand out in the street."

Besides the usual memorabilia, an unusual side of Arrowtown is recalled in an exhibit of the time when 5,000 Chinese mined the area. An exhibit called The Golden Cobwebs of the Otago Goldfields recalls those days of a different racial culture. The former Chinese settlement is now being excavated.

Many new souvenir shops have been added to Arrowtown but the neatest improvement is the takeover of the Stone Cottage at the main intersection by Janet Burton and Cynthia Balfour as a luncheon cafe.

The Stone Cottage is 110 years old and is modestly furnished with antiques of its day.

But Janet, Cynthia and their helpers perform magic in their little downstairs kitchen producing a marvelous assortment of quiches, crepes and deep "pie" dishes of bacon and egg, carrot and dill, chicken-corn-cheese, and ham-tomato-pumpkin. They do

their own fruit pies, raisin muffins and cheese scones as well.
"We keep changing recipes to keep ourselves from going around the bend," Janet said. The Stone Cottage is very popular. Try to get there early or late—for lunch only.

The Lady Navigator had to be dragged out of Arrowtown physically because there was a half-price sale in every shop in town that she felt was essential to her shopping research. She chewed on the driver all the way into Queenstown.

The Lady Navigator: "Nothing I do is important. Only what you do is important. I never get the time I need. But you take as much time fishing as you want. Even if it makes us late for a party. What kind of research is that? You should be more considerate and think of others. Me to start with." Etc.

The fifteen miles to Queenstown made for a long, long drive.

The Ever Popular Queenstown

One of the charms of Queenstown is its setting. Simply ideal visually. Sited around a couple of bends in the curvaceous Lake Wakatipu, the village is backed by mountains, giving it a unique self-contained alpine feeling. Across the lake the picturesque Remarkable Mountains offer a high, saw-toothed profile as a focus for postcards. (It is even better in the winter when the snow covered mountains are mirrored in the clear blue waters of the lake.)

In 1860, the site of the present Queenstown, now an exploding tourist resort, was a quiet sheep station owned by William Rees.

The finding of gold on the Arrow and the Shotover rivers changed the sheep farm into a gold supply camp where Rees sold prospectors needed goods and foods, eventually tearing down his sheepshed to build the Queen's Arms Hotel. That location is now occupied by Eichardt's Hotel, a popular pub.

Nearby Coronet Peak has long been a favorite of New Zealand and Australian skiers. It has also attracted ski instructors from all over the world during the July to September period which gives it an international flavor. As a result of the skiing, Queenstown was an early year-round resort town.

The addition of the Cardrona skifield and the opening of the Remarkables as the newest ski area has doubled Queenstown's popularity among winter visitors.

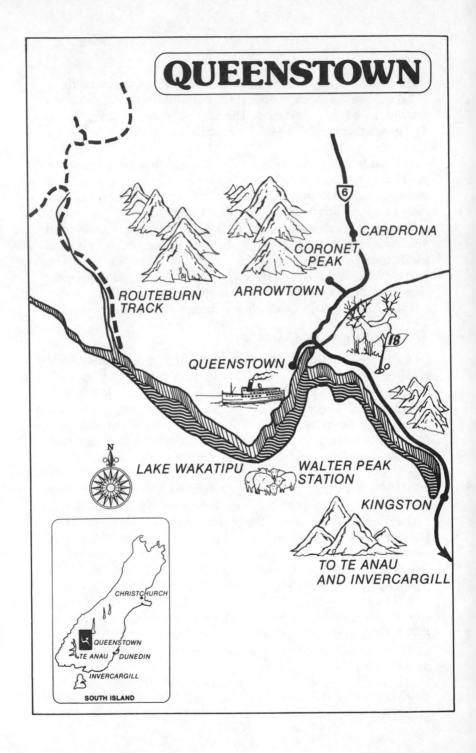

The year the Remarkables opened snowfalls were particularly light, leading local wags to call the new skifield "The Regrettables."

Our hotel reservations also proved regrettable. They were nonexistent. Everything in town was sold out. No problem. We steered Chilly Bin into the nearby municipal camping grounds, hooked into their electricity, put our plastic bucket under the sink outlet and strolled down to town.

The present hotel/motel inventory of 600 beds is being feverishly expanded. Rooms for over 3,000 beds were under construction or planned. Even THC is planning a new hotel—a 200-unit project on the lakefront.

Despite the frenetic development, Queenstown had no master plan. Land prices were spiraling out of sight. Speculators were buying so they could sell to the next wave of speculators.

One of the major problems that the city fathers faced was employee housing. The fast multiplying accommodations would require new employees but there already was insufficient affordable housing. Lack of suitable permanent housing will encourage temporary "hires" with the attendant decline in the level of service.

Still Queenstown enjoys an ever increasing popularity. We have heard of overseas visitors who have canceled a tour to New Zealand because they couldn't get a room in Queenstown. At the same time, we have heard that New Zealanders will no longer go to Queenstown because it is too expensive...but not by overseas standards.

Such popularity, of course, draws more attractions and more restaurants, more jet boats on the Shotover River, more rafting companies, and more helicopter operators.

You can buy a combination helicopter-plus activity trip of every description: heli-golf, heli-raft, heli-jetboat, heli-horse.

Several firmly established attractions draw deservedly continued support from visitors. One is the gondola cable car to the top of Bob's Peak and lunch at the Skyline Restaurant—owned by the same company that has put the cable car into Rotorua.

Near the bottom of the cable car is the Queenstown Motor Museum, a lovely collection of classics and oddities including several mint conditioned Rolls Royce and Bentleys. Many of the cars are privately owned and are on loan to the museum, being taken out on rare occasion by owners attending antique or vintage car rallies. All cars at the museum are operational.

The most prominent excursion is the *Earnslaw*, one of two steamships in the southern hemisphere to be powered by hand-shoveled coal. Her flumes of black smoke are enough to make any die-hard environmentalist cable Ralph Nader, but no one would dare. The "Lady of the Lake" has been chugging around the shores of Wakatipu as a vital communications supply link between country stations and Queenstown since 1912. The *Earnslaw* is just part of Queenstown.

Morning cruises, luncheon cruises, an afternoon cruise to a well known country sheep station, or dinner cruises are available.

If you love to see engines at work, stand on the walkway grill over the engine room as the ship gets underway to watch two firemen stoke the boilers—which take a ton of coal an hour. Watch as the engines begin to turn over with great sputters of steam while brass wheel handles are thrown this way and that. The fire shadows flicker around the engine room and the sound of the ship's bells go ding-dong. Good stuff.

Don't miss the *Earnslaw's* quaint bar forward either.

A plan to add a half-million-dollar vehicular ferry was announced as a sister ship to the *Earnslaw* by the same owners while we were in Queenstown. Their plan would transport cars or buses across the lake to Walter Peak Station where they would connect with the Te Anau highway via a secondary road, thereby opening an alternate route to Te Anau and Milford Sound. The route would be shorter, but rougher.

Jet boating on the Shotover River is exceptionally popular. Roaring around on a fast flowing river is a thrill. The authorities finally stepped in to establish controls following a fatal collision between a couple of jet-boat cowboys a few years back.

We pray for the same sort of regulations to control the dozens of river rafting companies before lives are lost as well.

Amid such juicy items as multi-million-dollar developments, a booming retail business, the establishment of the first non-gateway-city Duty Free shops in Queenstown, want to know what stoked the local populace most? The biggest news in upgraded Queenstown was the installation of a direct dial telephone exchange. No more telephone operators. Queenstown was taking a forward step into the modern world.

"You can't believe what some of our overseas visitors went through to make an overseas call," a travel authority told us.

If it worked in Rotorua with sheep, why wouldn't it work in Queenstown with cattle? The Cattledrome, established by the owners of the successful Agrodome in Rotorua, presents two shows daily, if you are into beef or dairy cows.

Another new attraction: a hang gliding simulator. You make a "free flight" but you are fully protected by a cable support system. Missed it. It's on the list for the next time. A Honolulu friend tried it and reported the experience to be safe and first rate.

What we didn't miss was dinner at Roaring Megs Restaurant on Shotover Street. That was great fun and included great food. My notes read "onion soup, homemade chicken liver pate, scallops with garlicky almonds and capsicums, kiwi fruitparfait."

Muttonbird was also on the menu.

"The muttonbird is the flying sheep of the South Island," Ray Drayton, the proprietor said. "Don't reach for the salt shaker. This is an airborne anchovy. It tastes like a chicken breast with sardines glued to its sides. And don't worry about going to the bathroom for a week."

Another new attraction at the waterfront jetty is Waterworld, an underwater viewing chamber where you watch giant rainbow and brown trout and quinnat salmon being fed along with longfin eels—and occasionally a diving duck.

It is forbidden to fish within a hundred meters of the jetty.

If you continue beyond the jetty on Marine Parade, you come to the Government Gardens, a peaceful peninsula with trees and bowling greens and tennis courts and flowers.

Across a short space of lake is another peninsula, Kevin Heights. Here are the most expensive homes, a good 18-hole golf course and a deer park, one of the first in the country.

The Routeburn And Other Nature Walks

Queenstown is the takeoff point for several walking tracks in the surrounding mountains. The best known is the Routeburn, a famous nature walk track traversing parts of Mount Aspiring and

Fiordland National Parks.

The marked trail can be walked in two directions, either starting from the Milford Highway and coming out at the Dart River which flows into Lake Wakatipu, or beginning from Queenstown.

You have a choice of walking it independently or with a guided group.

Two huts are provided by the Department of Conservation for "freedom walkers" who claim them on a first-come basis. Hikers are advised not to try the Harris Saddle in a storm or snow conditions unless they are very experienced or accompanied by a guide.

We signed on with Routeburn Walk Ltd., using their huts and bedding and fine guides, and permitting the company to supply the food and do the cooking.

After busing from Queenstown to Glenorchy, we stopped at the start of the track for a sandwich lunch after which we began a four-hour hike through a valley called Routeburn Flats filled with beech trees, then started a steady but gradual climb upward, ever upward. I should have been practicing on stairs at home, I thought. Routeburn Falls and the Routeburn Falls Hut was home for that first night.

Our party was small—a party is never more than fourteen—and our university graduate guide was also the chef. After walking all day with the chef, you don't sit down while she cooks alone. We quickly became a family unit with everyone pitching in. But it isn't mandatory.

The next day was nervous time. To reach the Harris Saddle we first had to cross a snowfield that slanted down the mountain. The edge of the snowfield ended in an abyss. If the snowfield slipped or we slipped, the result would be deadly.

We crossed the middle of the field carefully and slowly placing our feet in the tracks made by the person in front. Step by nervous step. (The imagination of a coward is a dreadful burden.) Once across that mine field, the ho-ho-hos and who's-afraids came easier.

At the Harris Saddle we crossed from Mount Aspiring National Park into Fiordland National Park and made a zigzag descent to Lake McKenzie were we spent two nights making side excursions during the day into the lovely scented forest.

During the next day's descent, an opening in the trees presented a panorama of the Hollyford River below. We had already done the Milford Track. Wouldn't it be fun to do the Hollyford?

By mid-afternoon we had reached Highway 94 to Milford, the point designated to catch the coach back to Queenstown via Te Anau.

The Routeburn Walk is a high mountain, sandfly-free, memorable adventure.

Routeburn Walk Ltd., P.O. Box 271, Queenstown, New Zealand.

Added to the many walks originating in Queenstown is the new Greenstone Valley Walk offering three-day or four-day treks with overnight stops at two architect designed huts. It covers the same general area as the Routeburn but follows the Greenstone River.

Greenstone Valley Walk, P.O. Box 568, Queenstown.

Overseas visitors who don't have the time to drive to Milford Sound but don't want to miss it—and they shouldn't—can take a sightseeing plane from Queenstown. You land at a small airstrip just steps away from the Milford Sound Hotel, take a boat trip out onto the Sound and return to Queenstown in a half day outing.

On a fair dinkum day, it is an exhilarating experience.

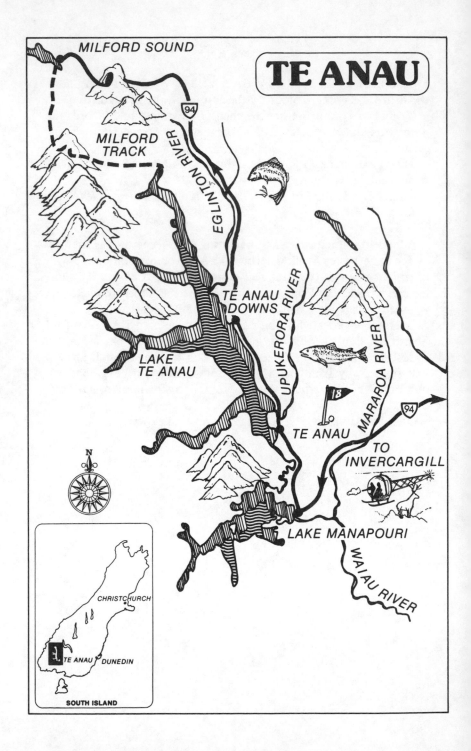

12. Fiordland

Blue Lakes . . . Tall Mountains . . .
Deep Sounds . . . Te Anau . . .
The Milford And Hollyford Tracks

The country leading to Te Anau is comparatively flat and dry but once you reach the lake and the village and look across to the deep green forests in the rugged, uninhabited mountains on the other side, you know you are on the edge of the wilds.

Te Anau is the headquarters for Fiordland National Park. With over 3,000,000 acres, it is the largest national park in New Zealand. In fact, it is one of the largest national parks in the world.

Size, however, it not its attraction. Rather, it is the grandeur of its scenery: magnificent cobalt blue fjords, majestic peaks, superlative waterfalls, hanging glaciers, mossy rain forests, pure lakes and snow-fed rivers. Just what Captain Cook speculated would be "beyond the mountains" as he viewed them from the sea.

I always think when I am at Te Anau that the lake runs east to west and that Milford Sound is due south. Wrong. The lake runs north and south and Milford Sound is due north.

Lake Te Anau is the largest lake in the South Island. The size of the lake is deceiving because it doesn't look large but what you can't see are the immense branches of water that disappear into the mountains.

To the south of Lake Te Anau is Manapouri, a very large, very deep lake (1,455 feet), considered as one of the most beautiful lakes in New Zealand. Habitation has not come to the shores of Lake Manapouri.

A small store at the lakeside village bearing the same name has rowboats to rent. Rowers can cross the inlet to a marked trail through the forest estimated to take three walking hours.

Of the various cruises available on the lake, one stands above all the others. By launch you go to the West Arm where a bus takes you into the hydroelectric dam through a tunnel that spirals 360 degrees down 800 feet—sensational ride—to the depths of the dam to see the seven giant turbines. The tunnel is wide enough to take two buses abreast.

A day-long tour extends the Manapouri cruise/dam visit by continuing on to the Wilmot Pass, stopping for scenic views at the summit, transcending rain forests to Deep Cove where passengers board a launch and cruise to Doubtful Sound on the west coast.

If you go, know that you will have driven the most expensive road in New Zealand. The road was essential to bring the heavy turbines, construction materials and equipment from the sea up to the dam site. It was built at a cost of *$5 an inch*.

All done to supply electricity to an aluminum plant at Bluff.

We've never done the whole-day trip but it is on our new priority list.

On one trip to Te Anau, we hired a young long-haired jet-boat jockey and fishing guide and went roaring down the Waiau River which winds between Te Anau and Lake Manapouri.

We'd stop and cast unsuccessfully then our jet jockey would roar off again.

Finally, I hooked my first river trout. The distance between the trout far down the river and my reel seemed to be about a hundred miles. I thought I had hooked into a mad whale. The drag on the long line aided by the rush of fast water made it feel like a ton, a jumping, flashing ton as it would clear the water trying to throw the hook.

When the giant, gorgeous creature was finally beached at my feet—ten minutes? . . . two hours later?—I was trembling with the physical drama of it all.

The jet jockey, hands in his pockets, said, "You get excited real easy, don't you?"

He was the only guide in New Zealand I didn't care for.

The village of Te Anau has not changed seriously for a number of years. New motels have been built, there may be a couple of new tearooms but, other than that, it is still a quiet town leaning on the visitor trade.

Floatplanes takeoff and land like giant dragon flies in front of the THC Hotel. Scenic flights also depart in light planes from the nearby airport. Fishing trips and fishing guides are arranged at a street-front travel office at the THC facility or at the Fiordland

Information Office across the street.

The most popular activity in Te Anau is a launch cruise to the Te Ana-au Caves. The early Maoris found a cave filled with a swirling river and strange lights in the caverns along the shore of the lake. They called the caves Te Ana-au or "Rushing Waters."

Not until 1948 were the caves rediscovered. Now visitors explore the glittering glowworm grottos by footpaths and aboard small boats.

It is first-rate and not to be missed. A good ten-pointer.

Walking along the waterfront under the tall bluegum trees down to the boat harbor at one end and the Fiordland National Park Information Center at the other is a short, scenic stroll. Pleasant. Park rangers can give you the latest information on long and short treks around Te Anau.

Opposite the park headquarters is a small trout viewing facility. The charge is 50¢ and is worth 10¢.

Cornerstone of the activity is still the Te Anau Resort Hotel with its perfect location facing the lake. The THC property, which always keeps changing things around, had added 15 spacious villa suites since we were last there. The villas, not cheap, are the first accommodations reserved, according to Bill Neilsen, the general manager. Each has a lounge, kitchen, bedroom and wood-burning fireplace. They were built near the pool area.

Two restaurants, two bars, a swimming pool, superb self-help laundries (several in fact) comprise the complex which, also, is the headquarters for the Milford Track, "the finest walk in the world."

Once we spent over six months in New Zealand, as part of a "Year of Saturdays" sabbatical, and we walked the Milford Track. It was a highlight, the cherry on top, of what was a delightful year of visiting other people's islands.

Our enthusiastic reports first in letters to friends and, later, in our first *Lost And Found* book, have been responsible for many of our friends taking the Milford Track, among them Carolyn Patterson, an editor with National Geographic Magazine. She and Geo's chief photographer did a splendid story which reached millions of impressionable Americans. One result is that Americans now comprise 25 percent of the walkers on the Milford Track.

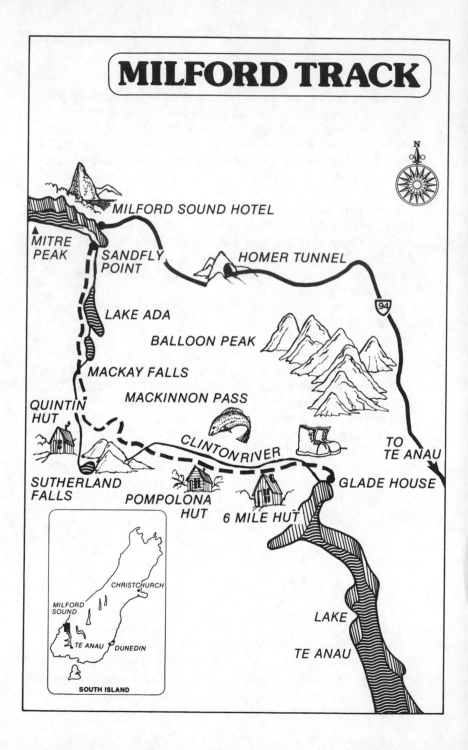

"You have to emphasize," returning friends have told us, "that it is not a walk in the park. The better condition you are in, the more you will enjoy it."

True. We had a lady who prepared for the Milford Track by walking her dog to the top of her garden. She didn't finish.

In addition, a few unathletic types returned with blood in their eyes and vengeance in their hearts because they had encountered floods, snowstorms, and other adverse weather conditions.

"It's all part of the fun of being in the mountains," we told them. They were not amused.

This southwestern tip of New Zealand faces the famous Roaring Forties and it brings gauge-busting amounts of rain and unpredictable snow flurries at any time of year. You do have to keep it in mind.

We were told of one lady from South Africa who signed on for the Milford Track and then canceled when she found out, to her horror, there were no porters.

Another was going to bring cocktail dresses and high-heeled shoes for a change of clothing after the day's hike.

Basically, the Milford Track is a five-day adventure.

The first day you meet around noon at the Milford Track office, part of the Te Anau Hotel, in your hiking clothes and with your backpack. If you don't have a pack or a rain cape you can borrow them from the Te Anau Hotel and turn them in at Milford Sound Hotel. Everything is wrapped in plastic bags which are provided by the Track. You are cautioned to limit yourself to 12 pounds.

The Track will also transport your luggage to the Milford Sound Hotel free of charge providing you clean clothes for the final banquet and the option of continuing on to your next destination without stopping at Te Anau.

Before leaving, you have your picture taken along with 40 other hikers. You don't think much of this at the time—*who are all of these funnily dressed people?*—but the photo becomes a cherished souvenir as these 40 strangers prove to be your closest friends before you finish the hike.

A bus takes you to Te Anau Downs to board a launch for the head of the lake. A half-mile hike brings you to Glade House, your first bunkhouse. Or rather, two bunkhouses: men in one, women in the other.

Each bunk has a pillow, a clean towel and, now, "duvets," eider-down comforters, which are warm improvements over the old army-type blankets we were furnished with.

Here you are supplied with a cotton sleeping. bag with an attached pillow sack for the bunk pillows at every camp. You pack your linen the next morning but leave behind the towel. A fresh towel is issued at every hut.

Separate facilities for men and women include hot showers, wash basins—and flush toilets.

Dinner is substantial and efficiently disposed of. Twenty-six minutes for soup, main dish, dessert and coffee.

After dinner, you are urged to stretch your legs before re-assembling for an orientation meeting in the cleared dining room. A short hike up the mountainside to a mountain stream called Glade Burn proves to be the ideal after dinner *digestive*. Bellbirds serenade you. The country is lush green.

At Glade Burn you dip into the clear running stream and have a sip of mountain water, and you then realize why no canteens are issued. There is no need. Fresh water is always within steps of where you are.

Phil Turnbull, for whom the meeting room at the Te Anau THC Hotel is named, is in charge of Glade House along with his hard-working wife, Betty, who runs the kitchen.

Each guest introduces himself and sticks a pin in the mounted world map to indicate his home town. Before the end of the season, the entire map will be covered with pins; hikers from every corner of the world walk the Milford.

Sixty percent of the annual 4,000 hikers are from overseas. This number of hikers is maximum, dictated by the present accommodations and the weather. The season is November 1 to April 1.

Another 3,500 independent "freedom" walkers annually take the Milford Track, backpacking their food and sleeping bags. This number is limited by facilities for overnight stays in the three National Park huts.

The Te Anau Hotel reservation computers handle all bookings for both operations. They also provide booking information.

Hiking the Track as a "freedom" walker is not entirely "free." Besides bus and launch transportation, there are hut fees—about NZ$50 total—half of which has to be prepaid to secure a reservation.

We remember Mr. Turnbull's word of advice: "Weigh your pack. If you are over twelve pounds, you are better off lightening your load. Anything feels all right the first couple of miles. After that, it is another story.

"We have scales outside in the hall. Anything you want to leave behind will be returned to the Te Anau Hotel where you can pick it up after the hike."

He then told a story we often repeat.

"In Te Anau, there was a little boy whose father, a friend of mine, was eager to take him on the Track. The little boy wasn't very keen about going. 'Can I take my pony?' he asked.

" 'No,' I told him. 'I'm afraid not. Animals aren't allowed in the park.'

" 'Can't I even take my dog?'

" 'No. It is against regulations. I'm truly sorry.'

"There was a pause, the little boy looking down at the ground sadly. Finally, he lifted his face and asked plaintively, 'But who do you tell your secrets to?' "

"Another piece of advice," Phil said to his new group of listeners.

"Take your time. The longer you take, the more you'll enjoy it. There is no group walking. You set your own pace. You have plenty of time to get to each hut on each leg of the walk."

There was an audible sigh of relief.

"One last word. It is the tradition that those in the top bunks serve tea in the morning to those in the bottom bunks." (The 'tradition' also proved a useful traffic device for cutting down the rush to the bathroom.)

"Breakfast will be served at eight in the morning, and you'll be off by nine. Lights go out at quarter of eleven. Good night."

We lingered to talk to Phil before turning in.

The pass, he told us, that made the walk possible was discovered in 1888 by a Scot Highlander, Quinton McPherson Mckinnon who later signed a contract to guide visitors over the track and also to carry the mail. The same year he signed the contract, 1892, he was assumed drowned on Lake Te Anau. Four years later his sailboat was found, still with the sails set, at the bottom of a shallow portion of the lake.

In 1908, the Health Department was in charge of the Track. The Tourist Hotel Corporation assumed the responsibility in 1955, refurbished the accommodations and established the Track's popularity.

"You label the Milford 'the finest walk in the world.' Why is it the 'finest' in your opinion?"

"It's the magnificent variety," replied Phil, without a moments hesitation. "You walk up the scenic river. Then you come out to an alpine glacier plain. Then you climb the Mackinnon Pass with its beautiful views, descend the other side in a rain forest to Sutherland Falls, one of the highest waterfalls in the world. From there, you follow the Arthur River with its spectacular waterfalls down to the incomparable Milford Sound. It is variety of the highest order."

The first morning, after receiving, or serving, a cup of tea or coffee, you have a hearty breakfast, weigh your pack again, compare sandfly bites and share insect repellents, and take off across the swinging bridge and up the Clinton River.

I can still picture it. The wide path, the green river dappled with patches of sun and shadow. If you stood very still, you could often see a large trout hanging in the current behind a big rock, occasionally darting out to grab a morsel but darting right back again to his waiting post, slowly undulating to keep his position in the river's current.

Why didn't everyone carry a fishing rod and catch trout, I wondered? Because, it was explained to me, if you catch it and keep it, you carry it.

The old Six Mile Hut—a lean-to really—is no longer a lunch stop. A major landslide in the '80s blocked the Clinton River, forming a lake which hikers now skirt until reaching the new lunch stop at Hirere Falls where sandwiches, hot and cold drinks, and soup on cold mornings, await the hikers. Another upgrade.

At the ninth mile, the trail comes out of the forest and in front of you is Mackinnon's Pass. My, it looks high.

At the eleventh mile—measuring from the jetty at Glade House—you arrive at the Pompolona Hut.

Where did such a name as Pompolona come from?

The story goes that Mckinnon, the pass discoverer and first guide, made a batter of sorts and fried it in the fat from mutton candles. A guest said it reminded him of an Italian pancake called 'pompolona' and from that time on the rest area was called Pompolona Hut.

Tea awaits the arrivees. But you shouldn't be first. You should enjoy the surroundings along the way. One small advantage of being first is that you get your choice of bunks and the first hot shower.

In 1983, a giant avalanche formed a dam above the hut, temporarily blocking the river. When the dam let go, a massive wall of water all but erased the old Pompolona Hut.

The destruction happened just eight weeks before the start of the season. Employing helicopters to bring in materials, a new enlarged camp was completed in time for the first party.

Today, there are four dorms instead of the original two—a luxurious upgrade for the Milford Walk.

Helicopters now also bring supplies to the huts.

Kea birds with their cheeky dispositions and raucous calls think Pompolona is their home. They have a reputation of sliding down metal roofs scaring the occupants to death.

Few dinners will taste as good as the one after the first full day on the Track.

Lights out at ten.

The next day is the day to pray for good weather.

The walk starts out easily across the glacier plain and you can see St Quinton Falls, Mount Balloon Avalanche Creek and Mirror Lake and Lake Mintaro on a side track which is a favorite resting spot. You will need the rest.

The climbing begins. A zigzag trail slanted ever higher and higher while the weather gets cooler and cooler. Alpine flowers grow alongside the path.

Reaching the top brings with it a great feeling of exhilaration. Hey, hey, I've done it.

The sweeping, majestic views of snow-topped peaks and wondrous valleys match your feeling of triumph.

On top, where there is a memorial cairn to Mackinnon, there is a new resting hut with radio communication to other huts—in case you have left behind a precious note book as I did. In bad weather hot tea, coffee and soup will be waiting. To underline how *bad* the weather can be, the new resting hut is the fifth one built on this site. Three of the previous huts were blown away.

Descending is tougher than ascending. If the main track is open, great. But the main track passes under the face of the nervous Jervois Glacier, and if it is more avalanche prone than usual, you take a path that is slippery, steep, rocky and jarring to every muscle in your body. Other than that, it is a lot of fun.

At the twentieth mile, you cross a suspension bridge over Roaring Creek and there before you is the lovely sight of Quintin Lodge.

Do not drink a cup of tea and head for bed. It is tempting to do so. But don't.

You must not miss the sheer beauty of the tall falls, Sutherland Falls, thirty relatively easy minutes away. To stand in the thundering noise and the mist of the Sutherland which drops 1,904 feet is one experience you will keep in your memory book forever.

And if you can join with others in the hilarious, drenching walk behind the falls, don't miss that either.

Quintin Hut, due for upgrading in the THC schedule, has a reputation for the best food on the Track. Maybe it is because the hikers are so hungry. Our party arranged for an airplane full of grog to be flow in, which eased many aches and pains that evening. We've heard the rumor that today wine and beer sometimes appear out of the forest which would be another distinctive upgrade in the system.

By the time you've reached Quintin Hut, the army of forty strangers has melded into a large circle of good friends. The divergent places of origin and different occupations make the group that much more interesting.

Thirteen miles lie ahead of you the last day and you can dawdle, but not much. You have a four o'clock rendezvous with the launch at Sandfly Point that you can't miss.

It rained continually on our last day but memories, now ten

years old, are as vivid as they were the morning after that sloshy, muddy, singing-in-the-rain 13-mile hike.

I remember the sides of mountains as sheets of waterfalls, as if buckets of water were being poured over giant washboards. I remember the roaring beauty of the Mackay Falls.

(When the two explorers, Mackay and Sutherland, first reached these falls, a flip of the coin determined that the falls would be named after Mackay. The name of the next falls naturally fell to Sutherland and the Sutherland Falls—the taller—are now world famous.)

The path around Lake Ada I still experience but even more memorable is the picture of a relentless rain raising the level of creeks we had to cross, ever higher and higher until, at the last, we were slogging through water almost knee deep rushing to its freedom in Milford Sound.

The signpost—and favorite photo spot—at Sandfly Point marking the end of the trail is a welcome sight. So is the new hut with an attendant serving tea, coffee and hot soup.

When the launch takes you across Milford Sound, you have a chance to drink in the beauty of the deep blue waters, the surrounding peaks and, of course, more waterfalls.

The Milford Track package now includes an overnight stay for every party member at the Milford Sound Hotel which is a vast improvement over splitting the group on "graduation" night, as in our case.

When you get to the hotel and go to your room and find your bags and take a deep bath and put on different clothes, the world is an exhilarating, wonderful place.

The family comes together in the bar. The hotel manager makes a brief congratulatory speech and hands out the Milford Track certificates and then everyone joins in the final banquet—also part of the package—which features good food, hilarious recall of incidents and much wine.

After breakfast the next morning is the saved finale: a proper launch tour of the Sound—in dry, warm clothes. The party over, some may stay on at the hotel, others fly out to Queenstown while most will catch the bus back to the Te Anau Hotel to reclaim cars.

The memory and the friendships go on forever.

Make no mistake. The Milford Track is the 'finest' walk in the world for most of us and certainly the most memorable.

Your travel agent has details, or write for more information or reservations to Milford Track, THC, Private Bag, Wellington 1, New Zealand or to Milford Track, Te Anau Resort Hotel, P.O. Box 185, Te Anau, New Zealand.

The only restriction is that children under ten cannot go—a rigid safety precaution because of the danger of flooding. The upper age level is 70 unless medical evidence can be shown of good health.

Freedom Walkers should write to the Te Anau address for reservations.

We did not repeat the Milford Track adventure, but we did revisit Te Anau and Milford Sound.

Another Way To See Milford Sound

Most of the tour buses you see in Te Anau are taking their passengers through Eglington Valley, over the divide, through the Homer tunnel, and down to Milford Sound for a cruise.

If the weather is fine, and if you have a car, drive to Milford. Make it a leisurely trip. Stop along the way. Have a quiet lunch at the hotel. Take the last cruise on the Sound, after the tour buses have departed.

However, if the weather is *iffy*, leave the driving chore to a tour bus driver, sit back and enjoy the scenery. It makes for a better day.

We stayed the night at the Te Anau THC hotel and experienced the luxury of the new villas . . . they are first class, certainly the best facilities in the THC chain and among the finest accommodations in upgraded New Zealand.

That night we had dinner with Bill Neilson, the manager, and his gracious and chic wife, Beverly. They drove us the next day to Lake Gunn Motor Lodge, halfway to Milford Sound, where we lunched with Gavin Fletcher, manager of the Milford Sound Hotel who drove us on to his hotel.

The Lake Gunn Motor Inn is a new facility replacing a well-known Cascade Creek rest stop destroyed by fire. For many years it has provided tour bus passengers tea, sammies and bickies, ice cream cones, postcards and restrooms.

The new motor inn has all of the bus stop requirements plus pleasant accommodations for fishermen who want to try their skills in the Cascade River and nearby Lake Gunn. It also serves as a base camp for much good local tramping. Cozy bar with fireplace. Cafeteria food.

The route through the Divide to Milford Sound was made possible by the Homer Tunnel, a monument to adversity.

The Homer Tunnel was started in 1935 with a labor force of men equipped with the most rudimentary equipment: wheelbarrows, picks and shovels. Isolated for six months at a time, the workers were endangered by avalanches which frequently stopped or destroyed the work and snuffed out lives. The first 'hole through' didn't come until 1940. The work was then halted until after the war.

In 1954, nineteen years after the work began, the first car drove through the tunnel. The initial estimate for construction in 1935 was $4,000. The final tab for the Homer Tunnel was $1,000,000.

Near the bottom of the winding road which Gavin drove like a typical New Zealander, i.e. flaps up and flat out, we stopped for a new look at "The Chasm."

The Chasm is a slot in granite. Its holes and pockets and water tunnels were carved by the cutting edge of the Cleddau River as it rages down to Milford Sound. The force of water sculpted many of the formations into rounded, smooth surfaces. A wooden and widened walkway has been built where once only a damp, sometimes slippery path existed. Even better, it is graded for easy walking and directs visitors through a one-way traffic pattern across the rock formations and the rushing river. A great improvement.

A short ride in the swift machine brought us to Milford Sound and the Milford Sound Hotel.

Upgrading at the Milford Sound Hotel has also been going on. All the upstairs rooms have been redecorated, a satellite dish for international television reception has been added.

What couldn't be improved is the awesome view from the front lobby looking up the throat of the beautiful Milford Sound with Mitre Peak overlooking the scene.

New boats are at dockside to take visitors cruising. We were advised:

(1) to take the smaller boat for better viewing

(2) take the 3pm tour after the tour buses had left, and
(3) do not take the luncheon trip. You should be out on the deck viewing and taking pictures instead of eating.

That evening before dinner we sat in the bar and watched the assembly of hikers who that afternoon had finished the Milford Track.

There was much laughter as the trampers compared notes and recalled experiences. Souvenir books of the trek were being shuffled among the group for addresses and phone numbers.

The standard greeting as fellow hikers arrived in the bar was, "I never would have recognized you."

We were most flattered that several in the group spotted us and came over to inquire "Aren't you the *Lost And Found* writers?"

The Kellys said we didn't emphasize the walk behind Sutherland Falls enough.

The Mouats recommended a farm they stayed at 20 minutes south of Rotorua.

The Dysarts were excited about their stay at Apple Tree Farm outside of Taupo where he learned how to play cricket and where they rode horses and mustered sheep.

The funniest story we heard came from a young couple who had booked overnight in a bed-and-breakfast home in Auckland. They checked in only to discover they were in a bed and brothel. Wrong kind of B&B. They gathered their things and sneaked out.

The Axelrods from L.A. thought the best buys in New Zealand were farm stays and practice rugby jerseys in Christchurch and the worst buys were leather goods.

At breakfast the next morning we met an American fisherman who was an investor in the Cardrona skifields.

He called the new four-passenger chairlift "the social chair" because two couples going up the mountain have a chance to meet and make new friends. "A great success," he said.

Wasn't it dangerous trying to get four people on a moving chairlift?

"It causes less trouble than a triple," he said.

His fishing guide was Roy Moss from Queenstown who looked and talked like the British actor Jack Hawkins.

How was the fishing?

"The pressure on the rivers is pushing the true fisherman farther and farther out," he commented. Roy has a first-class reputation. His address is Tadorna, Sunshine Bay, Queenstown.

Jules Trapper And The Hollyford Track

Having walked the Milford and the Routeburn Tracks, what our experience book was missing was the Hollyford.

Friends put us in touch with Jules Trapper, the owner-manager of the guided walk, and encouraged us to do whatever part of it we could even if we couldn't enjoy the whole Hollyford.

So it was we checked our luggage at the Milford Sound Hotel except for a small overnight bag, walked to the adjacent airstrip and waited for Jules Trapper to come for us in his magic airplane.

The Cessna 185 landed, turned at the end of the runway and taxied back to park among ten other light planes and two helicopters, most of which, if not all, were sightseeing craft.

Jules Trapper climbed out of the cockpit, a bearded, lean, energetic fellow with a brisk, comfortable manner. "As soon as I gas, we'll be off," he said, putting our small packs in the plane.

Next came a briefing of what he had scheduled.

"We will fly up to Martins Bay taking the scenic route. Martins Bay is where we have our second camp. Tonight it is filled with a group of trampers and new guides we have in training, but we'll have lunch with them and, afterwards, you can hike with them to the Seal Rocks.

"Then we are going to take a jetboat up the lake into the river to Pyke Camp, the first night's camp in the regular drill. We'll stay overnight, then get an early start tomorrow to another lake and waterfall, then jetboat back to Martins Bay, picnic with the others on the beach and I'll fly you back to Milford in time to catch the Te Anau bus.

"How does that sound?"

Breathtaking.

The Cessna climbed steadily in the sky and Jules turned south heading up the Arthur River and past Lake Ada to Sutherland Falls.

How different and how short the last day's trail of the Milford Track looked from the air.

Sandfly Point was in the wrong place from where I imagined it to be.

We could see the trail on the west side of Lake Ada and then the tiny huts of Quintin.

Sutherland Falls loomed before us and we flew over the tiny lake on top, Quill Lake, circled the bowl, and Jules put the plane on one wing as we returned to the Falls so that we could look straight down its cascading chute. Marvelous stuff.

Over a mountain range we climbed then descended to Milford Sound and followed it out to sea, rounded a cliff and headed north to Martins Bay.

"We have just done the scenic flight in reverse. Trampers—including 'freedom walkers' who do the Hollyford Track on their own, staying in park huts—have the option of flying out from Martins Bay. If our guests elect to walk out, they hike back to Pyke Camp, spend the night and walk out the next day. The cost of the plane ride is $20 extra. Everybody takes the plane."

Jules circled the small dirt airstrip. The hiking party just arriving from Pyke Camp got on the runway and waved and he had to go around again. We didn't know it but he was also peering into deer stockades in the vicinity where he occasionally corraled a stray buck or hind.

He later told us that he noted that a gate was shut and went back to find a buck. The fresh venison went into the pot that night.

"A hind could be worth $3.000. A hind carrying a fawn could bring as much as $5,000."

We landed on the dirt strip in a spray of pebbles and he taxied up to his cabins and parked under a tree twenty feet from his bedroom.

One of the trees was decorated with colorful crayfish pots; everybody referred to it as the "Christmas" tree.

The cabin was full of trampers waiting for lunch, fourteen in all. They came from America, Holland, Canada, Australia and New Zealand. In addition, there were the trainees along with the regular staff. Lunch was four different salads, cold lamb, beef meat loaf, cold beets, buttered bread, lemonade, tea and cake for desert.

After lunch the entire mob was herded into jetboats that flew over the water to a long lagoon protected from the ocean by a luminous sandbar. They dropped us on a rocky beach with guides to lead us past a National Park hut (14 bunks) and on to a peninsula filled with giant boulders.

The sweaty rock hopping was worth it after we encountered our first Fiordland crested penguins who posed for pictures as if they were professional models in tuxedo fronts and punk rock haircuts.

Farther on was a colony of fur-bearing seals.

"Don't get between a seal and the water," our guide said. "And watch where you step. A seal will blend right into the rocks. In the winter the bull seals will take off—no one knows where—leaving behind about 200 female seals and their pups to brave out the winter storms."

"Typical males," murmured the Lady Navigator.

It was a beautiful afternoon. Many of the seals were sporting around the rocks near shore but the majority were sleeping the afternoon away in the sun.

The Hollyford trampers would spend two nights in the Martins Bay hut exploring the area before flying, or walking, out.

Back at camp, Jules kept us in the jetboat, picked up another guide and we virtually flew across Lake McKerrow stopping briefly at the ghost town, Jamestown. Of the failed colony, only a gatepost and two apple trees remained. Today, when the apples ripen, members of the Hollyford staff harvest them to make "Jamestown Pie."

Jamestown was part of a development scheme to make Martins Bay a port from which to expeditiously ship the huge volume of gold from Otago to Australia. The plan envisioned the Hollyford Track as a shortened route from Queenstown to the sea. The lagoon over which we had skimmed to reach the seal colony that afternoon was to have been the harbor.

"The stakes were large," said Jules. "You have to remember that one river alone, the Shotover, was surpassed in its volume of gold only by the Klondike.

"But the road never came through. The sandbar in front of the lagoon made the entrance unsafe and the scheme collapsed."

We continued up the lake in the jetboat—exhilarating—and when the lake ran out we zoomed up the Hollyford River, following its bends and curves, flashing over even the shallowest parts of the river where we could see white gravel swirling just beneath the hull.

At a place called Jet Boat Landing we pulled in, tied up and hiked half a mile to Little Homer Falls, a scenic cascade of white water pouring down a hundred yards between two rows of green ferns and trees. Pretty, pretty.

We went back to Jet Boat Landing, slalomed downriver to the Pyke River Junction, went up Pyke River through fun-bumpy rapids to Pyke Lodge at the toe of Lake Alabaster. Sue, the cook, met us at the landing announcing that tea and freshly made cinnamon rolls were waiting.

The cabin was not large but adequate with a kitchen-dining room, two running water toilets and showers between the kitchen and the bunk rooms where fourteen bodies could sleep in the provided sleeping bags.

Chicken and cold beer was surpassed only by good talk.

Jules, the son of a successful car dealer in Invercargill, was an outdoor person who learned to fly at 20. An early crash left him with a small facial disfigurement which is partially covered by his beard.

He turned his back on the car business after two years and started the Hollyford Track in 1969 with an older partner who had since died.

In the early days, Jules guided, cooked, drove the boat, scrubbed the toilets and did the laundry. Three staff people in each hut now take his place.

It was not until 1982—and after an investment totaling $250,000—that he finally made a profit.

An integral part of the Hollyford operation is a radio network. Jules was in constant contact with Martins Bay hut, his office, and his wife, both in Invercargill. He mentioned that he was going to see a local production of "Fiddler on the Roof" when he got home from this current trip.

"Oh, we want to go, too," we said.

After we had determined that we would be in Invercargill at the time of the show, Jules got back on the radio to ask his wife to get tickets.

The next morning we motored up Lake Alabaster. It was alabaster perfect—not another soul on it—and not another soul would be on it unless it were by floatplane. You could only reach Lake Alabaster by jet boat up the river and Jules had the only jet boats. A huge, lovely, perfect lake—all our own.

We went to the far end of the lake and hiked a short distance to Barrington Falls. Again no one enjoys the falls except those on the Hollyford Track.

We fished a bit afterwards without success.

"Look over there," said Jules. An injured bird was limping around the shore, one wing extended and dragging. "That's a Paradise duck. No, it's not hurt. It's doing its broken wing act to draw our attention away from his family on the lake."

Sure enough, when we had drawn away, the 'broken wing' was mended and the duck took to the air.

Jetting back down the river and lake Jules pointed out Mt Madeline and Mt Tutoko, the tallest mountains in Fiordland National Park rising over 9,000 feet.

"Tell us what you usually do with your clients. What is the normal routine," we asked Jules.

"The normal routine is that you drive your car or take a bus to Marian Corner which is just above Cascade Creek on the road to Milford Sound. We have a van that picks up trampers from Marian Corner and takes them to the end of the Hollyford Road which marks the start of the Hollyford Track.

"They walk about four miles to Hidden Falls, have lunch, then follow an easy switchback trail until they come to Little Homer Falls. Here they are intercepted by a jetboat driver, escorted back to the landing, whisked to the Pyke River Junction and up the rapids to Pyke Lodge where they spend their first night.

"Normally, we take the party coming into Pyke Lodge on to Lake Alabaster that first evening. The next morning we jet them down to Jamestown—they love jetting on the river, incidentally. It is usually a firstime experience for most of the party. They then hike into Martins Bay from Jamestown, about a two-hour walk."

When we returned to Martins Bay camp, the hikers had already taken off for a picnic on the beach. Jules decided to "head them off at the pass" by taking a shortcut through a green-on-green estuary to a secluded cove back of huge sand dunes. We never found them but the detour permitted an exploration of the abandoned homesite of the original Martins Bay settlers. A few gate posts and stately old gum trees that looked strangely out of place were all that remained.

Raising cattle was the intended occupation of the two bachelor brothers who lived on the site. Once they had fattened the cattle, it took them three months to drive the herd through the Hollyford Valley and over the pass to market.

A tough life. One remaining letter reads: "Found dead seal on the beach and ate it."

As we buzzed the beach after an impromptu lunch at the camp en route back to Milford, we found the missing hikers just over the next sand dune. Highly mysterious. There were no footprints on that vast, empty beach!

We flew straight up Milford Sound to the strip just in time to make our bus to Te Anau.

Great experience and not expensive.

One caveat: the sandflies are prodigious. My hands were so swollen they looked like boxing mitts when I got back into the Chilly Bin.

Hollyford Tourist and Travel Co., P.O. Box 216, Invercargill, New Zealand.

13. The Southland

Deer Farms . . . Stage Plays . . . Stewart Island

When he came out of the new homestead, I thought we were back in Hawaii and looking at Tom Selleck. Well over six feet, mustached, unassumingly handsome . . . Simon Stewart was the owner of "Kotahi" and our host on an overnight farm stay.

The Lady Navigator: "I like it already."

We had ticked off of our "Desirable Experiences" list overnight stays at a horse stud farm, a dairy farm, an animal fattening farm. We had visited a goat farm even if we hadn't had an overnighter. Only the deer farm-stay remained to do.

The Queenstown Tourist Office made a telephone call to a new farm-stay company who, in turn, arranged for us to find Kotahi about 80km south on Highway 6 just beyond Five Rivers junction.

The short journey took us along the southern arm of Lake Wakatipu. At the end of the lake is Kingston, home of the famous Kingston Flyer. The steam railway makes several runs daily—summers only—over a short but scenic route in its second career as a local sightseeing attraction. Its old engine and restored cars are a delight for children of all ages.

Our next landmark was Garston, headquarters for a loyal band of fishermen devoted to the Mataura River. There is a small pub/inn that has almost as many devout followers.

We had no trouble finding Kotahi.

Simon, assisted by his 5-year-old son Daniel, helped us carry overnight necessities from Chilly Bin into the house over yet-to-be landscaped lawn.

Danny, wife, mother of a just-born third son and architect/designer of Kotahi, welcomed us warmly into an uncarpeted lounge for a cup of tea. A very pretty lady.

"My friends are appalled that I would have paying guests in an unfinished house, but I won't compromise on what I want . . .

and we can't afford what I want right now. Guests will help us afford our standards faster," Danny said without embarrassment. A very practical lady.

After tea, she toured us around the house, filling in word descriptions where no furniture existed or work was ongoing. She had designed skylights and bay windows, full sliding glass doors for maximum light.

"Wouldn't that be a problem during the cold winters of Southland?" we asked. She had built into the plans special protective covers and looked forward to testing them.

A very talented lady.

(The farm-stay rental organization had not seen Kotahi, although they had been urged to do so. We were the first overseas visitors the Stewarts had had in their new home.)

We settled into a private wing of the new home. The wing had been completed, carpeted and furnished. It came "ensuite" as they say, meaning "with private bathroom."

"We are just in the beginning phase of deer farming," said Simon. "I already have NZ$50,000 invested. Last May I bought ten hinds for $3,800 each and the rest is tied up in deer fencing, part of which is installed. When it is finished, I expect to have 40 acres capable of supporting 100 breeding hinds.

"The gestation period for a hind is eight to nine months. My deer are over at a friend's farm who has an established operation.

"Would you like to go and see it?"

"Oh, yes."

So we piled in the new four-wheel-drive station wagon and drove over to John Craigie's farm, another brand new ranchhouse with sliding glass doors, the kind of house you expect to find in California.

As we walked the fenced green pastures, John explained their layout.

"I have 100 acres in paddocks for deer. Half of that is divided into ten-acre paddocks in which the deer are rotated. We grow our own feed," said Craigie. "We also have 1,600 ewes on the farm."

We plied him with dumb questions, like, "how can you tell a good deer from a bad deer?"

"Many ways," said John. "You can judge their condition by their activity, their alertness. You look at body confirmations.

You wouldn't want a deer with funny feet or a malformed head, would you? You look for overshot or undershot jaws. That sort of thing.

"In 1978 I started the deer farming portion of my farm with nothing. Right now you are looking at 95 breeding hinds, seven young stags and five master stags. Along with the fencing, which cost $7,500 a mile, my deer farming operation represents an asset of about $500,000.

"There is not enough deer to supply the venison market."

As we approached a paddock with a herd of deer, they started to run and Simon spotted a fawn among the herd but as we got closer no fawn was to be seen.

"The fawn has been 'planted' by his mother," John said. "She will keep her offspring hidden for as long as ten days. Even though all of these deer are domesticated, that is, born in captivity, the ancient survival instinct still carries on.

"Deer farmers will provide cover in paddocks so that the mother can 'plant' her offspring to her satisfaction."

On a tour of the nearby sheepshed, John opened a large deep freezer and pulled out two sets of antlers.

"This is what we call 'velvet.' It brings high prices in Hong Kong and Korea where it is bought as an aphrodisiac. This one set, called a stick, will sell for $350. Velvet is a very important by-product of deer farming."

Is it painful for the deer?

"No, the law requires the use of a tranquilizer and a local anesthetic which is administered by a veterinarian."

On the way back to Kotahi we had more dumb questions.

"John measures his deer farm in acres instead of New Zealand hectares. And you do too. Why is this?"

Simon laughed. "You notice that we still measure our babies and our trout in pounds and ounces? Well, the same thing is true about farms. When a farmer tells you how big his farm is, he'll tell you in acres. My 3,000 acres sounds bigger than 1,200 hectares, doesn't it?"

Back at the farm over drinks and a gracious dinner of lamb with wine, the question and answer conversation continued to focus on farming.

"Our property goes from the road back over the hills in back of us. I started eight years ago with money from my family and $180,000 I borrowed from the bank. Paying interest on my loans is my biggest expense. That's why we haven't been faster finishing the house.

"I carry about 3,000 ewes and 800 replacement ewes plus 100 extra. I get 3,500 lambs a year. You have to estimate a three percent mortality rate at lambing time. Most of the lambs go to market but a number are kept as new stock, replacing the dry sheep which get unloaded. I also have about 75 breeding Herefords.

"During shearing time, three shearers will do 2,800 sheep in about four days, each shearer doing between 200 to 250 each per day.

"Southland farmers pay more taxes than any other regional farm group in New Zealand."

"Why?"

Simon laughed. "They make more money."

"Would you like to go along with me on my morning rounds before you have to leave?"

The next morning we climbed into his truck with his boy between us, two dogs in back and 'did the rounds.'

On the highway before cutting back into the property, Simon found two of his sheep outside the fence. Simon got out, opened a gate, whistled the dogs out of the back of the truck and into action. The dogs herded the sheep back where they belonged, jumped back into the truck and we continued the rounds.

As we slowly toured the property, Simon's eyes never stopped roving.

"What are you looking for?"

"Anything that is unusual. A ewe that is hung up somewhere or sick. Sheep that have problems lambing are culled out. A 'cast' sheep is one that is down and can't get up. If it is just before shearing time, it is possible that their wool will become so heavy with rain and mud that they can't get up. A black-backed sea gull can kill a cast ewe.

"I watch the lambs for the right time to tail them—that is cut off their tails so they don't get messy around the crotch. Today, we do it with a hot gas-operated searing iron that cauterizes the cut at the same time.

"The rifle in the car is for rabbits."

"How do you feel about having people in your house in the farm-stay program," I asked.

Simon gave a big grin. "Every guest is another yard of carpet," he said.

Simon and Danny Stewart, "Kotahi," 3 Road, Lumsden.

Showtime In Invercargill

The good news in downtown Invercargill was that they had acquired new Christmas lights. A benefactor in 1984 bequeathed $50,000 to the city specifically for Christmas lights to decorate the streets at the Yule season.

The bad news was that Christmas comes during the longest day of the year Down Under, and you cannot see Christmas lights until it is dark . . . and that didn't happen until after 10:30.

Invercargill is a prosperous farm city with wider-than-average streets named after rivers in Scotland and some stately old buildings.

By chance, while the Lady Navigator was shopping one of the newer upmarket boutiques, I found myself in the Provincial Council Building, the oldest building in Invercargill. In its lifetime, the venerable stone structure served as the Southland Provincial Council Chambers, the Masonic Hall, the Supreme Court, the City Traffic Department and the home of the Southland Board of Education. It is now a retail wool shop.

The St Mary's Basilica is a worthy ten-point visit just to see the Oamaru milk white stone.

Another landmark is the First Church which has an Italian medieval campanile rising above the trees.

You have to go to the Southland Centennial Museum to learn that Invercargill, built—and rebuilt—of fire-hungry timber, was known as "The City of Blazes," so often did it burn down.

Since we had invited ourselves to join the Trappers at the theater, we accepted their invitation to cocktails at their comfortable two-storey home facing the park where we met Jules' wife, Jenny, a handsome lady and a pilot in her own right.

The performance of "Fiddler on the Roof" proved to be outstanding due to the male lead—a sheep farmer—with a marvelous, if untrained, voice. The stage was curtain to curtain with people. A major production brought off in first-class fashion to an appreciative audience.

Sometimes our observations are challenged. In our original tome, we said of the Railway Hotel, a quaint Victorian stone edifice, "you wouldn't want to stay there."

A postcard of the Railway Hotel postmarked England bore the cryptic message: "Don't knock it until you have tried it."

Later, we heard it had a most popular restaurant. Gerrard's Railway Hotel was one of our first orders of research during Invercargill Revisited.

The restaurant was Victorian charming. Etched glass doors and decorations. Art Deco posters on the wall. The restored bar had old-time brass fixtures, polished wood and crystal lamps, all exactly right, and a portrait of the hotel in oil that I tried to borrow, buy or steal. Failed all three.

Because Thursday was the USA's Thanksgiving Day holiday, we arranged with the proprietor a traditional turkey dinner menu for our guests, Jenny and Jules, and a couple of their friends, Jill and Arthur Anderson.

It was a lesson learned in sticking to the food of the country. Our American roast turkey had the hardness of a kiln-baked brown brick, the requested small creamed onions were the size of apples and not creamed, the stuffing couldn't be cut with a knife.

But the local crayfish was delicious and the copious wine and port and conversation were better than dessert. Fortunately.

There was no pumpkin pie as ordered.

Not even a pavlova.

I voiced an objection to the sweet waitress who had thoughtfully put small American flags on the table, and she asked in her best mother-to-infant voice: "You want a peanut butter and jelly sammy for dessert?"

The best known restaurant in Invercargill at that time was Donovan's on the fringe of town occupying a 1916 stone house.

Its specialities were duck, venison and pheasant. "Pricey," we were told, "but first rate."

"Strathorn," said our motel owner, "just as good and not as pricey."

Other restaurants recommended by residents were the Homestead Family Restaurant—lots of frolicking children on weekends—Kitchners, and the Top of the Kelvin Hotel.

A word about hotels. In 1944, the thirsting public of Invercargill voted to end a 38-year period of abstinence and repeal its prohibition on liquor.

A condition was that the sale of alcoholic beverages would be controlled by a civic trust and all the profits would go to benefit the city. Today you find six hotels, six taverns, four bottle shops, four wine shops and two wholesale stores owned by the Invercargill Licensing Trust. It coins moneys which, in turn, is used for charities and community projects.

This Robin Hood concept has now been adopted by twenty other communities in New Zealand.

One of the hotels owned by the trust, in addition to the downtown Kelvin Hotel, is Ascot Park on the outskirts of the city. Ascot Park is a major convention center—and strategically located next to the Ascot Racetrack. (The city boundaries were extended to accommodate the new hotel-motel. There are advantages to being municipally owned.)

The hotel has a year-round occupancy of about 80 percent and is more profitable than a casino full of slot machines.

The tourists we have observed in this southernmost New Zealand city have mainly been New Zealanders attending conventions and/or race meetings. That tourism is alive and well is attested to by the number of hotels and motels—a total of 24.

The Southland Centennial Museum in Queen's Park has been greatly upgraded and, besides the usual, has many unusual attractions.

The first attraction is the tuatara, small cousins of the dinosaur, which look like foot-long lizards. Classified as "animals," the tuatara is unchanged after 200,000,000 years.

It is the oldest surviving original specimen of animal on earth.

Go to the Tuatarium, a unique skylighted enclosure built within the museum where the tuatara live in a recreated natural environment of wet forest. Meet Henry, age 100-plus, and the youngsters: Albert, 45, Lucy, 35, and Mildred, 30.

The ambition of the museum is that one of the ladies will become pregnant so that the cycle of birth can be witnessed and studied.

The keeper of the Tuatarium is L.C. Hazley, a nice young man who started his museum career as an after-school cleaner-upper. A janitor. He was utterly fascinated with the tuatara. He studied them, spent hours observing them, photographed them until, over a long period of time, he became a leading—if not the leading—authority on the tuatara.

On a recent trip to Washington D.C., he stopped by to confer with Smithsonian Institute scientists engaged in similar research. They wouldn't let him go, insisting that he conduct a series of seminars for all their tuatara keepers. (No, you cannot see a tuatara at the Smithsonian. They are not on public display.)

You can buy Hazley's booklet on the tuatara at the museum.

Naturally the museum devotes much of its space to Southland's regional history.

For example, we found the story of H.J. Pither, a world champion cyclist and would-be birdman who, on July 5, 1910, made a successful sustained powered flight of about a half a mile on a nearby beach.

Another local inventor built a monoplane of his own design, crashed it in a turnip paddock and was fined $4 for flying an unauthorized aircraft.

Ships and shipwrecks are part of the regional lore. Stranded sailors would make model boats and scratch messages on them, setting the pieces of wood afloat in the ocean currents, hoping the models would be found and they would be rescued.

One such scrap of wood in the museum reads:
"Ship Gen Grant wrkd Auckland Island may 14
10 survive on Enderby island Nov. 67
want relief"
Miracles do happen. The wood was found on Stewart Island and the sailors were saved.

A most ominous stone was found by seal hunters in 1832 at

Cape Providence with discernible scratchings on it reading like a first line in a Robert Louis Stevenson novel:

"Beware the Natives Plentey (sic) at Preservation."

You'll give good marks to the Southland Centennial Museum. It's another solid ten-point Non-Zip bonus visit.

We learned that a "hottie" was a clay bottle filled with hot water and put in the bed as a foot warmer, a predecessor of the electric blanket.

After visiting the museum, you must wander through the Queen's Park behind it. You can stroll through a splendid rose garden, a rhododendron garden, past duck ponds and little waterways and stop in the tearoom for a "cuppa."

On the west side of the Park are tennis courts, public swimming pool and the 18-hole, par-71 Queen's Park Golf Club.

If you are a collector of golf courses, you should know that you are only 25 miles northwest of the Tokanui Golf Club, the world's southernmost golf course. However, it is only a nine-hole course.

The world's southernmost 18-hole course is the Oreti Sands Golf Club, just five miles west of Invercargill.

Two short driving excursions outside of the city are worthwhile. One is to the west, to Riverton. Stop on the way at Anderson Park, a classic two-storey mansion set in a green estate, now an art gallery. A sure stop on city tours.

Riverton is a quiet town of yesteryear, the second oldest town in New Zealand and once an important timber town. With its town street of wood-fronted stores, you could shoot a motion picture set in the '20s and '30s era and never change a thing. It reminded us of Silverton, Colorado in the Rockies, once an important mining community. Take your camera.

To the southeast is Bluff, the most important port in Southland and the home of the famous Bluff oysters. The oyster season starts in March and ends no later than August. Catches are regulated.

Bluff Hill is a scenic lookout in good weather. You can see to the east Tiwai Point and the New Zealand Aluminum Smelter.

Look to the south across Foveaux Strait to Stewart Island and see Mt Anglem, 3,465 feet, the highest point on the island.

Here Cook made one of his two mapping mistakes in New Zealand. He stood out to sea passing the south end of New Zealand and didn't know that the land mass he observed was an island. He called it South Cape. Later the island received its present name after William Stewart who was an officer on the brig *Pegasus* which made a landing in 1809.

Foveaux Strait was named after the governor of New South Wales.

The Sweet-Forested Wonder Of Stewart Island

The first time we went to Stewart Island was in an amphibian airplane that landed on Halfmoon Bay in front of the tiny village of Oban and waddled up the beach to rest facing the South Seas Hotel, the only hotel.

The amphibian service out of Invercargill has been replaced by a small, twin-engine, turboprop airplane service that lands, after a twenty-minute flight, on a gravel strip scraped out of the top of a mountain.

The first time we went to Stewart Island we had nonstop rain in which we walked in mud-over-the-ankles all day. Slopping around in mud and rain does not make for the greatest day in the world, yet, even under those conditions, Stewart Island exuded an indefinable quality of tranquillity and beauty that said, "Hey, come back and try us again."

Perhaps it was because of its isolated location at the bottom of the world or its virgin wilderness unspoiled by throngs of people that we wanted to take up the unspoken invitation. Or, perhaps it was because of the friendly wood pigeon that whirred alongside us down one of those muddy tracks.

The first time we went to Stewart Island we didn't have the slightest desire to stay overnight. Reports of Stewart Island Lodge changed our attitudes for the second visit.

A van met the passengers at the end of the runway and drove us to the "terminal" in Oban, a one-room headquarters for a tour company.

Sam Nichols and Holmes, his five year old retriever, met us in a Land Rover.

Sam and his wife, Jane, are an attractive management team. They have the relaxed, confident air of people who could—and have—excelled in everything they have tried. Sam's horn-rimmed glasses lend a definite professional air, and he manages to convey a three-piece suit image even in his lodge clothes. He has a gentle, humorous, old-shoe personality. Jane is brown of hair, energized, younger looking than her about-forty years and has a contagious laugh you remember months after you've met.

Sam has been in love with Stewart Island since childhood.

Not really in love with his family's prosperous seed and farm machinery business in Invercargill, he and Jane took the plunge—an expensive plunge—to create a new lodge around the old family vacation homestead. Not an unnatural move for young entrepreneurs to take.

Holmes, we understood from his tail wagging, was all for it.

"We are really just finished," said Sam driving up a steep hill right behind town. "It took longer than we thought, and bringing everything over by boat from Invercargill cost a lot more than we thought."

Later, Jane told us that they had sold an 80-acre farm which she had operated while Sam worked in the family business. All of their capital went into the lodge project.

Sam showed us to our room in a new wing of accommodations that had four double bedrooms, each with private bath and large balcony overlooking Halfmoon Bay.

The central focus of the lodge—besides Holmes, a beauty of a flat-haired retriever—is the large living-dining room combination with a big picture window, a fine spot to hunker down with a drink and watch the dock and bay activities below. It, naturally, has a fireplace and big overstuffed leather chairs to encourage hunkering.

Sam interrupted my reverie and dog scratching.

"We offer choices. You can do what you are doing right now. You can hunt for Virginia deer. You can snorkel or scuba dive in water as clear as you can find anywhere and over populated with crayfish, scallops, mussels, pauas—that's like your California abalone.

"You can walk in the forests on several marked trails and along the shorefront.

"You can fish or sightsee on the *Toa Tai,* our 45-foot motor launch which we take out on a regular basis and have scheduled for this afternoon.

"What surprises most people is the fine weather we have in the winter, Stewart Island being so close to the South Pole. Halfmoon Bay is in the lee of the island and in a warm ocean current and it results in year-round, vacation weather."

Lunch was a delicious flounder sauteed in butter and lemon and served with a green salad. We began to feel right at home.

When the last piece of flounder was gone—I ate it—we went down to the dock, the industrial center of Oban where there is a fish packing plant and where many of the 62 boats registered in the islands's fishing fleet tie up at one time or another.

Besides the commercial ocean fishing, salmon farming such as we saw in the Marlborough Sounds is another big local industry. It is expected to reach a production level of 1,000 tons annually.

The broad beamed, comfortable launch *Toa Tai* tied up and we boarded. Several local friends had been invited to join us, including Ron Tindal, the ranking forest officer, the proprietors of the Horseshoe Haven, a major Stewart Island tourist accommodation center with six cabins, 20 tent sites and an 18-bed lodge, and three Maori ladies who worked on a part-time basis with Jane.

In retrospect, we called it the Blue Cod Caper. It was a fresh, first-time experience.

Twenty minutes after we left the dock we entered Paterson Inlet, a nine mile stretch of protected water that cuts into the middle of the island. Sam throttled down near an islet and said, "Let's get some lines overboard."

Weighted lines baited with fresh fish chunks were dropped to the bottom.

My line wasn't a minute over the side before I hooked into a fish, a nice sized blue cod. In the next hour the boat was in turmoil . . . boiling with action as our party lowered lines and pulled them right up again, cod dangling from them. We must have brought in four dozen fish, each weighing about two pounds.

"Is it like this all the time?" we asked Sam.

He just laughed with pleasure and said, "Of course."

(We still don't know).

Another expedition lay before us: exploring the little island of Ulva, a State Forest and Scenic Reserve and a sanctuary for flora and fauna. En route, we saw blue penguins, the smallest of the penguin family.

The white thatched Ron whose soft burr marked him as a native Scotsman led us first to the shoreline nests of cormorants, called the Greater Pied, one of four varieties of shag (or cormorant) found on Stewart Island. They dive 80- to 90-feet underwater to feed on blue cod.

Ulva Island is uninhabited although privately owned by a doctor and his wife who granted permission for the construction of a nature trail over rich natural vegetation. The trail, built of treated wooden slabs three feet wide, provides a dry walking platform over the mossy, often wet undergrowth, and, just as importantly, protects the area from excessive damage. The trail is well marked and numbered to coincide with an informational booklet available in Oban from what now—since the consolidation of overlapping departments—must be the Department of Conservation.

In the summer, guided tours are conducted by park personnel. Ron gave an idea of what a conducted tour was like.

What it is like is enchantment. We were standing in the middle of a green forest—so, it was another green forest—and he would point out a tiny shrub or a giant tree, an insect or a bird, and, magically, the interdependencies of the forest would come alive.

Here was a Monterey Cypress, 130 years old. There was a rimu, 500 to 600 years old.

Down alongside the path was a Kaka Beak Orchid which snapped its trap shut on passing insects.

Nearby, a silver-back Excited Dancer Orchid had tendrils that looked like flailing arms and legs.

Ron pointed out what looked like a tiny branch, out of which was growing a fungus plant. "That was once a caterpillar," he said. "It gets infected feet, dies, turns into a piece of what looks like wood and out of it comes a fungus growth.

"In 1907, seven Virginia deer were turned loose on Stewart Island. With all of this great feed and no predators, they multiplied into thousands, endangering the forests of Stewart Island. Inbreeding has reduced the size of specie to half that of its American counterpart. These weigh in at about 100 to 120 pounds. Very hard to hunt. We issue year-round licenses to reduce their numbers."

"Are they good for deer farming?"

"No," Ron said. "They die in captivity."

"Are they on Ulva Island?"

"Yes, but never for long. They swim across the open water—they can swim faster than you can row a dingy—probably attracted by the odor of desirable plants. We wait until the visitors are gone and then send in a team of hunters to spend the night. They hunt with lights. Not sporting, I know, but it is not sport to us. It is survival of the delicate, and rare, plant life on the island."

Back on the boat, small pieces of fresh cod had been fried to serve with tea. One of the Maori ladies had made "ginger crumble," a spicy cookie that was most palate pleasing.

We debarked at the Oban dock and walked over to the South Sea pub to have a beer to wash down the tea and watch the local fisherman have an afternoon pint. Hardy folk with hardy laughs.

Evening time, Jane's pet wood pigeon appears in the tree beyond the picture window. (The island is a music hall filled with the songs of birds auditioning.)

That night every bed in the lodge was taken. A party of pals from Alexandra gathered to spend the weekend at the Lodge. One of the guests, like Sam, was a lifelong Stewart Island visitor and much of the dinner hours was spent recalling raucous events. It was a time of hilarity.

Like the time they brought in the road show "Oklahoma."

"There were more people on the stage than in the audience. But it was a big occasion that called for a special paua supper involving 800 paua.

"Well, as you know, paua (abalone) has to be tenderized with the flat side of an ax and the problem was how to talk anyone into softening up 800 paua. The solution was easy. They took the tough shellfish up to the airstrip and ran over them with the airstrip steam roller. Did a quick, neat job."

Sam's friend chimed in with another. "You know, on the island a car is driven until it falls apart. Far beyond the time it is safe to have on the road. One commercial fisherman was warned repeatedly by the town's lone law officer to get rid of an ancient Austin that was beyond salvage. He never did. Finally the policeman blew up, 'For the last time I'm telling you to get that car off the road or you are going to gaol.' (That's jail.)

"The next morning, the car was seen sitting on a rock in the middle of the bay. It was good for a laugh for three months in the South Sea bar.

"By the way, you see those objects floating in the bay?"

"Lobster buoys?" we ventured, having seen them in Maine.

"Crayfish in New Zealand. Right. But visiting farmers on vacation are told they are sea pumpkins."

Several stories were told about local names. One fellow moved so slowly that he was nicknamed "Mort." He never knew why, but accepted it, never realizing the name had originated from "rigor mortis."

Sam is alternately "Sambo" or "Moose" or "Dog Nuts" or "Little Nuts." His father was "Nuts."

"Take your pick," he says.

Yes, there was a law officer on the island but no problems or vandalism occurred. "There is only one place in and one place out. Any mischief-maker knows he is going to get nabbed fairly smartly."

The next morning we took a tour of the island's twelve miles of road in the same van that brought us down from the airport. The van is part of Stewart Island Travel Scenic Tours & Taxi Service. Beryl Wilcox, driver.

We went from Horseshoe Haven to Golden Bay with half a dozen stops in between, including several observation points.

Tidbits of information included:

(1) Stewart Island has over 350,000 acres and a permanent resident count of about 450. Some 82 percent of the mass is owned by the Crown either in state forest lands or scenic reserves. Less than 3 percent of the island is privately owned.

(2) Maori tribes hold title to the balance of the land and own exclusive hunting rights for their prized muttonbird, the "flying anchovy" we found on the menu in Queenstown.

(3) Prior to refrigeration, the Maoris preserved the birds in seaweed kelp bags which imparted an unnatural salty flavor and, forevermore, established their "proper" taste.

Mutton birds migrate from Siberia.

(4) Sixty-two registered boats come to Stewart Island during the crayfish season working out of the Stewart Island Fisherman's Co-op.

(5) Crayfish were worth $60,000 a ton.

(6) Stewart Island has 667-square miles of land. Many beaches. No icebergs.

(7) Timbering for rimu used to be a big industry. Some 20 mills were located on Mill Creek.

(8) Sealers came in 1807. Whalers followed.

(9) There are telephone lines but no electric lines. Every house had its own generator.

(10) The name Oban came from the west coast of Scotland, near the island of Skye.

(11) If you go to Observation Point at dusk and see the last light in the sky, you will appreciate why the Maoris called the island "Rakiura" which means "heavenly glow."

After the van tour, we took the foot tour and walked from Thule bay to Golden Bay, then over the hill on the track known as Hill Walk and back down to town.

At the lodge we packed our few things, ate sammies for lunch and prepared to go to the airport. The weather was not brilliant.

"The weather report says a fog is coming in but you'll get out all right," said Sam.

"Once my mother and father and grandmother were over on a visit and we had a fog that wouldn't let up. Grandmother sat in that chair by the window for five days with her hat on her packed suitcase by her side. Mom and Dad moved the gin out to the kitchen.''

We wouldn't have minded the fog coming in for five days. Loved the lodge and loved the island.

The last rates we saw were about NZ$150 a day per person and that included accommodations, all meals and refreshments and boat touring. A different, remote, upgraded experience.

Write Stewart Island Lodge, P.O. Box 5, Halfmoon Bay, Stewart Island, New Zealand.

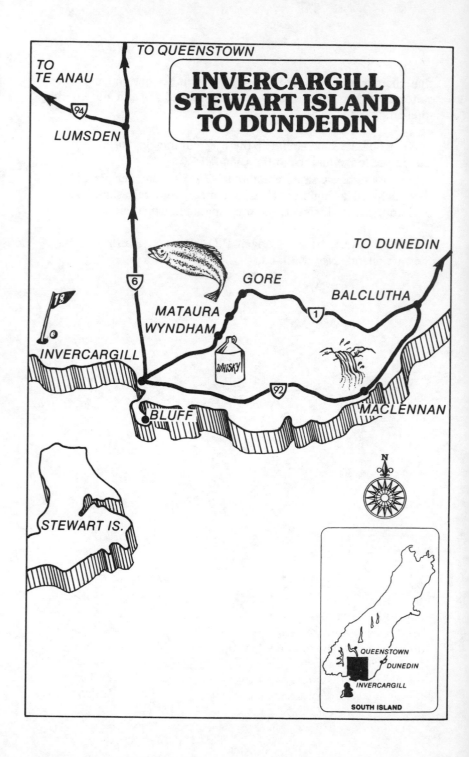

14. The East Coast Of The South Island

How To Get To Christchurch . . .
The North Route . . . The South Route
Dunedin And Timaru

Everybody goes to Christchurch.

Christchurch is a cameo of an English city, unique in many ways, the capital of Canterbury, a vast plain edged with alps and brimming over with produce and animals.

Because of its international airport, it is a hub where tour groups gather and head for Mount Cook, the Hermitage Hotel, Queenstown, a jet boat ride on the Shotover River, a trip one way or another to Milford Sound.

Many visitors will return to Christchurch via Dunedin on the east coast to fly on to Auckland or Australia or the United States.

Others, coming from the North Island, will drive from Blenheim down the Kaikoura Coast road to Christchurch which is the favorite scenic drive of many Kiwis.

Another favorite drive is the secondary Highway 92 along the coast and through forest parks between Invercargill and Balclutha. An AA official told us on a previous trip, "You must drive it. It is one of the last unspoiled drives in the country."

If you have time you can explore off-the-highway places with such names as Port Molyneux, Kaka Point, The Nuggets Lighthouse, Cannibal Bay, Jacks Bay and Jacks Bay Blowhole.

Above all you can't miss Purakaunui Falls. It is such a visual sensation that the front cover of our favorite reference book, *Wild New Zealand,* features the falls. We went there on a spring day and fell in love again. It had been misty when suddenly the sun broke through and we walked through the silver beech forest, down a yellow sun-splashed path . . . the world as sweet as it gets from a fresh rain bath. We came to the platform facing these picture-perfect steppes of rock covered with sheets of frothy, tumbling waters. Hand holding time. God's in His heaven and all's right with the world.

Having done Highway 92 once, we decided we had to follow the

261

easier drive route of Highway 1 through Gore, Balclutha to Dunedin brushing by the Hokonui Hills, an area once known for its moonshine whiskey during a time when making your own wee drop was considered an inalienable right by Scottish settlers.

On the fringe of these famous hideout hills is Edendale, known for dairy cows and cheese. Mataura and Gore draw international fishermen who long to tie into a record-breaking brown trout that live in the Mataura River running along much of the highway.

Another tourist attraction is Peggydale. A few miles south of Balclutha, this major souvenir shop-restaurant-cafeteria facility sits atop a knoll surrounded by pretty gardens.

"You'll see a bloke sitting on the porch in a wheelchair watching the tour buses go by. If a bus doesn't pull in and stop at Peggydale, the bus driver will hear about it. He's famous," we were told.

"He" was Bill Jones, the man in the wheelchair. Partially paralyzed in a mining accident, Bill and his wife, Peg, started a little gift shop by the side of the road several years ago.

Bill is also the brother, we found out later, of Norman Jones, a Member of Parliament, who is known as "the mouth of the south."

"Yessir," a citizen from Gore told us, "when there's something stirring, old Norman, he's about."

The location of the Jones' gift shop turned out to come at a strategic place in the tour bus itinerary where the older passengers needed a pit stop. Restrooms proved to the the key to Peggydale's success.

Today it's a major tourist center, open seven days a week, specializing in New Zealand natural fiber clothing, sheepskins, leather and suede goods, souvenir items, woolen rugs, boots, knitwear . . . and lots of clean bathrooms.

The separate restaurant can hold several bus groups and also serves as a dinner meeting place for Balclutha activities.

Balclutha, where you turn off to Highway 92 southbound, is near the mouth of the Clutha River and is a center for local farming, mainly sheep. Over 1,500,000 sheep are processed here annually. That represents a lot of lambchops. (Clutha means Clyde in Scotland and Balclutha translates into "by the River Clyde.")

What we remembered as a simple road in and out of Dunedin

had become a fast traffic motorway. We got lost and almost by-passed the city.

Nobody should by-pass Dunedin.

Dunedin is a kiss of Scotch candy.

Founded by religious rebel Scots of the Presbyterian church, funded by miners' gold, decorated with noble buildings and enriched with a famous medical school, it is the Edinburgh of the South.

The initial colonization plan was based on the Wakefield scheme, an agricultural society with everyone in his and her place, but instead it became a pastoral society i.e. sheep in the pasture instead of crops in the field and the Wakefield concept collapsed.

They make chocolate and whiskey in Dunedin. How could you not love such a city? When coffee is roasting in the Gregg's plant and its aroma mixes with chocolate simmering in the Cadbury plant, its enough to make you sing out loud. You find that medley of odors in the vicinity of the railroad station—one of the country's grandest Edwardian buildings. Gingerbread in stone. Turrets and battlements, stained glass windows, mosaics on the floor, rococo tiled walls and ticket windows, polished wood and polished brass.

Nearby are the Law Courts embellished with battlements, a royal coat-of-arms at the entrance together with a figure of Justice with drawn sword and scales, unblindfolded. A noble building worthy of the law.

If that is not enough, across the street and down a block is the Police Station built in 1895 and modeled after New Scotland Yard in London.

The Law Courts, the Railway Station, the Police Station, all within a block of each other make a happy trinity of yesteryears' architecture.

The Lady Navigator, who is forever rearranging things, wanted to move the functions of the three buildings into the nearby Cadbury chocolate plant and move the making of chocolate bars into the Railway Station, bonbons into the Law Courts and chocolate-covered cookies into the Police Station. Daily tours and free sampling, of course. She thinks like that.

Actually, you can tour Cadbury's Chocolate Factory afternoons, Monday through Thursday, except summers from mid-November to mid-February. Phone: 741-126.

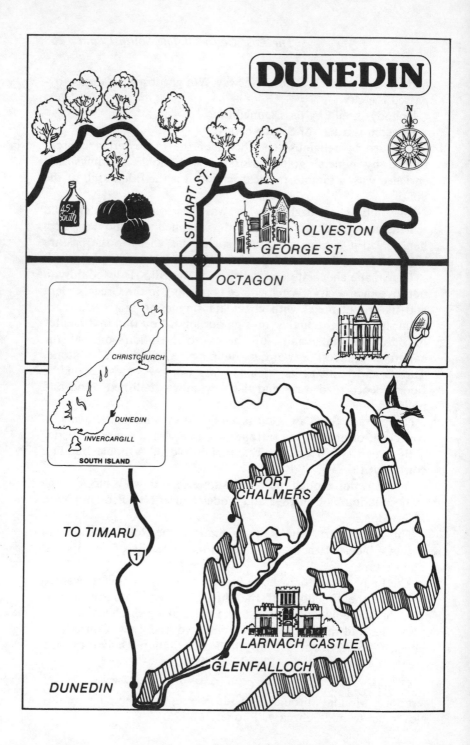

Another tour of a different nature is through the Speights Brewery, the major regional brewery with a final visit to the boardroom where free ale is offered. Monday through Thursdays also. Small fee. Reservations advised because numbers are limited. Phone 779-480.

If an overseas visitor who had time for only one activity in Dunedin asked our counsel, we wouldn't hesitate. "Go to Olveston."

Olveston, the former mansion of the Theomin family, was left to the city complete: exquisite furnishings and fine art in place and a trust fund to guarantee its maintenance. A magnanimous gift.

What great taste the owner had. A businessman who traveled everywhere, Mr. Theomin created a museum-in-his-own-lifetime in the 35-room Jacobethan house which reflects refinement, good judgment and the graciousness of the turn-of-the-century era. Of course, having a gracious amount of unlimited funds helped.

The home is maintained as though the owners were still in residence.

The dining room is set for a formal dinner, placecards at each setting. The guest, you can imagine, are sipping sherry in the drawing room, waiting to be called in.

Visitors tour the dining room, the billiard room, the Great Hall, the library and the drawing room (no dressed-for-dinner guests are there), the bedrooms and bathrooms, and marvel at every turn. The Delft pottery, the walk-in silver vault, the valuable collections in ivory, jade, silver, and pewter, the Persian rugs, clocks and ornaments, the original canvases including avant garde art . . . all awe even the most blase tourist.

We've toured many estate/mansion/museums around the world and Olveston is one of the most satisfactory. What was especially pleasing was the pride the guides had in their manor. Olveston, you felt, was *their* house.

You can tour the estate only with a guide. Free. Reservations take precedence over unreserved visitors. Call 773-320. 42 Royal Terrace.

Second only to Olveston in tour priority is the estate/mansion/museum called Larnach Castle. Located on the Otago Peninsula about twenty minutes from the city, on 35 acres of a high plateau, Larnach Castle is at first appealing, in large part, because of the character of its builder and the drama surrounding his life.

William J. M. Larnach was born in 1838 in Australia. He was at one time a bank manager in Australia and came to New Zealand to manage the first Bank of Otago.

How did a bank manager in a such a small community afford such an incredibly expensive domicile? His wife was Eliza de Guise a French heiress with a dowry of £85,000, a lot of money in the 19th century.

The neo-Gothic exterior of the four-storey structure, started in 1871, took three years and the toil of 200 workmen. Another twelve years were spent on the interior by European artists and craftsmen imported to lay the tile floors, sculpt the stone staircases, and carve the ceilings, decorative wall paneling, doors, windows and cupboards. The main sculptor worked in the castle for eighteen years.

Woods from all over the world were used. Fireplaces are of Italian marble. Belgian tiles, Roman tiles, English tiles and Venetian glass decorate different rooms. Bricks from Marseille that cost six pence each were brought in to floor the stables.

Lavish gardens were embellished with pergolas made with French glass sheltering walls. There are glass houses for fruit, smokehouses for meats, hot houses for flowers. The 40,000-square-foot castle required a staff of forty-six in its days of glory.

On our first visit to the castle in the mid-1970s, it was borderline between being completely gone and barely surviving. The estate had been taken over by a young couple, Barry and Margaret Barker who dreamed of restoring it to its former glory.

We doubted seriously that their efforts could surmount the problem of saving the castle much less improve it out of cash box receipts alone.

Lo and behold, they are winning.

The grounds have been tidied up and are now profusely floral. Individual rooms have been restored and are partially furnished with period pieces in keeping with the style and the elegance of the castle's heyday.

It isn't just the things that show that have concerned the owners. Major structural renovations have been required.

Margaret Barker appeared in the entry to escort us around the property. She pointed out a turret that had been reinforced with steel beams, and talked of the expense of repairing a leaky roof.

As an example of things that do show, she led us to the second floor which had been re-tiled with handmade, commissioned tiles from Stoke-on-Trent in England, the home of Wedgewood, Minton and Spode.

The castle draws ever nearer to the 19th century splendor of the original days of Larnach. Private parties in the ballroom help finance the restoration.

So does income from a "castle-stay" program. The Barkers converted an old Colonial Farm Building in back of the castle into private bedrooms and the loft of the stables into bunkrooms for young people on adventure tours. The latter might have amused Larnach because, in a reversal of its character, he called the castle "The Camp."

Picture this. Despite the fact that The Camp was just thirteen kilometers from the city, it was nonetheless an awesome commute for the banker, by horse. Or, rather, horses. Larnach had matched teams of blood horses—six greys and six blacks—and you can imagine his leaving the estate in his carriage behind the thundering clatter of twenty-four hooves.

His death was just as dramatic. Surrounded by financial troubles on every side, nagged by a personal scandal never clearly defined, Larnach committed suicide in Wellington's Parliament Building, shocking the country.

Over a cup of tea with Margaret Barker who has lavished brawn and big bucks on Larnach since 1967, and whose family has resided there during the entire time, we asked "What was your motivation in starting this project?"

"I sort of forget now," she said tiredly. "I think it was because we thought it would be a great place for the children to grow up in."

Open year round from 9am to 5pm; summers until 8pm. Small charge.

A trip out to the Otago Peninsula calls for a visit to the famous Royal Albatross Colony. Hours of tours are strictly controlled and you must pre-buy your ticket. Contact the Visitor Information Centre at the Octagon in the middle of the city, just off George Street, the main street of Dunedin.

As you drive along the Otago Peninsula, you will be looking down on Port Chalmers, Dunedin's deepwater port, and from the earliest days an important element in the city's economic health.

Here the first settlers, 344 in number, arrived in two ships, the *John Wickliffe* and the *Philip Laing* in March and April 1848 as members of the "Lay Association of the Free Church of Scotland." They had broken away from the Established Church of Scotland to establish a new start in a new country, removed from the bitterness of religious differences.

The harbor was always important but when gold was discovered in Otago, the annual arrival of 60 ships jumped to over 600.

From Port Chalmers, the first frozen meat was shipped to England on the refrigerator ship, the *Dunedin*, in 1882. It followed naturally that New Zealand's first freezing works for processing lamb and beef was established there.

The return along the waterfront of the peninsula takes you by Glennfalloch Gardens, famous for its rhododendrons and woodland setting. A small chalet to the side serves tea and lunches.

We went into the chalet to have a bit of lunch. Almost all of the tables were full. As we approached the counter, a man came over to us and asked, "Are you here for lunch?"

When we replied in the affirmative, he said, "Join us. We are on a tour and some of our members didn't show up and there is plenty of room. Be our guests."

So we sat down to lunch with members of the Royal Servicemen's Association of Gore and traded stories.

At the Visitors Information Center in Dunedin you also find all of the pamphlets you need and make local tour bookings. We liked the sound of the Great Guided Walks of Dunedin Unlimited which has three different inner-city walks that show and explain the highlights of Dunedin's history, architecture and gardens. They even have keys that can get you into otherwise off-limit secret corners.

On your own, you should visit the Otago Museum. Very well done. We spent a rainy and windy afternoon there among exhibits that ranged from American Navajo Indians to 18th century watches.

Being Polynesian oriented, we found the Pacific Collection, containing some of the finest examples of Oceanic art in existence, of particular interest.

On display is one of the strong ancestral enigmatic stone figures from Easter Island. (We didn't know they could be removed.)

We saw a splendid Gilbert Island warrior dressed in an armor of woven coconut fiber with a stomach guard of fish skin and a weapon made of sharks' teeth.

From the Marquesas, there was a tortoise and clam shell crown with an interior lining of red and blue trade beads.

The rare and the curious: the pintle and rudder gudgeon saved from the *H.M.S. Bounty* burned and sunk at Pitcairn Island.

A Maori Warrior in a dogskin coat was outstanding.

Another place to visit—you need a car or a taxi—is the Art Gallery at Logan Park. The Gallery has a major collection of the works of Frances Hodgkins (1869-1947), one of New Zealand's most renown artists. On a previous visit to Dunedin, the Hodgkins paintings were in storage to make room for a motion picture industry exhibit.

We were, therefore, delighted to find a room almost full of her work. A charming watercolor of the circus vans arriving in Dinar, Brittany . . . a tender scene of a woman and child in watercolor and charcoal . . . a still life in oil showing strong impressionistic influences . . . red sails in water color . . . portraits in oil. All in all, the work of a flexible, sensitive artist who succeeded in different styles.

Internationally famous after her move to Europe, Frances Hodgkins was born and raised in the genteel fashion of far-off Dunedin.

Another famous New Zealand artist you find on exhibit at the Art Gallery is C. F. Goldie whose delicately sympathetic, often ironic portraits of Maoris has to be seen and appreciated.

To own a "Goldie" is the cherished ambition of many New Zealanders.

Still another "must" place on your tour list is the Early Settlers Museum, just down Anzac Avenue from the railway station.

Outside in a huge glass case is *Josephine*, a double-headed railroad engine with two cow-catchers, two spotlights and two "straight-shooter" smokestacks. It could go either direction.

The walls of the museum are lined with somber, solid pioneers of the district. Each portrait subject looks at the camera with the cheerful countenance of a person about to be shot right between the eyes.

My favorite object in the museum is a beautifully ornate bank writing desk, partitioned to give clients privacy while they filled out bank forms. A knob on the top of the mellowed wood octagonal upright desk dialed in the correct day and month.

Another favorite is a polyphon. You put 20¢ in a slot and you get a musical piece recorded on a metal disc and driven by a clockwork mechanism. This predecessor to today's stereo tape deck was used in an arcade that opened in 1875. There's another one in the Wanganui museum.

Also you'll find a doll collection and costumes of the times, among other curiosities.

Dunedin is proud of its Botanic Gardens at the north end of the city with flora from many parts of the world, also an aviary and teahouse and another statue of Peter Pan. New Zealand gardens are fond of Peter Pan.

If you are in New Zealand in September or October, beware. You are in danger of catching Rhododendron Fever. Every year it starts in the North Island sometime in September and moves south as the weather warms. Most towns and cities across New Zealand are affected by it. The Botanic Gardens of Dunedin, in full bloom in late October, has a Rhododendron Dell with one of the most varied collections of hybrids and species anywhere. One hybrid is named "Lovelock" after Jack Lovelock, the 1936 Gold Medalist runner who was born and schooled in Timaru but who lived nearby.

If you are a collector of sporting trivia, and a golfer, you should play the Otago Golf Club, the oldest club in New Zealand, having been founded in 1871.

Called Balmacewan because of its location, you will find after the tough par-5 11th hole that the means to get to the 12th green is something you've never seen on a golf course before: a rope tow! You press a button, grab a moving rope which helps pull you and your trundler up the hill.

"Oh, yes," a member told us. "We used to have a tractor and a cart down here to take you up the hill—but with the price of help these days . . . ."

Maybe some day they'll have a quadruple chairlift like Cardrona's to transport a foursome simultaneously.

Another excellent course is the St. Clair Golf Club, a hilltop, scenic layout with undulating fairways and a heavy border of trees. Open to visitors Mondays, Wednesdays and Fridays.

For tennis, you can call the Logan Park courts and see if you can get a court. There should be space because the club has 25 hard courts and 12 grass courts.

A modest expansion of accommodations is taking place in Dunedin. While it is not much more than an overnight stop for visitors, the city receives heavy traffic from South Islanders because of its major hospital, part of the University of Otago's medical school.

The weather was rainy and we didn't want to stay in the Chilly Bin. Several drive-bys were required before we eventually found a new motel, the Commodore, whose last empty unit was designed for handicapped visitors . . . a shower made to accommodate a roll-in wheelchair, faucet handles at hip level . . . wider doorways . . . pull-up bars at other strategic places.

One of our unsupported rule-of-thumb tenets is that university towns are apt to have more imaginative restaurants than non-university towns.

For example, in Dunedin there are French restaurants. I wished we had tried 95 Filleul at 95 Filleul Street, or Ragano (seafood), Pot Pourri (vegetarian), The Huntsman for steaks. La Scala still leads the list of Italian restaurants. There are also Hungarian, Indian and Chinese restaurants.

Blades would be among the top half dozen, and friends included Aggies as "the best in the city."

We took our Wanaka friends, the Coles, to Sunday night dinner at a "family restaurant" which made the Listener-Montana survey list of "best in the country." It was a charmless disaster. One should never go to a "family restaurant" on a Sunday night unless one also has screaming, scampering children because the place will be filled with screaming, scampering children. Too, the food will be served cafeteria style and will be well picked over—the kids come early and are hungry—and it is generally tasteless.

Breakfast with Champions

The last important town on the East Coast northbound to Christchurch is Timaru, a port town with Victorian hotels that overflow with Kiwi summer visitors. A three-week Christmas festival fills every bed in town.

For such a laid-back city is has a surprising reputation for producing champions in almost every field of sport including horse racing.

Phar Lap, the most famous race horse in Down Under history, was bred and born as "Lightning" in Timaru before being shipped to Australia, being renamed and going on to glory.

Bob Fitzsimmons, who won the middleweight, light-heavyweight and heavyweight world boxing titles, built his physique in his father's Timaru blacksmith shop. He had 354 fights of which 350 were in the boxing ring and four in the matrimonial ring. Won all the first, lost all the second.

Still another: John Lovelock, a progenitor of New Zealand's successful distance runners, set the world record for the mile and the 1500 meters in the 1936 Olympics held in Berlin. He was presented with a oak tree sapling by Adolf Hitler which was planted—and is still growing—at his alma mater school yard, the Timaru Boys High School.

Timaru has a handsome church, St. Mary's Anglican Church, with crenelated stone tower. Beside it is the Pioneer Museum in a modern building which has been closed each time we have been in Timaru.

Probably one of the most handsome restaurants in New Zealand is the Custom House Restaurant. It has taken over the old Custom House which has the graceful lines of a classic Grecian temple and is particularly dramatic when floodlighted at night.

The town's pride should rest with the local art gallery, named Aigantighe, Welsh for "welcome to our house."

The contemporary building was constructed by a wealthy Mackenzie Country sheep station owner as his retirement mansion but, under the pressure of the feminine members of his family, it became the headquarters for the local art museum.

Its collection is extensive and valuable, including two Goldies: "The Last of Her Tribe" and "Cast of the Cannibals."

A recent enlargement of the museum has allowed for more

exhibit space and more exhibits. We were enchanted by a traveling exhibit of the amusing cartoons by Tom Scott, one of New Zealand's top political and social satirists.

The Public Relations Office in Timaru sells the town as the headquarters for activities in surrounding rivers and mountains, including trout and salmon fishing, skiing in the Alps, rafting down the Rangitata Gorge, farm stays, hunting and a thousand walkways.

"What's the highlight activity?" we asked.

"Trips on Air Safari. They really give every customer the red carpet treatment."

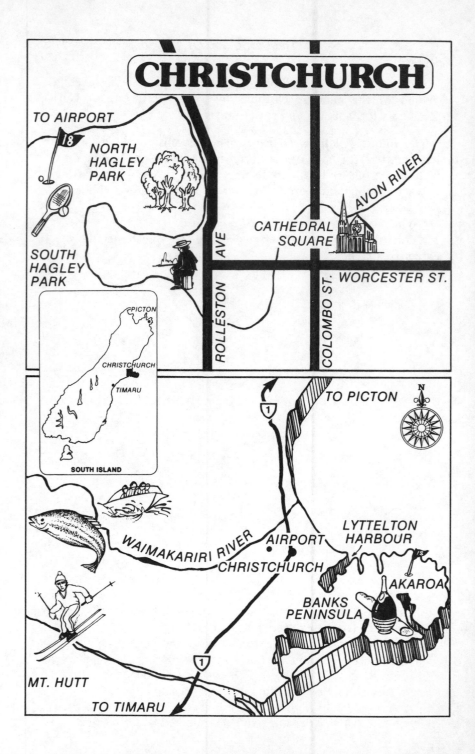

15. Christchurch, The Most English City— True or False?

Wizards and Cathedrals . . .
Canoeing On The Avon . . .
The Best Fish Soup . . . The Arts Centre

Christchurch, for all of it surface reserve, is slightly mad.

It is, for example, the only city in the world which has an Official Wizard.

Behind all those pretty flower gardens and neat homes laid out in neat squares, despite its reputation as being more English than the English, disregarding its founding as a Church of England Settlement, there lurks behind this facade a certain degree of a Gemini's split personality with schizophrenic overtones, a city with a certain number of nuts in its fruitcake.

If you have any doubts, go to the square in front of the Cathedral at noontime and watch its true personality slip through the cracks.

As the Cathedral doors open and close, the sound of liturgical music might be heard in start-and-stop snatches.

Outside, there will be carts selling fruits and flowers, university students in jeans and jogging shoes intent on getting pedestrians to sign a petition for or against today's hottest issue, and, in dramatic contrast, a gaggle of very properly disciplined schoolboys dressed in blazers and straw boaters striding along purposely. There might be a juggler, a couple of heavily bearded gentlemen already heavily into the muscatel counterbalanced by gloved matrons in Queen Mary hats, a passing policeman who takes it all in with a benign glance, pigeons and people sitting on steps munching luncheon sammies and enjoying the air.

At one o'clock, a character in a long black flowing robe, his long black hair framing an aquiline face and black eyes, climbs upon a stool or ladder and begins his day's outrageous diatribe on whatever has come into his head that morning.

It is time for The Wizard.

He draws an immediate crowd. His daily harangue is interrupted with frequent objections and questions and derisive comments which he enjoys as much as a salamander enjoys eating insects. He ridicules his would-be persecutors, he destroys his questioners, he dices, minces and mashes his detractors before swallowing them with an ostentatious smacking of lips. Oh, he is evil.

Oh, he is a delight . . . and a joy to the citizens of Christchurch who relish his doses of insanity because he mirrors their secret personality.

I had a chance to chat with the Wizard privately. In public or in private he is always on stage. There is no casting aside of character. He is always The Wizard.

"Well, I belong here. The south has a happy heritage of wizardry, but it wasn't easy as first. In 1974, there was a fight between the City Council and myself because only monarchists really appreciate a wizard.

"I hate people being moral about things. They should play the game and not cheat with moral crusades, with moral concepts.

"I said to the Council 'I would like to be your local wizard. I stand up to students and puncture their little egos. I have stopped punks from rioting and straightened out rich kids and their parents which I learned to do in Sydney at the University of New South Wales. There, the vice chancellor made me the university's official wizard.'

"So the Promotional Council, being promotionally minded and not stuffy like the City Council, made me the official wizard in Christchurch.

"Oh, I do more than just talk in the square. I do spells and things. For example, when Air New Zealand's new Boeing 767 came to Christchurch on its inaugural flight I invoked the blessing. The president of Boeing was there and he was quite taken with the Wizard, I must say, until it was time for the plane to leave. The plane was on the runway ready for takeoff when it had to come back because of a mechanical.

"I understand that in the Boeing plant in Seattle there is a blowup of me with a line saying, 'Don't let this man anywhere near our aircraft.'

"Another time I accompanied the Canterbury Rugby team to Auckland for a game and put a curse on the Auckland team which then smashed Canterbury something like 33 to 3. Terrible. Tragic. I had failed. I put on sack cloth and ashes and resigned and went into the hills. I was never going to come back.

"Well, the town was up in arms. 'Please, Mr. Wizard, come back,' they pleaded. They held a big rally and gave money and sent messages. What could I do? I came back.

"Oh, I do ravings. My eyes go funny. My followers like that. But, in reality, I'm going for truth. Now, your American government is not in good taste. You can't have a good looking government without style, costumes, slogans with everybody acting his and her parts. China is appalling. Japan is feudal.

"For example, I have my own army. Alf's Imperial Army, a special group with white pith helmets and red jackets. Oh, my yes, we hold regimental messes where everybody dines and drinks and gets smashed and breaks up the furniture and toasts the Queen and brawls on tables and all that sort of good thing.

"There is also a fire brigade, the Fort Custer Fire Brigade, which is strong on brass things. Over in Hamilton there is McGillicuddy's Flying Claymores, very artistic. It's catching on.

"You see, the university jeans and T-shirt students are very conventional. The dear children like to get dressed up in something decent, like pith helmets and red jackets.

"I'm an artist in a sense. I am a living work of art. They are thinking of putting me in a crate and sending me over to Tasmania for a Wizardmania event. You see, the world needs me.

"I have to go as cargo because I can't have a passport as I don't believe in papers. I refuse to fill out forms and questionnaires. Your balance in life is destroyed by government documents. If you fill out government papers, you become part of government, you see.

"They tried to get me to fill out census papers but I refused. The first time I got away with it on a technicality. The second time I was on a yacht twelve miles out to sea. Hah! They missed me again.

"My family is not too friendly to this idea of my saving the world . . . and all that sort of thing.

"Actually women run the world. I use the feminists for support. No reason why women don't deserve more than men. They do more. Males show off but don't do very much. We can learn a lot from animals. Especially the lion. She hunts. He eats.

"Actually the American red Indians are very good role models. Wear fancy feathers. Smoke pipes. Don't work. We need to go back that kind of original, reasonable, primitive concept.

"Let me explain my theory of the world."

I backed off from the flood of words, pleading no more time; late for a luncheon date with the Lady Navigator.

She hunts. I eat.

The Wizard understood that.

The serious side of Christchurch began in December 1850 when four ships filled with English settlers arrived at the deepwater harbor just over the hill from what is now downtown Christchurch. The names of those first settlers and the ships have been embedded in brass in the sidewalks around Cathedral Square.

The weary travelers who had been at sea for two months marched over the rough track from that port—today the port of Lyttelton—to the site of the new city where a small stream wandered lazily through the meadows.

Founding of the Church of England Settlement was based on the same theory set forth by the New Zealand Company. A cross-section of all classes of society were unplugged from the English countryside and replugged into colonial life. Neat and tidy.

The streets and districts were named after bishops and churches. The little river was christened The Shakespeare until it was found to have been named the River Avon by prior Scot settlers.

Construction of the Cathedral was started in 1864 which, considering the ecclesiastical nature of the founding company, should have been rushed to completion. It was not finished for thirty seven years.

Access to the port assumed priority. A road was completed over the pass in 1857 and a railroad tunnel was completed in 1867.

A gold star should be awarded posthumously to the original surveyors for the city who set aside a large reserve of land in what is now the green heart of the city. Hagley Park—actually North Hagley and South Hagley Park as they are separated by Riccarton Avenue—are filled with tennis and lawn bowl courts, rugby fields and cricket ovals, cycling lanes and polo grounds, a golf course, botanic gardens and, of course, the River Avon.

The English heritage of Christchurch is clearly evident in many of the handsome Gothic buildings, starting with the Cathedral.

Even the Canterbury Information Centre and its parent, the Chamber of Commerce, are housed in a government building dating back to 1887. The building carries the shield of the city with the motto: Britons Hold Your Own.

The ladies at the information desk were holding their own . . . conversation, that is. They would flunk any courtesy test, a rare occurrence in upgraded New Zealand. They acted with the disdain of political appointees.

Across the Avon from the Chamber of Commerce are the first Canterbury Provincial Government Buildings, a complex of stone Gothic structures dating from 1859 and considered to be the finest examples of Gothic architecture in the country. They have been preserved as memorials to the city.

You must visit the Council Chambers, circa 1865, a gem of a building with its stone carvings, stained glass windows, press and public galleries, and a barrel ceiling extensively decorated.

By contrast, look across the riverbank to the modern Town Hall built at a cost of $5 million. A steal. It boasts an auditorium, a theater, conference facilities and a restaurant. Fronting Town Hall is the spectacular Ferrier water fountain. Night lighted, it looks as if it were made out of fine lace. Daytimes, the spray of the fountains gives it the appearance of two dandelions gone to seed.

Another contrast is New Regent Street not far behind the Cathedral. One side of the street is devoted to a series of buildings of Spanish architecture, red tiles and all. Not quiet in keeping with the Christchurch character. But then, what is?

While there are many new hotels and motel in Christchurch, as throughout New Zealand, the popularity of the city and its status as an international gateway for visitors make reservations necessary.

We rolled into the city, our last stop, intent on turning in our faithful Chilly Bin and looked for a convenient motel within walking distance of the city. It took us an hour and a half of hunting. Those we wanted were full, and those we could get into, we didn't want.

Finally, on a recommendation of a motel owner whose place we liked, we found the off-the-street Akron Motel on Bealey Avenue. Just right. A modest motel owned and managed by Ron Kiesanowski and his wife, June. Neither ever stopped working; both provided us—and every guest—with all sorts of help.

It was Ron who observed that Newmans might be delighted to exchange the campervan for a small town car, which made sense. No sooner said than done. He knocked on the door with a cheery "Good as gold, they will pick up the van tomorrow morning." Good people.

(We repeat: when you get a four-star motel operated by the owner, you get reasonably priced, superior accommodations and service to match.)

Across the street at 82 Bealey Avenue is Eliza's Manor House, run by John and Roz Smith. An outstanding bed-and-breakfast operation, according to the Al Myers family of San Francisco.

We emptied our home-on-wheels with regret and gratitude. It had never given us a single mechanical problem, had provided camping facilities when we needed them, hot meals and afternoon tea effortlessly. We had traveled over 6,500 kilometers in over six weeks without worrying about a hotel reservation. Our cost for oil and diesel was just over US$300. A great affordable experience.

It had not been that long—no more than a couple of years—since we were last in Christchurch, but new restaurants has popped up like weeds in a newly planted garden.

Our best find, thanks to Barry Turner of Air New Zealand, was Pescator downtown. Excellent food. Good wines. The creamy fish soup created by the owner-chef, G. Spiteri, was the best soup we had during the entire trip.

An evening adventure was Chambers Restaurant in what once was the Canterbury Public Library. The library occupied the site from 1863, this stone building since 1901, until it outgrew the premises.

It was a BYO establishment and our neighboring table was filled with an office Christmas party. The party attendees didn't bring a bottle—they bought a portable reefer filled with beer, booze and several wines. Wild.

In keeping with the library tradition the evening menu was labeled Chapter Two. The pre-theater menu, for earlier and faster dining, was labeled Chapter One.

Three restaurants passed the critical time tests of a discriminating antique dealer who passed them on to us. Sign of Takahe, he noted, "was sort of touristy, in an old home in the Cashmere Hills." Of Scarborough Fair, "tell Graham that you are a travel writer and a friend of mine. He'll fit you in." We did. Graham didn't. "You'd be lucky to get in Tiffany's on the River. We weren't lucky."

Chun Wah II was recommended by everyone for Chinese food.

A cluster of Gothic Buildings on the townside border of North Hagley Park includes Christs College, the Canterbury Museum in back of which is the McDougall Art Gallery. Across the street are the ancient buildings of the University before a student population explosion necessitated its transfer to a new, barren center of study on the outskirts of town. The former premises now encompass the Arts Centre.

Behind the museum, taking a sizable piece of Hagley Park, are the 75 acres of the Botanic Gardens which can be toured aboard the "Toast Rack," an electrically operated vehicle. A small charge will get your sore feet on board.

We always make a pilgrimage to the museum because it is constantly expanding and upgrading its exhibits. A fund drive to finance a major renovation was underway. A sum of $15,000 had been raised by the staff to bring the building up to earthquake-proof standards. I bought a brick for the new edifice for $10.

I also was given a short voluntary guided tour by a staff member to see new additions.

In the recreated pioneer village, for example, I saw in the blacksmith shop an iron skid once used on a wagon carrying wool to market from a high country sheep station in the winter. The ski was attached to the wheel which converted the wagon into a sled of sorts.

The guide also pointed out a rare lintel—the part over the doorway—carved in wood, he said, in the early 19th century in the Maori soft metal period when they used low grade iron before they used steel chisels. There are only two other such lintels in the world. One is in the British Museum. The other is in the Peabody Museum in Salem, Massachusetts.

The lintel in the Canterbury Museum was in Devonshire, England where it was bought for a few pound sterling by a South American millionaire. The South American's daughter was kidnapped and, to help pay the ransom, the father sold many of his art objects. The museum bought the lintel in 1978 for $81,000.

I saw a portrait of New Zealand Company's creator, Edward Wakefield, which the guide said was done by two artists. One artist painted the man, the other did the dogs at his feet.

Upstairs there is a well-known exhibit area devoted to the Antarctic discoveries. When Ernest Shackelton tried to reach the South Pole in 1907, one of his hopes for success rested on a motorized sled. It failed dismally. The old, awkward wooden sled in on exhibit near a sleek modern light metal sled which was successfully used in the second crossing of the Antarctica in 1980. Shackelton's sled was a good idea born too soon.

The museum now has a Maori carver at work in the Maori Hall.

The morning of our departure we went down to the Antigua Boatsheds at 2 Cambridge Terrace and rented a canoe and paddled up the Avon River between rows of willow trees, among ducks and ducklings. A pleasant way to enjoy an hour in Christchurch.

In truth, the plastic canoe was a bit ratty but the Lady Navigator closed her eyes and imagined herself in a paisley frock and a wide brimmed straw hat, occasionally dipping her long stemmed red rose in the river while I alternately paddled and plunked at my mandolin.

We intended to follow the canoe ride with a carriage ride that leaves from the front door of the Canterbury Information Office and pretend we were rolling through the English countryside or en route to our country mansion in Surrey . . . but the carriage had gone to a wedding. Next time. It goes on the list.

Several tours can be taken in the environs of Christchurch.

During one trip we took a jet-boat up the Waimakariri River and fished—not very successful fishing, but it was an exciting day.

Another time we drove out to the Banks Peninsula, an all day trip which, in retrospect, was not worth the time but we were drawn by the curiosity of visiting the one place that the French had started a colony before selling out to the New Zealand Company upon learning that their claim to New Zealand land had been pre-empted by the Waitangi Treaty.

The French colonists stayed. In the pleasant Victorian village of Akaroa, half of the street names are in French and the other half in English. One street is named after the French Catholic Bishop, Pompallier, another street is named after the Anglican Bishop, Selwyn.

The Banks Peninsula is Captain Cook's only other mapping error in New Zealand. He thought that the landmass was an island, naming it Banks Island after the expedition's gentleman botanist.

You should make a trip to Lyttelton through the road tunnel, the longest tunnel in New Zealand, which was not put through until 1964. Clinging to the side of the hill, it reminded us of Sausalito, California opposite San Francisco.

Golf courses surround Christchurch. Throughout Canterbury, there are 42 courses. Most welcome visitors and some have hire clubs. We have played Waitikiri, a little more than three miles north of the city, and also, more enjoyable, Russley which is the golf course you pass coming in from the airport. Russley is the site of many national and international tournaments.

Because the city is so flat, it is a good place to cycle. There's a Rent-A-Bike at 84 Worcester Street.

Christchurch is also a ski center because Mt Hutt, a major ski complex, is within commuting distance. There are no mountain accommodations at Hutt and the nearest village of Methven is limited in rooms and amenities.

Mt Hutt has a vast skiing area that reaches to almost 7,000 feet. T-Bars and a Triple Chair service 700 acres of downhill skiing, mostly for the intermediate skier. The ski school is staffed by 55 internationally qualified instructors.

Japanese ski teams use Mt Hutt for training.

A Leopard Coachline leaves daily from the downtown United Service Hotel and takes slightly less than three hours to reach the Mt Hutt car park.

Our last visit before leaving Christchurch was to the Arts Centre opposite the museum.

It was a Saturday and the Summer Market was on. It's a goodie. Over 60 stalls were selling handknit sweaters, bakery goods—we immediately plunged into the bran muffins—leather goods, carved wooden bowls, jewelry, antiques, bric-a-brac, junk-a-junk and herbs and plants. The Lady Navigator was in her element and I knew we had a problem because we had a plane to catch.

When the Lady Navigator makes up her mind, the lovely lady has all the flexibility and malleability of a tractor coming down a muddy hill.

The Lady Navigator: *"We are going to see everything."* Jaw sets firmly. *"This is for My Chapter On Shopping."*

There was no need to answer. The memory of Arrowtown was still with me.

"Everything" included a coffee shop, two restaurants—the Restaurant Sorbonne and the Dux de Lux, a gourmet vegetarian restaurant,—the Cornerstone Pottery, the music rooms, the Academy Cinema, Banks Peninsula Folk Club, more music rooms, ballet rooms and a couple of dozen craft shops. One rug weaver took 22 minutes.

The Arts Centre covers almost five acres. The ancient neo-gothic buildings, while grand in concept, are beginning to look worn and torn. Tatty, would be the word.

Every charity and do-good cause was given space after the university moved out in 1975 and the property has been becoming increasingly frayed ever since.

Now there is a director for the project who knows the things that need to be done to move the Arts Centre forward instead of letting it slip backward.

We hope the city fathers realize that they have a tremendous potential for a unique attraction which would be the envy of the rest of New Zealand and a first-class drawing card for the city. It deserves priority support.

If they have troubles with funding, call in the Wizard.

Yes, we made the airplane. Barely.

The Lady Navigator: "Poo. We had hours."

16. Found And Treasured

Best Buys . . .
High Fashions At Reasonable Prices
A Nation of Craftsmen . . . Places To Shop

Poo. I was right. Scads of time!
We could have spent another hour at the Arts Centre instead of just *sitting* in the Christchurch airport terminal.

I could have visited the toy woodcarver, the cane and stained glass craftsmen, the print maker . . . there were dozens of talented artisans I missed.

Christopher Doig, manager, wants the Arts Centre to become the largest permanent showcase for artisans as well as the largest cultural and community center in New Zealand. His criteria for leasing space is that the people who paint, weave, mold, blow, stitch, carve, cut and assemble each item in the permanent showrooms also be the people who sell them.

"There is something very satisfying about seeing how an artist creates his product," Doig said.

Right on target.

Hugh Bannerman of Dilana Rugs (Italian for "of wool") is the perfect example. We wandered into his workshop and walked around a half-shorn carpet as deep as clover just before harvest. It was, indeed, fascinating to see the hand grooming in progress . . . the varying depths of woolen pile at each stage. Part of the carpet was, seemingly, finished. Some sections had been shorn but not clipped, some clipped but not yet carved, and a small portion, in the final stage, had been sculpt.

You appreciate an item a lot more when you personally witness just how much work goes into it.

Didn't it distract him having people wander in asking dumb questions?

"It's a better option. I set up this public workshop to attract customers, thinking New Zealanders," he said. "Most of my commissions have come from North American interior designers."

Interior designers know a bargain when they see one.
His all-wool, all-handmade rugs and wall hangings are heirloom
pieces. They are also ceremonial gift pieces. The New Zealand
Prime Minister commissioned one to give to the Prime Minister of
India.

At any price, they would be a bargain—they are that well
designed and expertly made. At NZ$280 a square meter—US$150
at the time—they were a near steal.

The Saturday bonus at the Arts Centre, April through October,
is a courtyard fair of 65 (and growing) exhibitors. It has all of the
zest and color of a medieval "faire," plus some pretty special
craft items.

Next time we go to Christchurch, I'll leave Him at Cathedral
Square with the Wizard.

But I have leapt ahead—chronologically—of my shopping discoveries.

I cannot imagine starting a visit to New Zealand without first
rushing out to buy that ritualistic loaf of Vogel's multi-grain
densely-textured bread and a pack of richly satisfying Toffee
Pops, those most delectable Cadbury chocolate covered
"biscuits" filled with caramel. Either, or both, go with the bottle
of cream-laced sweet milk the hotel has so thoughtfully stashed in
the refrigerator.

Our New Zealand shopping starts at basic levels.

When we first started journeying to the land of milk-and-Toffee
Pops, we didn't think of New Zealand as a shoppers' Shangri-la.

Fashions were, frankly, a bit frumpy. Well made, but frumpy.
Souvenirs showed little imagination, and all pottery was brown.
Abundant, but brown.

Shopping hours were limited. Except for emergency medicines,
you could buy nothing more exciting than an ice cream cone on
weekend afternoons. Few stores accepted international credit
cards and "getting it at wholesale" was as startling and
incomprehensible as flying to the moon for a romantic dinner in
June.

Things changed over the decade. There is ever increasing broad-
er shopping opportunities on weekends. Even ultra staid Dunedin
courageously embraced the trail blazing trend in 1985 when

Carnegie Centre, the city's outgrown library converted to boutique shopping, remained open the first Sunday of every month.

Fashion of the highest type sprung to life seemingly overnight, as unexpected but effective as Jack's proverbial Bean Stalk. The evidence is on the street. Stylish Kiwi "birds" stir the feathers of my Best Friend and kindle a lot of admiration and a modicum of envy in my consciousness.

Quality has always been a requisite of New Zealand manufactured apparel. Now, there's a strong sense of elan. Maybe it is because such houses as Pringles of Scotland, Pierre Cardin of France, Jag of Australia, among many, franchised their lines for manufacture in New Zealand. They provide the designs and/or patterns, sometimes the fabric, and the local partner provides everything else to market the line.

Or maybe it is the result of New Zealanders' travels abroad. Or an influx of immigrants with fashion savvy. Or a change in educational emphasis. Or an expanding tourist market. Or a combination of all of these.

Whatever the cause, there's a keen awareness of what is going on in the world fashion capitals spiced with a noticeable degree of individuality and originality among the fashion designers.

The Japanese are buying everything in sight. Shopping Guide Services are available in most major cities. Duty free shopping has been deregulated, permitting new operators across the county to sell in competition with established duty free shops in the gateway cities of Auckland, Christchurch and Wellington.

Plastic, the credit card kind, is accepted by merchants everywhere. You bet.

Best Buys

Today, there are excellent books on New Zealand available in bookstores. History books, fact books, guide books, picture books. Great souvenir or pass-along items to take home, relatively easy to pack, but, more importantly, they add so much to your visit. (Two printed-in-America guidebooks you might find helpful are *The Maverick Guide To New Zealand* by fellow Hawaii resident Bob Bone, ably assisted by his Kiwi wife, Sara, and Elizabeth Hansen's *A Woman's Travel Guide To New Zealand.)*

For the average shopper, New Zealand provides obvious answers to the souvenir question: sheepskins and wool . . . or something made from both.

There are handknitted or machine-made woolen sweaters, the newer—and softer—mohair blended apparel, blankets and rugs, hats and slippers, socks and gloves, fabrics and yarn in a spectrum of beautiful colors, and, coming on strong, woolen art as in wall hangings and/or "paintings."

Check any wool purchase for the Woolmark logo. The use of this swirled line black and white trademark, perhaps the world's best known textile insignia, is vigorously policed in the New Zealand marketplace. Its presence virtually guarantees quality.

You'll find myriad wearables and curios fabricated from the skins of sheep at most affordable prices. And, in the high fashion arena, designers have tanned it to the weight and suppleness of fine wool, dyed it in vibrant high colors and even batiked it.

For the discerning shopper, there are choices beyond those by-products of New Zealand's number one industry.

Andrew Thomson, hotelier to the jettiest of the jet-set, nudges interested guests towards antique jewelry and silver, saddlery, art and ceramics. Persian rugs, for some reason he doesn't understand, are better buys in New Zealand than in the Orient. He also recommends polo ponies—just the thing you need. Or a race horse. Shares are sold through the Stock Exchange.

His wife, Pip, a pip of a lady, introduced me to a spate of fashion designer names.

Why buy a wardrobe in New Zealand? The fashions are singular, the quality of both fabric and workmanship superb, and the prices are a fraction of the international big names in the fashion industry.

When a smart public relations lady we know from Los Angeles comes to New Zealand and spends almost $700 and takes home a suitcase of never-seen-in-L.A. fashions, you know something is going on.

For example, labels bearing the names of Rosaria Hall, Patrick Steel, Barbara Lee and Margaret Milne use fine fabrics, nod to the fashion capitals of the world, but set their own distinctive trends.

As we roamed the land we asked other good friends and business associates what they buy and why it was of good value. We compiled an impressive list of "best buys" and sources for finding them. Some are luxury items. Others utilitarian. Some are available in other countries but most are not, which is just one more *good* reason for visiting New Zealand.

Among our finds were silk or tissue thin woolen lingerie, exquisite jade jewelry and sculpture, ski and cold weather apparel, winter sports equipment and summer camping gear, a lot of quality souvenirs, including a resurgence of traditional bone carvings. And, of course, antiques.

But let us start our grand tour in the shopping capital of the country.

Auckland

Nearly one out of every three New Zealanders reside in Auckland. That statistic alone accounts for the fact that, except for one-of-a-kind crafts and some antiques, you can buy anything that is available for sale in the country in Auckland. It's the marketplace.

On Andrew Thomson's tip, I stopped by the Customs & Queen Street store of Walker & Hall to ask Win Charlesbois, a New Yorker turned Kiwi: "Why is antique jewelry considered a good buy here?"

Walker & Hall have been a major force in the antique and jewelry business of New Zealand for many years.

"Because," said Win Charlesbois, "there is no sales tax on handcrafted or antique jewelry and individuals paying with travelers cheque or cash get a ten percent dealer discount. That's the same discount the store gives to 'trade' customers, jewelry buyers from America mostly who, back home, add a sizable 'middleman' markup."

He got my attention instantly.

"There's no duty, no tax, no restrictions on exporting antiques," my informant volunteered. The company maintains its stock of antique furniture, silver, cutlery in its original store at 33 Anzac Avenue.

Mr. Charlesbois also claimed Walker & Hall is able to sell cultured pearls at the lowest prices in the world as a result of the 1986 New Zealand tax reforms.

We found the two-level pricing system at the Walker & Hall curious. Pieces priced under $3,000 are sold in the Shortland at

Queen Street store. Higher priced pieces are kept at the Customs and Queen Street store, just two blocks away.

In between those stores, you'll find the Great Northern Arcade on Queen Street. Two good reasons for stopping are the Canterbury Store and an art gallery, New Vision Ceramic Arts.

For every broad shouldered man frustrated by the shortage of size 44 or larger sweaters in New Zealand stores, God created the Canterbury Stores. Rugby was the genus of the Canterbury line seventy years ago, and rugby players came big even then. They started in "jerseys" (that's sweaters in American English) and in recent years, the "world's toughest activewear" manufacturer has branched into yachting and leisurewear.

One of the most popular Canterbury styles is called the rugby practice shirt. It evolved when a factory worker sewed remnants leftover from various rugby team shirt orders into a single jersey. The kaleidoscopic hallucination captivated the young and the young-at-heart. Mismatched striped sleeves, front panels, back panels and collars in total disharmony, boldly went where no striped shirt has gone before, to the top of the Hit Parade. Its price captivates, too, just half that of the legitimate team jerseys.

There are Canterbury stores in most major New Zealand cities now. I'm told the U.S.A. label for these "sweatshirts" is Merona. Whatever the name, they are a lot less expensive in the land of their birth.

If it were not located in a shopping arcade, the New Vision Ceramic Arts could pass as a small museum. Both its interior design and its contents appeal. Each art object receives museum presentation.

A couple of blocks up Queen Street, heading away from the harbor, there is a Liberty of London fabric shop. Actually, the store officially is Barker & Pollock, but the L.O.L label is prominently displayed. Viyella and lawn fabrics are specialities of the English fabric maker, and the B&P selection is larger than any of the other L.O.L outlets we found throughout New Zealand. With the escalating price of Viyella—they expected the next shipment to double—B&P should consider moving out of the C.M.L. Arcade and into a bank vault.

Tisdale's, also on Queen Street, confirmed what we had heard repeatedly from avid fishermen: the New Zealand Kilwell graphite rod is of world class design and quality.

"As good as Orvis," was one exalted claim. The Rotorua-based Kilwell makes, under franchise, both the Hardy's of England and the Fenwick rods and reels, but markets its own gear at about one third the cost of the franchised brands.

Further, add this bit of gossip: a former Kilwell's executive branched out into his own company in the late 1970s. His Wyn graphite rod, quite similar to the Kilwell but priced lower, and the U.S.A. Berkley line franchised to Wyn have the endorsement of scores of local enthusiasts.

The point is, if a trip to the land of trout-filled lakes and rivers is in your future, combined with a need of new fishing gear, wait to shop the New Zealand products. You'll get top quality and save money.

O'Connell Street

"Whoever Said Money Can't Buy Happiness Didn't Know Where To Shop" is a popular bumper sticker in Hawaii. You can buy a lot of Happiness on O'Connell Street in Auckland.

O'Connell Street is a quiet corner back of the main street, Queen, just two blocks long, wedged between the American Consulate and Freyberg Place where brown baggers munch sammies in the sun.

Smart little boutiques, shoe salons, and designer work- and showrooms occupy the narrow cobblestone street.

Until the mid-1980s, the area belonged to the legal profession and ground floor tenants were their commercial services. When the courthouse moved out of the neighborhood, the attorneys followed, and the services followed the attorneys, leaving a lot of landlords in a quandary.

O'Connell's juxtaposition to the heart of the city and, undoubtedly, its distressed rental rates made it ripe for takeover by the arty. The fashionable following of the nearby fashion shoe stores on High Street, John Greer and Dadley's, may have tilted its fate towards a designer enclave.

Plums, the salon of wedding dress and evening-wear designer Kevin Berkahn, claims to have been the first fashion kid on the block. He now has lots of company. Among others, there is Adrian Winkellman (elegant classics), Doris dePont (casuals), Zou Zou (day and evening wear), Monsoon (men's).

Neighbors on High Street just around the corner add to the

image: Trelise Cooper's Limited Editions, and ZZZZ, a trendy men's shop, among them.

At the upper end of O'Connell and around another curved corner, on Chancery Street in Chancery House, is Patrick Steel's designer service showroom (great cotton knit sweaters).

While catering to private clients, Patrick and most of the other boutiques sell from a line of ready-to-wear which is individually fitted to each customer. That's right. You see something you like—it will be in a size 10—you order it in the proper size, or in a different color or different fabric, or modify it to your tastes, and the shop whips it up for you.

If the designer makes up a selection of clothes in sizes 12 and 14, these are the first to go.

Americans should remember that the British sizes prevail Down Under. The British size 10 is equivalent to the American size 8. If you forget this equation, prepare to feel very fat, very dowdy. (Once—somewhere—I saw a store named "Big and Beautiful" but pride prevented my walking under that sign, through the door. They probably had my size.)

Remember, also, if custom tailoring appeals to you, sufficient time for fittings must be factored into your stopover in Auckland or Christchurch. Wise is the woman who shops before heading out to other destinations and saves enough time on the way back through for final finishing.

It is in Christchurch where you will find some of the freshest looks in fashion. There is Barbara Lee, one of New Zealand's pioneer "hauts" who calls her shop in the downtown mall, Panache. Rosaria Hall, whose fine fabrics and innovative designs I personally adore, may have given up her boutique in exclusive favor of supplying retail stores around the country and Australia. Her prices, we understand, have climbed the pinnacle of popularity with her.

In Auckland, Hall's clothes are featured in Fay Steele's boutique in Manurea, a residential district about twenty minutes from downtown.

O'Connell Street doesn't hold an exclusive on rarified fashions. There is Parnell, the haunt of Marilyn Sainty, who designs "keepers," Blanche Maude for upmarket casuals, and Colin Cole, the darling of Auckland's matrons.

Marilyn's boutique, Scotties, sells both the Marilyn Sainty and the Tutto label, clothes that "have staying power," in the designer's words.

Colin Cole is a flamboyant camp of a fellow who poses in long capes but who, in reality, is father to six or seven children and is, probably, the most expensive designer in New Zealand. He has a large loyal following finding their way down the secret corridor to an unmarked door to pay $600 for a christening gown. From such humble beginning, mightier prices grow.

The Cupboard, one of the first boutiques to open in Parnell Village, still offers good value for price. The designer/owner, whose name I failed to record, has the same flair and classic feel as Adrian Winkellman, but a lot more empathy for your pocketbook.

My only complaint with Parnell is the lack of taxi stands. Trying to get back to your hotel is unnecessarily burdensome.

The Not So Haut Spree

You don't have to pay the price of the custom-designed apparel to get quality fashion in New Zealand.

Julie Steele's Fashion Tour of Auckland's apparel and accessories manufacturers is a morning, or afternoon, well spent. The bargain loving former school teacher can get it for you wholesale and make the "getting" a memorable field trip.

The basic tour stops at two women's wear, two knitwear and one shoe factory. Julie sizes up the interests of guests on each tour group of eight or less, then adds other outlet stores accordingly. It could be men's shirts, kitchenware, linens, luggage or any number of other products. Except high fashion designer workrooms. None are on her tours.

Each stop lasts about twenty minutes. It is a time of frantic pawing and pulling stacks and piles from racks and tables. Even the tour organizer buys.

"Oh, my, yes. I'm my own best customer," she confesses ruefully.

When I took the tour, two pencil-slim Sheilas kept our group waiting an extra ten minutes while they wildly tried on everything from the 6-8 size racks. Depositing armloads with the cashier, they dashed to the size 12-14 rack, hurriedly picked out six dresses, and muttered "For Mum, that'll do."

A store manager of a chain was overheard telling her companion, "These prices are the same as I pay with my store discount." It made everybody's day.

Factory discount tours abound in other parts of the world, but Julie Steel's was New Zealand's first.

"I came from Opotiki on the East Cape—it's a very small town—where buying anything wholesale was unheard of. The teachers at my first job introduced my to the factory outlet stores during lunch breaks. It was a new world.

"When friends and family came to town, a tour of the factories was the first thing I shared with them. It just grew from there."

The half-day shopping spree gives you an overview of the quality and style of the New Zealand ready-to-wear market. The tour costs under NZ$15. Your bonus is in the experience itself. It is like being in group therapy with Imelda Marcos. You say you are only an observer. You need nothing. You already are over-packed.

You buy!

Fashion Tours is a member of the Auckland Tourist Industry Association, entrepreneurs conducting small groups on wine, walking, historical, cultural, and city tours. Phone: 396-896.

Other Shopping Alternatives

If lower fashion and its accompanying tab is more your style, head for Karangahape Road.

Karangahape Road at the top of Queen Street, is sometimes called "The Strip," more often just "K" Road. It is noisy. It is buoyant. It is a tad sleazy. It is ethnic. It is the historic Bargain Road of Auckland.

But it is not a place to be after dark.

Sheraton Hotel is the only visitor accommodation within walking distance of this vibrant mainstream shopping road of Auckland, but city buses converge on "K" Road from every direction. Just as the city's multi-racial people do.

Note: Sheraton got into the shopping act by opening a small seven-day shopping mall adjacent to its location at the corner of Karangahape and Symonds.

Then, there's the Victoria Street Market, Auckland's phoenix in every sense of the meaning.

Rising, as it were, from ashes to live again as a people's marketplace, the old "destructor" buildings—you read about their history in the Auckland Chapter—flourish with the good life. It's an impressive, if gregarious, "second career."

What makes Victoria Street Market work is its variety. There are trendy restaurants and bars, ethnic and specialty fast foods to munch while strolling around the daub-bricked courtyard crowded with crafts and trademen's carts cluttered with everything imaginable.

But the courtyard action is but the tip of the iceberg.

Shops and boutiques of every persuasion occupy the inter sanctums of the sprawling complex. The Fruit Shed offers produce and herbs previously unknown to New Zealand. We bought sweaters for family and friends, some of which were the wrong size. No problem. Exchange was easy.

Weekend entertainment is the icing on top. Packed on Sundays. You will be swamped by stampeding sippers and shoppers.

Albert Street Market, a more modest find-a-bargain shopping emporium, also stays open seven days a week. It is the successor to the Cook Street Market and the predecessor to the Name-Of-Whichever-Street-It-Moves-To-Next Market. Thirty-five regular stall vendors sell handcrafted art and apparel, and bargain-priced clothing in a building that is under option to a highrise developer. Weekends, their numbers swell and overflow onto the adjacent parking lots.

No food or beverage concessions are permitted inside the building but its location, between the diversified dining of the elegant Regent Hotel and the Customhouse, provides libation and culinary opportunities.

Next door, The Customhouse, architecturally French Renaissance, served the city for more than 80 years. Vacated in 1973 when the new Customhouse was completed, it took nearly a decade to save it from demolition. Now operative as an arts and entertainment center, its craft stores, restaurants and bars open six and a half days weekly. Sunday hours: noon to 5pm.

The Museum Shop

Our last official shopping destination in Auckland, other than the obligatory bookstores to scan the newest literature on New Zealand, is the War Memorial Museum Shop. The object of our affection is their jade collection, although the range of books and quality gift/souvenir items tempt, especially some of the new bone-carved jewelry, new to our best buys list.

What the museum shop features is jade carving as an art form. Greenstone is jade, factually speaking. But, editorially speaking, it is just greenstone in the hands of souvenir makers, becoming fine jade in the hands of an artist.

Donn Salt is a jade carver.

Others, too, come to mind: Neil Hanna, John Edgar, John Sheehan, Hepi Maxwell and Neil Brown. But it is Donn Salt who carved my amulet which absorbs my *mana*, my spirit, as I wear it. It was Donn Salt who released a head of a woman from its encasement of a greenstone block, the magic of which is mysteriously glorious. It was Donn Salt from whom the Maori arikis commissioned a gift of jade for Prince William of Wales.

He does stunning work. Every time I have visited the Auckland Museum Shop, there have been lovely examples of his artistry.

Buying at the source, and meeting the folk behind the product is an adventure.

Here is what we found unique in different parts of the country.

North Of Auckland

Glendara Galleries on Highway 1 between Wellsford and Dome Valley is a workshop and showroom for regional woodcrafters. Here we found a wide selection of Kauri products—and some of the best we saw. The Japanese streamers flying freely overhead marks the location.

Another 4-star ranking goes to the art and craft cooperative, Origin, on State highway 10 between roads leading to Kerikeri and Waimate North.

We visited Origin early in our second-time-around all-points tour, which is my only excuse for breaking the McDermott Cardinal Shopping Rule: "When you see something you really like, buy it." I passed up a batik suede vest that was as supple as fine woolen and tie-dyed in the Indonesian tradition. The designer was Muriel Wright. I still regret the loss.

I try never to make the same mistake twice. On a tip from a friend, I telephoned Bonnie Dickens in Kerikeri, "Bonz" to her friends and customers of handknitted sweaters in fashion colors and with-it designs. Bonz is in the vanguard of the country's newest cottage industry. She designs each sweater, provides the wool and/or mohair and pays home knitters to produce one sweater every ten days. She is fussy about quality and tough on non-producers, but has knitters standing in line to work because she pays top dollars.

Ms. Dickens was in Auckland, but her companion met us at the Kerikeri Post Office, led us to her house to inspect the entire collection. We were overwhelmed by the hot bright abstracts, the cool geometrics, the cable and bobble knits, the Arran and Fairsles. Natural wools. Mohairs. Blends.

And the quantity was incredible.

We'd expected to see a dozen sweaters at the most. There were dozens of each of thirty designs. It looked more like a factory storeroom than a handknitter's workshop.

Then came the history of Bonz, the "cottage" industry. Bonz, the former marketing professional for a kitchen equipment company in Auckland, seeing friends off at the airport was wearing one of her own designs. Two American tourists asked her where they could find something similar. She took them to a shop at the airport terminal and was aghast to see how old-fashioned all the sweaters were. Bonz decided to take her marketing talents out of the kitchen.

"When was that?"

"Just a year ago."

"Is business good?"

"Good? She did $80,000 in her first year and hopes to top $100,000 by the end of the year."

Just your average small cottage industry.

You will find her designs at better craft stores throughout the North Island—maybe even the South Island by now. In Auckland, Bonz sweaters are sold at the Great New Zealand Shop and in the Sheraton Hotel.

Hamilton

When the name of Hamilton is mentioned, I think of Woolrest.

Hamilton sired the Woolrest, the original improved-upon-natural sheepskins that hospitals around the world have used to help long-term patients avoid bedsores for many years. Improved upon because everybody knows sheep do not grow to the size of a kingsized bed.

Woolrest takes long, thick, shaggy fibers of pure wool and tufts them into a thick pure new-wool woven base. This fits over the mattress, under the sheet, and induces heavenly deep sleep. It is cool in summer; warm in winter. Something to do with the natural fibers absorbing its own moisture which I don't understand fully. What I do understand is that it works and if any defect is found within five years, Woolrest will make it right.

The price of NZ$289 for our king-sized Woolrest represented a 50 percent savings over the USA price.

I love my Woolrest and, by affiliation, I love Hamilton.

Cambridge

Cambridge was my favorite tea stop en route from Auckland when we called Taupo "home" for six months in 1976. We could knock off a cuppa, five antique stores and a couple of craft shops in fifteen minutes, thirty if something caught our fancy. The leafy umbrella of stately old trees guiding the motorist into towncenter gives it an old world charm. It is even better now since a bypass siphons off the transport and lumber trucks from the secluded village.

It was in Cambridge that we first learned that antique dealers buy in England and Europe to supplement inventories acquired from local sources. While their prices have increased since 1975, they are still sane, probably lower than you'd pay abroad in spite of the freight they obviously pass along.

Remember, there is no tax on antiques.

Articles from local estates have increased perceptively, one dealer reported, since the New Zealand currency was permitted to float freely, spiraling interest rates to dizzy new heights and creating a recessionary economy. You don't know whether to clap for joy as a buyer, or weep at the plight of the sellers.

The courtesy of the New Zealand shop clerk is legendary. You can rely on being cheerily bumped along to another store. "No, we don't have that pattern but Mrs. Sheldrick at Colonial Heritage probably does."

The recommendable crafts store in Cambridge is Jakobs, whose store policy is to buy exclusively handmade items.

Rotorua

Rotorua, being one of the primary tourist destinations, is a blurr of shopping opportunities. Show me a tourist attraction, and I'll show you a souvenir shop. Even the pluckiest shopper tends to feel weak in the knees.

The rare opportunity of Rotorua is its Maori arts and crafts. While you will find these everywhere, the place to begin is the New Zealand Maori Arts and Crafts Institute, more commonly known as Whakarewarewa, and more likely to be called just Whaka.

Created by an act of parliament in 1963, the Institute teaches young Maoris their birthright cultures. Woodcarving came first because "carving was our way of passing on history and legends," says Clive Fugill, head carver. The Maori had no written language.

Then came greenstone and bone carving. The highly successful program has graduated more than sixty master carvers. Their work, some as fine as you will see in historical museums, is available in the Institute's retail shop, the only place we have ever seen a greenstone *mere* for sell. The flattened teardrop weapon once prized by the warrior is now prized by heritage collectors, especially in greenstone.

Incidentally, it is illegal to export an historic artifact without the written consent of the Minister of Internal Affairs, an action taken to stop the erosion of Maori objects by overseas acquisition.

We also found quality Maori art at Scholes Gallery in The Little Village across from the THC Hotel, and a superb collection of natural fiber and skin apparel at the Natural Dash in the Mid City Shopping Centre. "Investment buying" describes the selection of color-coordinated suedes and leathers, silks and wools. It's another way of saying "expensive."

Across town, under the shadow cast by the Skyline gondola, is the only souvenir shop that sells nary a Maori gift, I dare say. Hillside Herbs opened in the colonial-styled complex in 1985, a cottage industry fostered by rejection.

When Lorraine Nowland applied for a job at the bank she was

told she was "too old."

"When life gives you lemons, make lemonade," is a tenet of her faith.

She made lemonade by selling teas and seeds and dried herbs imaginatively off a cart at the waterfront. Her "cart" was a 1910 gypsy caravan built in Reading, England, which garnered attention. Sales boomed.

The move to Fairy Springs Road gave Lorraine and her husband, Jeff, two acres in which to plant a medicinal herb garden, a culinary herb garden and aromatic shrubs, roses and fragrant herbs used in the making of potpourri, including 13 varieties of lavender.

Demonstrations are held twice daily on the use and culture of herbs but "most sessions are rushed to a screaming finish because the women cannot wait to get back to the shop to buy the vast assortment of dried herbs, shampoos, teas, plants and every conceivable herb-crafted item."

It is a most fragrant experience.

Taupo

Another theme-oriented sales emporium south of Rotorua, almost in Taupo, is the Honey Centre where glass-encased bees busily buzz about their business making honey for their queen. Customers just as busily buy those honeys in every form you can fancy, from health foods to soaps, candies to candles, energy tablets to antibiotics, shampoos to hand creams. Just name it.

"The fruit-and-honey combinations are popular items," said Dawn Jansen, leading us to the tasting bar. It was hard making up gift boxes from selections of honeys flavored with kiwifruit, loganberry, strawberry, orange, mango, apricot, spice apple, banana, even peanut butter. The honeys are mailed around the world, frequently accompanied by honey pots from around the world.

Mr. Jansen gives demonstrations with the bees whose glass hives are vented to permit them outdoor access. "One of the hives will always be almost full to force the bees to swarm, a dramatic phenomenon to watch."

After learning about the bees, you can learn from the potters spinning pots, the lapidarist carving or polishing greenstone jewelry, or the Maori woodcarver in separate rustic sheds around the compound.

Napier

We stopped at a wine store in Napier to restock. Between the sherry tasting, flagon filling counter and the cashier's counter we encountered an exhibition of exquisite sculpture. The artist, Edgar Mansfield, was "the first sculptor from New Zealand to achieve recognition in Europe and England or to have one-man exhibitions in England," according to a review from "Sculpture International" dated 1968.

A bookbinder and abstract painter as well, Mr. Mansfield's work is in permanent collections of the British Museum, Victoria & Albert Museum, Auckland Museum and at libraries in a dozen or more countries.

We asked the wine merchant on duty how the works of a man of such artistic achievements happened to be here, in this wine shop.

"Oh, the owners of the shop are Mr. Mansfield's exclusive agents."

The name of the shop was, after all, Winecraft Gallery. You never know where you'll find a gem.

Sheepskin factory tours are offered throughout the country, presenting visitors the opportunity to see the tanning and manufacturing process. None is more formally organized than that of Classic Decor of Napier. Two tours daily. Coach parties by arrangement. Factory outlet store hours: 7:30am to 5pm Monday to Friday, and 9 to 4 Saturdays.

The array of fuzzy products boggles the mind. Bed covers, mattress covers, carseat covers, bicycle seat covers, foot covers, and golf club covers are but a small part of the inventory available in colors called cloud, ash, chocolate, harvest, white, gold, cream and honey . . . and priced from $5 to $500.

Warehouse shelves are stacked to the ceiling with natural and dyed sheepskin rugs in every size, shape, depth of pile and price range.

You and your credit cards are welcome at the factory in the Napier suburb of Pandora. Last year, over 20,000 visitors toured the premises.

Norsewood

South from Napier on State Highway 2 is another factory open to tourist inspection. We didn't get there, but ask any Kiwi about Norsewear and he will attest that the all-wool knitwear for outdoor people is among the best in the world, if not the best.

You must buy a pair of Norsewear socks for your fishing.

Norsewear's snowflake label identifies sweaters with traditional Scandinavian designs in tribute to the pioneers of Norsewood, a group of 483 men, women and children who sailed 108 days from Norway in 1872. The Pioneer Cottage Museum details the settlers' hard times, and their perseverance.

New Plymouth

If no self-respecting New Zealand tramper would be caught in the bush without his Norsewear socks on, no resident of New Zealand would admit that he didn't own a Swanndri bush shirt. The "Swanni" is the national dress.

On the South Island it is called a "Lammie," as in "lamb tending."

Made of new wool and also lined with wool, the olive drab or boldly checkered red-and-black bush shirts, hooded or collared, are the mainstays on which the company's reputation was founded a quarter of a century ago.

"You'll never suffer hypothermia wearing a Swanni," a fishing guide told us. "Nor will you ever be cold, even if you get soaking wet. The two wools lock in your body warmth."

High praise from a professional who knows.

The Swanndri factory is just north of New Plymouth in Waitara, but, sorry, they do not cater to tourists. Our Taranaki host arranged a tour and an introduction to Swanndri's managing director, Denton Webb. After explaining that the company is owned by Alliance Textiles, the largest in Australasia, and how quality control is maintained at every level—Alliance owns the spinning, knitting, weaving mills that make the wool and the largest apparel manufacturing company as well—he escorted us through the factory.

We saw Swannis in every color: bright orange made exclusively for the road maintenance crews, deep forest green for the national forestry service personnel, and new experimental camouflage pat-

terns to appeal to a younger market.

"What do you call this style?" I asked, fingering the cuff of a zipper-front jacket in a soft muted plaid.

"We call it Model 105. It is our runaway best seller this year."

We never found the entire Swanndri line at any one store but the original bush shirt and Model 105 are sold at sports outfitters and apparel stores everywhere. Look for the swan emblem on the breast pocket.

Wanganui

If blankets or car "rugs" are on your shopping list and you are motoring south, schedule a stop at the Wanganui Woolen Mill's shop. Operated primarily for employees, but open to the public, it offers a 20 percent discount.

Wellington

Downtown shopping in Wellington is convenient. It is concentrated.

Before the Eighties, bluntly speaking, it was downright dowdy. Cosmetic surgery has helped a lot in the past half decade.

Along the "Golden Mile" from Courtenay Place to the Railroad Station via Lambton Quay, three new shopping centers have debuted. A drab department store was converted into small, individualistic, energy-charged stores, considerably brightening Lambton Quay. Art galleries and craft stores, some fifteen at last count, are centered on Courtenay Place. The tourist newspaper, *Capital Times*, carries a Craft & Gallery Guide of the downtown area.

Cuba Street Mall, even if it has expanded, retains the feel of a neighborhood village surrounded by city. Skin Things is a neat leather goods store. Its hot-on-hot colored polished suede and lambskin apparel was a notch above other leather goods. Their factory is in Wellington and, while you will find some selections of the label "Skin Things" in better stores around New Zealand, the Cuba Street showroom is their only retail outlet.

The shopper's bonus is in being able to see the wide range of styles, colors and sizes available.

Interesting note: small-sized leatherwear is hard to find. Reason: the petite Japanese are shopping like vacuum cleaners.

Kelburn Village, a stroll from the Skyline Restaurant, is an interesting shopping diversion. Trendy stores in historic village buildings. We wandered into a children's wear store called Edward & Emma, a "keeper" we might have missed except for our Hawera friends, the Murphys, who know the owners.

Fran Brown of Wellington decided there was a place in the market for well-made, color-coordinated or dyed-to-match—yes, higher priced, too—children's clothes made of all natural fibers. Her winter fabrics are Liberty's Viyella and the best New Zealand woolens, summer fabrics feature Liberty's lawn. She commissions handknitted sweaters that are extremely popular with overseas visitors, especially grandmothers.

In less than five years, she had opened franchised stores in ten New Zealand cities. She will have more. Mrs. Brown is selling classics.

She is also selling size 14 girls' clothes to small ladies, especially to those petite Japanese.

One of the best shopping experiences in Wellington is offered by The Out & About bunch. Three women, wives of prominent businessmen with strong diplomatic contacts, banned together in 1984 to cure their own 'empty nest' syndromes by providing personalized service to visitors. Their efforts are ranked successful by everybody.

Tourist authorities recommend them highly. The State Department retains their services regularly to entertain wives of visiting dignitaries. The women have filled their days with interesting people from around the world and, at the same time, give their clients a flavor of Wellington they might otherwise miss.

Personalized is the word for this service. The Out & About ladies are equally at ease conducting a morning of shopping and tea at a Wellington home for one person, a tour of the harbour and waterfront for fifty or more, or a visit with local potters or craftspeople at work for four or less.

Costs vary according to size of the group and length of the tour, ranging from $15 an hour (walking tour) to $50 an hour (car, driver and lunch included).

The "best buy" bonus is a new friend. Pick your action in Wellington and write Out & About, P.O. Box 3701, Wellington. Or phone 729-726.

Picton

The Creek Pottery, open seven days a week, claims to exhibit New Zealand's largest range of pottery.

Blenheim

Stock up on bargain wine at Hunters and the Montana Winery.

Nelson

We heard it repeatedly: "There are more potters per capita in New Zealand than in any other country in the world."

Seventy-three of them reside in Nelson.

"Nelson is recognized by the Queen Elizabeth II Arts Council as the heartland of the nation's crafts. There's more here than just pottery."

It was Peter Heath, district tout, hoisting the provincial flag.

"Part of it is the clay—best in the country. We export it to other areas, you know. But a larger part of it is because of the quality of our lifestyle, our temperate climate, sunny days—the highest number of sunny days in the country." (Still a larger reason could be due to a government subsidy given the unemployed who produce arts or crafts!)

Peter estimated over 200 craftsmen—spinners, knitters, weavers, glassblowers, ceramists, jewelers, and leather or wood carvers—dot the lushly green rolling backroads in the district.

Over half of the potters welcome guests to their workrooms and galleries. The Nelson Potters Association publishes a where-to-find-them guide and map. Or, for an overview of Nelson pottery, visit the Clayworks at 123 Bridge Street. (Read about the fascinating building in the Marlborough Chapter.)

Nile Street and South Street hold a dozen cozy colonial cottages specializing in made-in-the-area crafts.

We visited the South Street Gallery opposite the Rutherford Hotel and shopped the Wool Store run by owner Jillian Moss who was looking for a "kitchen sink substitute."

Ms. Moss is a lady who obviously enjoys her vocational liberation and her clientele. In a different twist on the handspun "cottage industry" success story, Jillian buys the output of sixty knitters in the area and sells them exclusively in her shop. Supplementing the originals are three quality manufactured labels:

Mahana, Oglivy Originals and High Country.

Asked why she did not stock mohair sweaters, she answered "because the fluff gets up my nose."

Around the corner on Trafalgar Square and behind the Rutherford is gold- and silversmith Jens Hansen. He and his associates create distinctive contemporary jewelry, or accept commissions to design especially for you. Excellent work.

Westland

The ancients prized greenstone for making cutting tools and weapons, the moderns for jewelry and souvenirs. Its fibrous composition of intertwined minerals gives it strength and durability. Even steel will not scratch the best greenstone.

New Zealand's jade comes from the area around Greymouth and Hokitika. Or rather, it comes from the fault line of the Southern Alps, the result of heat, pressure and mineralization. Earthquakes and floods have bounced boulders of nephrite down the wild, wild rivers that feed the Tasman sea, depositing them in hidden terraces, along beaches and into the sea. Ocean currents have carried fragments as far north as 25 miles.

Samples of such alluvial boulders are displayed in factories in Hokitika—and Auckland—where craftsmen transform them into every sort of curio. Diamond saw slices frequently reveal colors that pale in marbled tracings from bottle green at the core to elusive yellows at the outer rind.

No longer in plentiful supply, jade now is the object of prospecting in the mountains throughout every summer.

"The mother lode was discovered within the last decade. Prior to that, only alluvial jade was found," said Ian Boustridge, master jade carver from Greymouth, highly recommended by the PR officer, seconded by the motorcamp owner.

"In summers, prospectors take portable saws to cut rocks into chunks so they can be lifted out by helicopter.

"A boulder of jade is like a piece of timber. It has grains. The pancake form has a single grain; the square-shaped boulder a double grain, but it is uncarveable."

How did he get into jade carving?

"When the antique bottle craze hit New Zealand—I was sixteen—we hit the goldmining areas. When you begin finding alluvial boulders of greenstone, your priorities change quickly.

"My high-school pottery teacher introduced me to the book Jade Country and one thing led to another. After school, I went to work for a greenstone factory in Hokitika, learned the basics, then decided there was more satisfaction in carving one-of-a-kinds."

How large are the ranks of jade carvers?

"Probably twenty total, but only half a dozen are worth their salt."

Donn Salt was in that honored handful. It was at Ian's that we saw that unusual head carved by Salt, a thank-you gift for some professional courtesy. The head was a pale grey-green, the color of glacier water, which is also the color of whitebait. The Maoris named it *inanga*, whitebait.

Subsequently, we met locals by the score who said they preferred inanga to all the other New Zealand jade colors.

Ian identified and classified them as:

Kawakawa — a rich medium-green popular with the factories as jewelry, thus more frequently displayed in stores.

Kahurangi — a pale green and the most commercial.

Kokopu — the word means speckled trout; this color has intricate marbling and is highly prized.

Flower — there is a bit of stone left in the jade during the slicing process, which adds a distinctive characteristic.

Ian Boustridge's freeform spiral carvings are modern tinged with just a hint of Maori traditional art. He sells through the National Museum in Wellington and the War Memorial Museum in Auckland. But, if you are in the neighborhood and genuinely interested in acquiring a piece of art—not a curio—write to him. 25 Coates Street, Greymouth, 6048.

Arthur's Pass Road

The Woodworks at the village town of Kumara on the western side of the Pass sells items made mostly of rimu. Entrepreneurs moved from Christchurch to gain access to more tourists.

On the eastern side of the Pass, at Arthur's Pass township, Oscar's Haus sold handcrafted trinkets by children in the community during the Christmas season, another ingenious idea.

Their handspun or knitted items tended to be for alpine wear, logical since their elevation is at 3,500-plus feet.

Geraldine

A route priority of the South Island tour was via Geraldine to call upon the one and only source for natural black sheepskin slippers.

Our first pairs of cozies were bought at the Black Sheep Shop in the Bay of Islands. No longer.

"We cannot get them from Lynn River, the manufacturer in Geraldine," the manager told us.

We were determined to get to Lynn River.

Wouldn't you know. We arrived in Geraldine on Sunday!

Fairlie

The Farm Barn, just west of Fairlie, is a splendid tea stop unless there are dozens of tour buses on the premises.

Its 360-degree circular cafe-gift shop that is sited on the crest of a hill presents a 360-degree view of the Southern Alps and the Canterbury Plains. It offers a 360-degree selection of Kiwi-made giftware as well.

Twizel

In the construction camp that grew up to be a township, at a craft store called High Country Agency, we found distinctive souvenirs made in the area. A massive chess set carved from the heart of punga featured Maori chieftains as the king and queen and kiwi birds as pawns. Never saw another like it.

Wanaka

Our quiet little secret hiding place on the South Island has been discovered.

Adjacent to Helwick Street, the main shopping thoroughfare, is a new shopping mall, Pembroke, selling health foods, Chinese cloisonne and oriental rugs.

At the top of Helwick Street is one of the most visually satisfactory nurseries you will ever encounter. Wanaka Floral Studio & Garden Shop welcomes you with a cascading waterfall over river rocks and pebbles. Above the garden path and through lush plantings is a gift shop featuring floral motif items.

Wanaka has its share of artists documenting the changing seasons in a part of the world that God blessed. Two of them are Truda Landreth and Hilda River.

Landreth murals are so realistic you find it hard to believe upon closer examination that they are executed in wool. She works on commission against a twelve-month waiting list.

Hilda River's studio is on Russell Street just above town. A landscape artist whose popularity with the locals stems from now gone forever scenes since the damming of the Clutha River, she is equally popular with tourists for her reasonable prices. She tells of the couple who came back from Queenstown to buy still more paintings, exclaiming they could buy eight of her paintings directly from her—priced from $25 to $300—for what they had to pay for one painting at Queenstown galleries.

"I'd rather give the price discount to my customers than pay it all in government taxes," she told us.

Arrowtown

The entire village is a tea-lunch-museum-shopping stop. *It is if you can get your Driver to stop!*

Queenstown

How big is shopping in Queenstown?

The Japanese buy so many bulky woolens and sheepskins that outbound 747s resembled pregnant dirigibles on departures. To cope with the happy problem, Air New Zealand instituted a once-a-week air freight service to Tokyo, temporarily separating people from their packages. The hassle-free service provides shop-to-home delivery.

A byproduct of this "Orient Express" is same-day cargo service from the South Island to California, for transshipment beyond. A dandy way of getting new acquisitions home.

How big is shopping in the remarkable resort cradled by the Remarkables- Harris- Thomson- and Eyre mountain ranges?

The first non-gateway city duty free store opened in Queenstown. Until 1985, the DF stores operated only in Auckland, Christchurch and Wellington under exclusive contractual agreements with airport authorities.

According to new licensee Richard Sellens, "Queenstown is the perfect place for a duty free operation because the city gets 50 percent of all visitors to New Zealand and they stay an average three-and-a-half days."

Auckland, he says, gets 80 percent of all overseas visitors but the average length of stay is one day.

"The point is, when tourists get to places where they can relax, they open their purses."

The trouble, at least initially, was that although legislation permitted new DF shops to open, no legal provision was made permitting them access to bonded depots at the air terminals, making delivery of the goods at flight departure time virtually impossible. Those rights belong exclusively to existing concessionaires whose contracts expire at staggered intervals beginning 1988.

We found above-average merchandise in The Spinning Wheel (woolens), Grahams (men's wear), Marquise (New Zealand designerwear), Cherri M (moderate priced women's apparel), Bill Lacheny Sports (winter sportswear).

The street legend of Queenstown is a portrait artist who has been at it for nineteen years, first in Paris then Montreal and San Antonio and, since 1976, in Queenstown. He and the *TSS Earnslaw*, the vintage steamship, are the only Queenstown subjects ever honored on a national calendar.

John Parsons works as a commercial street artist from October to May, earning about half his annual income in January cranking out a pastel portrait every half hour. The rest of the year he paints oils at home.

"My real work," he calls it.

"Where are your oils on sales?"

"They're not. I have the largest collection of John Parsons originals in the world. When I'm dead, they'll be worth millions."

That's one approach to wealth.

Mossburn

You can miss Mossburn driving to Te Anau if you blink. You can miss the Wapiti tannery and manufacturing factory even as you look at it. Don't think "factory." Think store. Little store.

Joan F. Allison has a line of conservative leather fashions that are tanned beautifully and reasonably priced.

Invercargill

To say it is orderly, it was planned by Scots, and it is conservative is redundant. It is all the above plus the favorite shopping town for women throughout Southland and Fiordland because of its Scots-fair prices and friendliness.

Example: While browsing in the A. J. Boult upmarket women's store, Image, I asked if they had a tailor who could replace a zipper in my Driver's trousers. No, but the Boult men's store, Gustave's, could. The manager volunteered to take the trousers over personally. You know that's rare.

The recommendable craft stores are Gallery 5 on King Street and Westside Gallery on Dee Street. The Wool Court, an historic courthouse building, carries so much wool yarn that I was prompted to ask if every woman in New Zealand knits.

"They are encouraged to," the sales clerk said. "In 1984, the government spent a lot of money campaigning to interest the young women in the craft."

Was it successful?

"My yes. There are so many people willing to buy sweaters for re-sale these days, kitting is becoming a national industry."

Later, in Dunedin, when we lunched with the busload from Gore, I polled the women for knitters. Yes, everyone knitted. They estimated that 90 percent of all New Zealand women knit, but agreed that only a small percent knit on commission. "Most of us just can't be bothered," summed up one lady . . . and all the others nodded affirmatively.

Stewart Island

The Fernery is a rare discovery, worthy of being franchised in every national park throughout the world.

Ron Tindal, the Forestry Officer, and his wife Elspeth, the innovative retailer, deserve recognition as "national treasures."

Handmade products are themed after the infinite varieties of fernery that grow on Stewart Island. Ferns are imprinted on note cards, books, prints and paintings. Peter Beadle's art is outstanding. There are silk and linen handscreened scarves, shirts and dresses, tablemats and napkins sprouting fernery designs in delicate shades by Susan Salmond.

Perhaps the most enchanting items are the miniature fern terrariums. The art of terrariums was discovered quite by accident in 1830 when a London doctor, Nathaniel Ward, put a moth chrysalis in a large jar loosely covered by a glass lid. A tiny fern appeared months later. It grew without fresh water and unattended for 19 years.

A class-act touch: Each item's price tag is written on a leaf.

Inscribed on the leafy price tag of a terrarium containing a Prince of Wales Feather fern is "Rear a Royal Babe."

Balclutha

Peggydale is one of the most successful souvenir shops in New Zealand.

Its inventory includes something of everything produced in New Zealand plus leatherware made in its own factory. Open every day of the year—yes, even on Christmas.

Dunedin

Chocolates and antiques we discovered as special buys of Dunedin on our first trip there more than a decade ago. Silk lingerie and custom-tailored leatherwear now join them.

The tour of Cadbury's Chocolate factory, one of the largest processors in the world, remains at the top of my all-time favorite shopping tours due, mainly, to sampling privileges.

"Dunedin is the antique center of New Zealand," says Trevor Plumbly, a dealer at 466 George Street, the author of *Antiques and Things* and a TV commentator on the business of antiques.

You are reminded that wealthy Scots settled the city and that the gold of the South Island flowed through Dunedin in the last century. Plumbly has priceless pieces appear on his desk regularly, the most recent was a George I coffee pot in mint condition.

In addition to Plumbly's, downtown there is Christie's at 453 Princes Street, and in suburban Caversham a covey of antique stores.

CDL & Company, as a buzz word for fine hand-stitched silk lingerie, somehow lacked glamour. So, they called the line "Butterflies" and it flutters on fancy hangers in pricey boutiques and better women's wear stores throughout New Zealand, in Australia and England.

Born of scholarly connections, the smooth idea belongs to Dr. Cooper, the "C" in CDL & Company and a professor of economics at Otago University.

"Michael travels extensively, and because he seeks pretty packables to bring home to his wife, the idea for lingerie was hatched over drinks with still another couple, the Langdons."

Wendy Douglas was providing background about this cottage industry from her executive perch at an ironing board in her living room. We were surrounded by elegant samples of "knickers" and "teddies" (panties and nightgowns).

"We laugh just thinking about the scene at Heathrow airport when Michael's suitcase popped open, dropping knickers all over the tarmac on one of his combined sales-and-lecture trips."

"We're so small that Joy, the designer, and I still dye the lace to match the silks and satins and crepes in the preserving pan over the kitchen sink," she howled.

The finished product is gorgeously feminine.

When I admired a suede jacket worn by our friend, Phyllis Cole, she volunteered to take me to her tailor. I almost declined, thinking that most visitors would never stop long enough during a holiday to have leather apparel custom made.

Z.K.F's Suede and Leather Clothing, upstairs at 8 Moray Place, is a small showroom watched over by a giant Hungarian talent who, after a heart attack, ceased manufacturing to return to one-on-one tailoring "at prices that are one-third that of the rest of the country."

P.S. You can be fitted in a day.

Dunedin's shopping action is around or near the Octagon, including Carnegie Centre, the converted library that now serves as an art and crafts, entertainment, and dining gathering place.

Christchurch

Christchurch is home of the Canterbury jerseys that I raved about in the Auckland section. The biggest selection of these made-to-last-a-lifetime sweatshirts, shorts, and pants for men, women and children can be found at Canterbury Tails in the Canterbury Centre.

Other sturdy products made in the Canterbury Plains to suit the ruggedness of the Southern Alps—or the Himalayas—are outdoor camping equipment, clothing and accessories. A Macpac line of jackets and overalls made of "fibrepile" was especially recommended for outdoor enthusiasts because it absorbs less than 19 percent of its weight in water (always a factor in New Zealand), dries in 15 minutes or less yet retains 80 percent of its insulation when wet. Also recommended were parkas made of Gore-tex, a laminated fabric ideal for "very wet" weather.

The Kiwis have taken tent-making to an artform status. Whether it is the mountaineer's one-person tent or a large family sized two-bedroom/lounge/verandah affair, there will be value for money in a Sunshine Leisure purchase.

Arthur Ellis, a company that makes down sleeping bags, has even come up with a model for people like me who cannot sleep without poking a foot into the fresh air, but like to snuggle in a double. Two zipped together accommodate the hot foot. It is exclusively at McEwings, 97 Cashel Street.

Most of the shopping emporiums are near Cathedral Square. There is Shades Arcade on Hereford with its appealing boutiques including the Clothes Horse where Rosaria Hall's clothes may be purchased, and Wool Design, specialists in naturally dyed yarns. (They use flowers, plants and roots for dyeing.)

Across from Shades on High Street, in City Mall, you'll find Panache, the Barbara Lee designer boutique. Another highly respected custom designer, Judith Malcolm, is just off Hereford in the same vicinity.

If you are interested in designer leathers, seek out Avanti 31, the Caroline Moore shop on Chancery Lane around the corner from Noah's Hotel. She's a whiz with supple leathers and suedes.

Visitor publications throughout the country will lead you to crafts galleries, shows or periodic fairs. The artisans are just as eager to find you, as you, them.

There were craft buying opportunities layered over craft buying experiences during our last visit to Christchurch. In addition to the newly discovered Arts Centre, the annual New Zealand Crafts Show, a private enterprise copied from American counterparts, was in progress. It brought in out-of-the-district exhibitors. There were potters from Nelson, a famous bone carver from Marlborough (Norman Clark of Flat Creek), an international award-winning porcelain dollmaker (Robyn Hayes) who sold one beauty for $2,000, batik dyers on silk . . . pewter sculptors, woodturners, jewelers. And some 75 others.

Backers Fiona and Toby Dunkley schedule annual shows in Tauranga, Hastings, Palmerston North, Hamilton, Wellington, and Auckland also. Read the local visitors publication.

Incidentally, the New Zealand Antique Dealers Association also holds exhibitions in major cities twice annually. If antique-ing is your interest, ask about its dates. It is worthwhile.

The best antique store "find" in Christchurch was Garden City Antiques, with two outlets: a shop at 192 Papanui Road; a warehouse at 200 Fendalton Road. Go to the latter. It is more fun, has a bigger selection and prices are cheaper. It is packed to the rafters and overflowing into the owners' backyard. In addition to fine, elegant pieces, Wayne Wright stocks rustic, if not primitive, folk artifacts . . . like six-foot-wide double oxen yolks in hand hewn, heavy wood.

One of us couldn't live without it!

One of us wondered how in the world we would get it home, and what in the world we would do with it after we got it home.

One of us is a shopping researcher.

One of us is an impulse buyer.

The wizard is right, you know: "She hunts. He eats."

17. What To Know Before You Go

You will enjoy New Zealand so much and engage in so many activities that you are apt to forget what a small country it is.

Less than 1,000 miles from tip to toe, as slender as a pair of slippers.

You are never more than 80 miles from either the Pacific Ocean on the east or the Tasman Sea on the west.

New Zealand is about the size of Colorado and shares many of Colorado's features: alpine mountains, snow-fed rivers, ski resorts and trout fishing.

The country is divided into two narrowly separated islands, the North Island and the South Island, both of volcanic origin. The North Island still experiences some volcanic action.

Abundant rainfall creates lush pasturelands throughout the country. Heavy fertilization makes them greener and the grazing of millions of animals keeps them as trim and neat as a freshly mowed lawn.

Huge herds of cattle (10,000,000), flocks of sheep (130,000,000 at lambing time), and substantial smatterings of deer and goats and pigs form the economic backbone of the country.

The human animals number only 3,000,000.

When the Polynesians arrived by ocean-going canoes in a migration from what are now the Cook Islands and the Society Islands (French Polynesia) around the 11th and 12th centuries, the land was already inhabited by another race of Polynesians whose occupation was hunting the *moa* bird, a giant now extinct ostrich-like fowl. These earlier Polynesians are now referred as the Archaic Maori or Moa Hunters. When and where they came from is not known.

Kupe, the Maori counterpart to Capt. James Cook who "discovered" the islands for Europeans, was supposed to have preceded the second wave of Polynesians by a century or two, returning home to "Hawaiki," the homeland, to report on the

islands which he called Aotearoa, the "Land of the Long White Cloud."

The second wave of Polynesians, known as the Classic Maori, brought with them knowledge of fishing and agriculture. Their staple diet was a tuberous root called *kumara*, a sweet potato.

The word "native" is never used in describing a Maori. He or she is a New Zealander.

The Europeans came as settlers in the 19th century. Mostly of English descent, they are colloquially known as *Pakeha*. Today, the Pakeha outnumbers the Maori about nine to one but the Maori population is growing at a much faster rate.

There is no surface racial tension in New Zealand. According to newspaper reports you'll read, other island groups working in New Zealand—Samoan and Tongan primarily—seem to get into a fair share of trouble with the law, usually due to excessive imbibing. Violence was unknown ten years ago. Today is is not uncommon.

An interesting sidenote is that over 400,000 of the country's population is foreign born and over 100,000 New Zealand-born people live and work in Australia.

New Zealanders are a quietly proud people, sensitive to their isolated environment, and, in the past, have had a strong tendency to belittle themselves. Fortunately, this tendency is disappearing. The people's attitudes reflect a new personal and national confidence.

Another change we found is in service. You can't take young people off of the farm and make them excellent service people in the visitor industry overnight. It takes training and exposure.

There is obviously a lot more training today. Hotels and restaurants are a thousand percent better than they were ten years ago. The competent, friendly service found today is a definite plus toward the upgrading of New Zealand.

Weather And What To Wear

New Zealand is a country where you can take your bikini and your fur coat and never know from day to day which one you are going to wear.

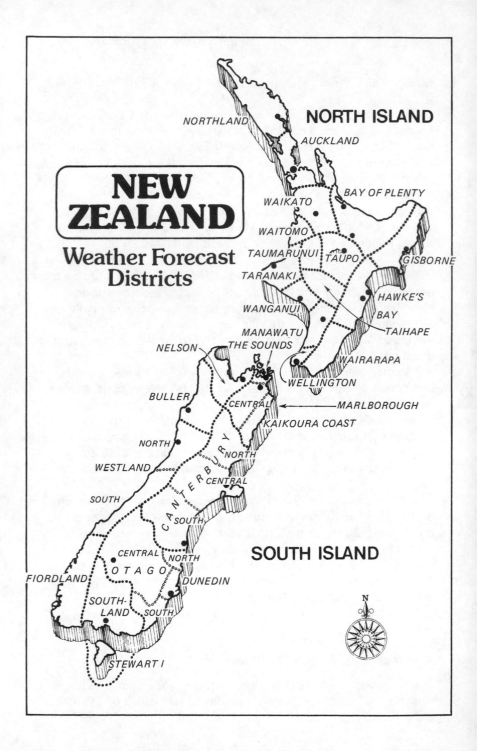

Generally, the climate is mild but with extreme variations. It can be beautifully balmy one day and wind-whipped freezing the next. The generous amount of rain is what makes the countryside so green and appealing so you should never be too far away from an umbrella and a raincoat. My favorite garment is a fishing oilskin with drawstrings at the waist and a hood which I bought in an Auckland sporting store.

Fabric raingear doesn't ward off New Zealand rain. Also, in wet weather, jeans don't dry easily, nor do tennis shoes. Woolen clothes and leather footwear are recommended.

Count on buying a handknit wool sweater. Great buys in newer, smarter styles. And thick 100 percent wool socks.

Business wear is formal although in the summer you will see a large number of males in walking shorts and, *de rigueur*, long socks with short sleeve shirts and ties.

The older ladies in cities tend to dress formally for shopping. Gloves and purses and hats, you know. They make a lovely sight. The young matrons are Sydney-New York chic.

Dress in the evening in private homes may be informal but don't count on it. Dining out in the evening usually calls for a jacket and a tie. New Zealanders do not dress in bright colors.

Because so much time is spent out of doors and so much time is spent walking, your wardrobe should focus on warmth and comfort. Go with a comfortable hat and waterproof walking shoes and—our newest find—silk thermal underwear. It's wonderful.

But, even in autumn, the hearty male Kiwi may be wearing shorts.

Sitting out at the edge of the Tasman Sea like two huge aircraft carriers, the North and the South Islands are at the mercy of the west winds that blow in from Australia. It can be as glorious in the winter as in the summer . . . and as miserable in the summer as in the winter.

You'll find, like everybody in New Zealand, that you pay extra attention to the media weather reports.

You know that New Zealand, being south of the Equator, has reverse seasons from the Northern Hemisphere. Summer is from December through February. Autumn is from March through

May. (New Zealanders do not use the word "Fall.") Winter is from June through August. Spring from September through November.

When is the best time to go to New Zealand? Anytime.
(Secretly, however, we are going to plan our next trip for February through March, even April.)
The weather is measured in Celsius, not Fahrenheit.
If it is 0 Celsius, you're freezing. If it is 20 Celsius, you're comfortable. If it is 40 Celsius, you're boiling.
Everything in New Zealand is on the metric system.
Study the weather map and learn the regional names. You'll find it is a good investment of time.

Travel Formalities And Other Niceties

"Whayya mean I need a visa?" I said to the passport control officer at the Auckland airport.
We had been coming to New Zealand once or more every year for the last dozen years but I had forgotten that stays exceeding one month require a visa in American passports. Embarrassing.
The officer stamped our passports for a 30-day stay and allowed us into the country.
As we planned to stay over two months, our first order of business the next day was a trip to the Immigration Department in downtown Auckland. We filled out the necessary papers, showed our return tickets and a bundle of travelers checks, and our passports were stamped for a three-month stay. Six months maximum.
To stay longer than six months as a visitor or if you want to migrate to New Zealand, you should contact the Department of Labour, Private Bag, Te Aro, Wellington or visit the nearest New Zealand Diplomatic or Consular Office.
If you come from Australia, Canada or one of the other Commonwealth countries all you need is a document of identity and a clean shirt. Stay as long as you like.

Customs Regulations

The general standard of Customs found around the world applies in New Zealand: one carton of cigarettes, one bottle of spirits.

Because New Zealand is an agricultural country, there are definite restrictions on imported foodstuffs. No plants or vegetables or animal products are allowed. An Amnesty Box is prominently displayed in the Immigration Room at the airport.

Before you deplane upon arrival from an international flight, the airplane cabin is fumigated and passengers, despite the long flight, must sit for five painful minutes while the suspected fleas, flies and insects dutifully expire.

In past years when we have entered New Zealand with golf equipment, we have had to undergo a thorough agricultural inspection where even the soles of our golf shoes were cleaned. The last time we entered the country, however, we were waved straight through. "How come?" we asked an agricultural inspector. "Sometimes we do, sometimes we don't," he said with a shrug.

No sidearms are allowed. If you are coming to hunt and bringing your own shotguns or rifles, you must have a permit for either weapon and register your rifle.

Electrical Current

New Zealand electricity is 230 volts, 50 cycle, alternating current and is not suitable for the American 110 volts direct current. Most hotels and motels do provide 110-volt a.c. sockets for electric razors.

If you are traveling with a lady who won't leave home without electric haircurlers—the bane of any male traveling companion—you will need a transformer unless the appliance operates on dual voltage. In any event, you will need a converter three-pin plug for the New Zealand electrical outlets. The three-pin plug is an oddity which is not easily found in America. If you cannot find a three-pin plug, a two-pin plug with two flat prongs slanted toward each other like the sad eyes on a stick figure doll will work.

Your Health

Medical facilities are of a high standard and fees at private facilities are nominal compared to the United States. There is no free medical treatment offered to visitors unless the visitor suffers a personal injury in an accident. If you get hurt, irrespective of fault, you will receive free medical and hospital treatment, or payment for expenses.

Chemists (drugstores) are everywhere and there is a week-end/holiday rotation system among chemists to provide for emergencies. The on-duty store schedule will be posted on every chemist's door.

Tipping

Tipping is the exception and not the rule.

When we first arrive in Auckland, we are still in the American habit of scattering coins and bills, confetti fashion, among all we encounter. Then we go off into the country and by the time we return to Auckland we tip *nobody*. You are a seasoned New Zealand traveler if you do the same.

Cash and Credit Cards

Understanding New Zealand money is not a problem to Americans and Commonwealth countries. The New Zealand currency is a decimal system with dollars and cents.

Fortunately, the acceptance of credit cards has expanded. We found that we were almost always covered between either our American Express or Visa cards. Many merchants also recognize Bankcard, Diners' Club, Masters, JTB, among others.

Holidays

Unusual national holidays are Waitangi Day (February 6), Anzac Day (April 25), the Queen's Birthday (first Monday in June) and Boxing Day (the first weekday after Christmas).

Each of the eleven provinces also celebrates separate anniversary days.

The summer school holiday occurs from mid-December to the end of January. During this period, it is wise for a visitor to have reservations for accommodations and many of the activities.

Communications

New Zealanders are readers.

Daily newspapers are everywhere. The largest newspaper is the *Auckland Herald* with a circulation over 200,000 followed by the *Auckland Star* with about 125,000 readers.

Women's Weekly is the most popular magazine. A TV/Radio guide is combined with excellent articles in a publication called *The New Zealander Listener* put out by the Broadcast House.

The TV is government owned and controlled and is rather sad. Limited funds limit the originality and American reruns are a large part of the viewing diet.

Good radio, culturally balanced, mostly government operated.

Internal Travel

There is a government controlled rail and bus service which has a network of lines throughout the country. A good way to save money, if not time.

Another transportation money saver is to buy Air New Zealand and Mount Cook airline tickets for internal air travel *before leaving home*. Substantial reduced fares are available throughout the year and special incentive fares are set during trough periods. Check your travel agency.

The Sporting Life

The sporting life in New Zealand has to be its biggest attraction. Nowhere in the world will you find such a tightly concentrated variety of sports activities of such quality.

We'll quickly highlight what you might like to know about the more prominent sports before packing for New Zealand.

Fishing

Probably Zane Grey, the famous Western fiction and sports writer of the mid-20s, lit the fire under the international reputation of New Zealand's fishing.

It is a reputation still intact although the fish are fewer in number and smaller in size.

It is all comparative. I have a friend from Cape Cod who caught a three-pound trout in the Hinemaimai River near Lake Taupo where we had a summer cottage and, as he was preparing his fish for dinner, he turned around from the kitchen sink and said, "You know, I never caught a trout before I couldn't clean with my finger nails."

In New Zealand, you have to throw back a trout that you would consider a trophy in a New York stream.

Trout fishing is one of the better imported sports to New Zealand.

In pre-European times, there were few freshwater fish of any consequence, excepting eels.

The English, whose tradition is to take their sporting games with them wherever they go, corrected the lack of freshwater fishing by importing brown trout from Tasmania in 1867. (The English also imported the rabbit for hunting, with disastrous results.)

Genus of rainbow trout in New Zealand was a single shipment of ova from the Russian River in California in 1883. At that time, a captured hen (female) was stripped of her eggs which were then overlaid with the sperm or sperm glands of a jack (male), and packed in living moss which was cocooned in layers of ice and charcoal several feet thick.

The box was shipped as cargo in a refrigerated container. The ova, still in a frozen state upon reaching Auckland, were hatched and raised in a stream in a four-acre reserve of the Auckland Domain which had been donated to the Auckland Acclimatization Society in 1867 for the raising of imported grasses, bushes, flowers and song birds.

These first rainbows were the progenitors of such a pure strain that they are still the base breeding stock for rainbows that are sent all over the world today—including back to the United States.

The superb unpolluted water and abundant food in New Zealand lakes and rivers proved ideal breeding grounds for the browns and rainbows. Their giant size and excellent condition and their reputation as fierce fighters made New Zealand a mecca for anglers around the world.

The size and number of trout have been reduced in the last fifty years but the fishing is still of a standard un-realized almost anywhere else.

For example, in the Taupo district where fishing is permissible year round, the annual harvest by anglers exceeds 600,000 trout. The average weight today is slightly under four pounds.

You have to know there are twenty-six different fishing districts in New Zealand, each with its own Acclimatization Society, each authorized to issue its own license, each with its own "home rule" season.

Generally, trout may be fished from the first of October to the end of March, excepting Lake Taupo and Lake Rotorua which are open all year long.

The dedicated fisherman should consider buying a month-long Visitor's License which allows fishing in any of the twenty-six districts. The license must be purchased at a New Zealand Tourist And Publicity Office.

If I were an expert fisherman and planned to fish throughout the country, I'd write Barry Jaggar, Hunting and Fishing Officer, NZTPO, Private Bag, Rotorua for current information and regulations. He can also organize your fishing itinerary, including hotel-motel-lodge reservations, transportation and guides.

If you are like me, a maladroit amateur fisherman who wants to go home with a picture of a fat trout dangling from your hand—and who doesn't—you will want a guide.

The guide, licensed and approved by NZTPO, has all the equipment you will need except for warm underwear and socks. He'll provide all the necessary ground transportation whether limousine or four-wheel drive. Arrange for a jet-boat or a launch. He can sell you a one-day license and, in all probability, will bring lunch and morning or afternoon tea.

The guide knows where the fish are, what to fish with, where not to fish, when to throw the fish back.

For the novice and the expert alike, he has another great value. He has keys. He has keys to paddocks leading to otherwise inaccessible streams, paddocks belonging to farmers who trust him, knowing he will always lock the gates and leave the livestock undisturbed. He can go where few other fishermen can go. If you want a shot at stretches of river which are comparatively virgin, you need an experienced guide to open gates.

Fishing on streams feeding into lakes and 300 yards from the mouths of lakes and many other areas are reserved for fly-fishing. Fly-fishing produces more fish in New Zealand than any other method. There is not a great deal of spin fishing in the country.

The increasing numbers of anglers is producing a strain on the fish population and there is more emphasis on releasing landed but unharmed fish and, in isolated areas, using barbless hooks.

Rainbow trout dominate the waters of the North Island. Browns are available but harder to catch. In the South Island, the brown trout is more numerous but still wily.

Salmon are found only in the South Island and the runs up river from the ocean start around the first of the year and continue into March.

New Zealand salmon come in monstrous sizes. They are generally fished at sea mouths with heavy-gear surf rods using metal spinners on baited casting reels.

Surf casting is also productive from almost any shoreline in New Zealand.

Big game fishing is at its best in New Zealand in the late summer (February-April) and is concentrated on the East Coast of the North Island.

If you take a map of the North Island, you can locate the principal sport fishing ports by moving from north to south down the east coast, Whangaroa, Bay of Islands, Tutukaka just north of Whangarei, Mercury Bay on the Coromandel Peninsula with fine fishing off Great Mercury Island and Tauranga and Whakatane in the Bay of Plenty where the principal fishing grounds are off Mayor Island.

Striped marlin are the most prolific of the swordfish followed by the black marlin. Mako shark and tuna are also frequent catches.

Visitors can join individual big game clubs at fishing centers for a minor fee which will include use of the club facilities.

Golf

If you are never far from water in New Zealand, you are never more than a five iron from a golf course.

Due to the English/Scottish heritage, golf courses spread like rabbits in the country with some 325 registered golf courses, public and private—mostly private, but accessible to the public. Many private clubs, with times reserved for members, cater to visitors.

While driving through the country, it is not uncommon to see signs at the entrance to golf clubs saying: "Visitors Welcome."

The standard practice is to carry a letter from your home club as an introduction. We have never found this necessary. When it was a major club we wanted to play, we have simply called the club secretary, identified ourselves, and, always, were welcomed and given a suggested starting time.

Even the green fees for major clubs is minor compared to

international standards. Often, in clubs in the country there is only an honor box. The player is asked to fill out a card and attach it to his bag, and drop an envelope in a box with the requested few dollars.

Carts are called *trundlers* and spikes are called *sprigs*.

Do not expect to find motorized carts. There aren't any.

"The only aid the visitor will not find available is the motorized trundler," reads a government pamphlet. "They are not used, except by the occasional member who has been granted permission to use one, on medical ground."

Nor will you find caddies.

The standard ball used in New Zealand is the small English ball and the tees are usually plastic.

Without exception, New Zealanders like to walk, enjoy the camaraderie, bet modestly but consistently, and play *briskly*. None of this sighting, sighing, practice swinging, wiggle-waggling, walking away from the ball, etc. They get up to the ball, hit it, and charge forward.

A sign before the first tee at the Centennial Course in Taupo sums up the New Zealand attitude: "You should play this course and have an enjoyable game in less that 3 hours."

We have played over 20 courses in New Zealand and enjoyed them all for their scenery and, when we have picked up a Kiwi, for their companionship.

(The only exception to this is Titirangi in Auckland where I have been invited twice to play in the prestigious Air New Zealand/Shell Pro-Am Invitational Tournament. In two rounds I never made a par. The last disastrous round was played with Lanny Wadkins, an international star. I finished the eighteenth hole by shanking my approach shot into the parking lot across the street. I crossed the street, recovered the ball and slunk into the clubhouse by a circuitous route and hid. I haven't been invited back since.)

One thing a visitor will find—again very English—is that sports are seasonal and one doesn't play a lot of golf in the summertime.

Few courses have sprinkler systems and the fairways go hard and brown.

Golfers play summer games such as cricket and tennis or head for the water and their boats.

Note: dress on private courses is very correct. It is considered bad taste to wear short socks with golfing shorts. You should know that knee-length socks are a must.

Hunting

As said before, under Customs regulations, sidearms, i.e. revolvers and pistols, are illegal and entry is prohibited. Firearms must be declared and an "entry permit," good for one month, obtained from the police at the airport. There is no charge for the permit. Shotguns do not need to be registered.

What has attracted the international hunter to New Zealand is the alpine chase for tahr and chamois.

The deer population proliferated during the war when seasonal hunting ceased. Their vast numbers were devastating the forests until government-appointed hunters were employed to dramatically reduce the herds.

When it was found that the venison was highly prized in Germany and commanded astronomical prices, professional hunters moved in to hunt by helicopter.

Now deer farming is an emerging major agricultural industry. Feral deer—wild deer from the forests—are even more valuable as breeding stock but the guns today shoot nets from helicopters. The captured live animals are transported to farms throughout the country.

You still have the amateur Kiwi hunter in the field "dressed in his gum boots, shorts and woolly socks and his Swanni? tramping the mountains at nine miles an hour," says Simon Dickie, our favorite outdoor authority.

The amateur is competing against the professional and the professional is competing against the professional. It is not the place for an overseas amateur sportsman and his popgun.

It is not recommended by the government authorities to contemplate hunting in New Zealand without a guide.

Two choices are open: hunt on a safari ranch where results and top trophies are guaranteed, or hunt in the wild with a guide where results will depend on luck, the skill and fitness of the hunter.

Simon Dickie of South Pacific Sporting Adventures, P.O. Box 682, Taupo, offers excellent hunting with selected guides.

"What should hunters bring with them?" we asked Simon.

Simon talks quickly and directly to the point. He is not a man who wastes time. "We tell visitors that we can provide him or her with everything required except woolen clothes, socks and sturdy, lightweight boots.''

"How do you describe the hunting?''

"The wilderness area of the North Island provides challenging hunting for what we call the true 'Fair Chase' hunter. Our native forest lands are unique to New Zealand and provide adequate protection for the animals that live within their confines. It is a supreme challenge to hunt game in these forests. If the hunter is to succeed in taking the animal of his choice—that being the ultimate in 'Fair Chase' hunting—the hunter must be determined and skillful.

"Is it tough physically?''

"It's no stroll in the park. If you choose to hunt our sika or red deer species, you need to be in good physical shape. You have to spend several hours each day creeping though the forest in true Indian fashion, as quietly as possible, while traversing a variety of terrain from flat and rolling to steep and rugged. Quite often, we'll cross small streams many times during the course of the day.

"It also requires intense concentration, being a supreme challenge to any hunter, with most kills being made at close range.

"Much of our 'Fair Chase' hunting is carried out on Crown and State Forest Lands where no trophy fee is payable.

"We also offer a number of hunts on private land which has not been subjected to ceaseless hunting pressure. Your chances of success are much greater and, in some cases, assured. If you take a trophy animal on these private lands, a trophy fee is levied.''

According to the 1986 state schedule, a hunting guide for one day, including vehicular transportation and all equipment, was NZ$400 for one person and $500 for two.

To reach more remote areas, fixed wing and helicopter transportation is available at a variety of rates as are meals and overnight options.

That's the North Island. On the South Island we were recommended to Gary Joll of Lilybank Safari Park at Lake Tekapo, near Mount Cook, who controls a 2,000-acre hunting reserve. We talked to Mr. Joll when we stayed overnight at Lake Tekapo.

Lilybank is for the hunter after a classic trophy animal. The guest hunts for, and pays for, a particular kind of animal, the amount of pay varying according to the trophy animal the hunter is after. No trophy. No pay.

A limited amount of hunting for waterfowl and gamebirds is available in New Zealand.

The season for duck, swan, pheasant and quail opens the first Saturday in May. Licenses are required. The duck and swan season lasts for only three weeks. The pheasant and quail goes on for two months.

Rabbits, wild pig, opossums are considered pests and a license to hunt them in not required.

Shooting Australian cricketers and English rugby players, from what a visitor reads in the daily newspapers, is often considered desirable but not sporting.

As in fishing, for additional hunting information and guide services, write the Hunting and Fishing Officer in Taupo and give him some parameters of your ambitions, abilities, budget and time. He has the sources to "jack it up" for you, as they say in New Zealand.

Skiing

The appeal of skiing in New Zealand is that it occurs in July, August and September, being on the south side of the Equator. So if you are a true ski bum, tired of looking at frying bodies on beaches and longing for the flurry of snow and the sight of your own breath against a chilled air, head for New Zealand.

When it is trout fishing time in the Rockies, the snow is flying in the Southern Alps.

There have been dramatic advances in New Zealand skiing facilities in the last decade.

The single ski area on the North Island is in the Tongariro National Park at the south end of Lake Taupo. The tallest mountain of the North Island, Ruapehu, has skifields on its north face called Whakapapa where the THC Chateau provides gracious accommodations, and on its southwest slopes called Turoa.

We skied Turoa the first season it was opened and found it most enjoyable. Good chair lift and good runs above the timberline.

Interesting aside: in Southern Hemisphere countries the timberline ends at 2,000 feet as opposed to 10,000 feet in Northern Hemisphere countries.

On the South Island, the traditional fields have been at Mt Hutt outside of Christchurch and Coronet Peak outside of Queenstown.

Now there are major fields at Lake Tekapo, Treble Cone near Wanaka, Mt Cardrona between Wanaka and Queenstown, and at the Remarkables across the lake at Queenstown.

There are about twenty club ski areas in addition with rope tows and T-bars and platters.

Perhaps the most dramatic upgrading in skiing is heli-skiing.

For the expert skier there are now a lot of great options on the South Island. I say "expert" because the terrain and the fresh, sometimes deep, powder snow of the areas you are dropped into by helicopter require more than an average intermediate skiing ability. I don't care what the operators says.

Also there is a rare experience available: taking a ski plane to Tasman Glacier on Mount Cook and skiing down.

Queenstown has the brightest apres-ski action.

With skiers able to choose between Coronet Peak, the Remarkables and Mt Cardrona—plus helicopter skiing in the wilderness—and accommodations of all types and at all prices, with an abundance of bars, discos and restaurants, Queenstown draws a large crowd of bright young people looking for other bright young people in the evening.

Note: while there is excellent skiing in New Zealand, do not expect to find the amenities of Colorado or Switzerland or of the ultimate, Deer Valley—my dear—in Utah. There are no mountainside accommodations at the base of the ski runs or top-of-the-lift restaurants. Trails are not manicured and marked like California skifields. You can't ski in and ski out of your hotel as you do at Courchevel or Snowmass.

On the other hand, lifts and ski rentals are, at most, half of what you pay in America, including ski lessons from an international corps of instructors. They follow the snow to New Zealand. When I first skied Coronet Peak in 1975 there were thirty ski instructors from nine different countries.

River Rafting

The most spectacular growth in the sporting field has been in river rafting.

Because New Zealand is honeycombed by large rivers finding their way to the sea from lofted mountains, white water adventuring is a natural.

You now find river rafting companies everywhere—fifty during a 1986 census.

Therein lies a problem.

Many of those rivers are wild or turbulent with steep gradations and many river rafting companies—no, most river rafting companies—offer Type 5 rapids.

Type 3 is a to-be-taken-very-serious and dangerous rapid. Type 4 is very dangerous.

Let me share with you what a guide book to the Deschutes River Canyon in Oregon says about Type 5. "Extremely Dangerous. These rapids require technical maneuvering in strong hydraulics. Rapids may be extended some distance. Standing waves and midstream obstructions or suckholes present serious hazards to equipment and life. Novices and many experienced boatmen should line boats through or portage around."

When I asked one New Zealand operator why he promoted Type 5 rapids, he laughed and replied, "Our objective is to scare the pants off our passengers."

He is not going to have a chance at my pants.

The crux of the problem is that there are too many weekend operators who own a raft but not necessarily the experience to operate it safely. They will take a group under any conditions to make a buck.

The inevitable happened while we were in Queenstown. After a heavy rainstorm, an operator took a raftload of people on the Shotover River when the water level was considered dangerously high . . . beyond an industry approved level for safety.

An American tour guide was tossed into the water. It was fifteen minutes before he was pulled from the water, not breathing, technically dead. They were able to revive his breathing, fortunately, and, according to the news report, he suffered no bad after effects.

The other river-rafting operators called for an investigation.

We talked to several experienced, well financed operators and they all agreed that the present fifty companies will be reduced by half over the next few years. Our hope is that the weeding out of incompetents will take place before they take the lives of any passengers.

The message to us was clear. If you want to go river rafting, go with the one with the most experience.

Spectator Sports And Others

New Zealanders, a conservative people, are slightly horse mad. Every day somewhere in this small country is a horse race. Flat racing or trotters. Auckland alone has three tracks: Ellerslie and Avondale for racing and Alexandra Park for harness racing.

Over 390 days of racing are scheduled at some 260 meetings.

Our impression after driving through most of New Zealand is that if there is a garage in a village you will also find a golf course. Two garages and you will find a race track.

Breeding and selling outstanding thoroughbreds is a national industry. Yearling sales attract international buyers who spend millions of dollars to get New Zealand horses for racing abroad.

We've heard that New Zealand horses are better because of the lime in the grass.

Oh, yes, we mustn't forget greyhound racing.

Betting on horses and greyhounds at off-track offices known as TAB shops (Totilisator Agency Board) is another national sport. TAB offices are found throughout the country. Annually the betting in TAB shops exceeds NZ$500,000,000. Profits from TAB go to the NZ Racing Authorities Amenities Account and Stakes Subsidy Scheme and are distributed to the racing, harness and greyhound clubs to boost race clubs' prize money.

And then there is rugby. It is a national religion.

You should try to see a rugby game if you are in New Zealand during the March-to-October season.

To be picked for the national rugby team, the "All Blacks," is an honor with a greater weight than that of prime minister. The "All Blacks" represent the country at home and abroad, defending the national rugby honor against Australia, England and France.

The summer sport is cricket. The concentration of the nation is centered on test matches—national matches—with Australia and England and India and others.

New Zealand does well in rugby. Cricket is another matter.

I was in Christchurch the morning of a third and deciding match against Australia and went into a barber shop to get a small trim. The barber started discussing the fine points of the previous afternoon's match and I got sheared, drenched and tailed while he nattered on.

New Zealand won that afternoon but it took three months before I stopped looking like an army recruit.

There is motorcycle racing, midget car racing and Grand Prix racing and many motorboat, big and small sailboat events.

Add to the list rowing, water skiing, softball—lots of soft-ball—soccer and surfing, lawn bowls, croquet and, oh, yes, bridge. New Zealanders are dotty-potty over bridge and there are bridge clubs and tournaments everywhere.

New Zealanders' enthusiasm for sports is reflected in the dis-proportionately high number of world champions it produces in relation to its small population.

Bob Fitzsimmons in boxing, Sir Edmund Hillary in alpine climbing, Jack Lovelock created a heritage of winning the 1,500 meters in the 1936 Olympics which has been passed down through Peter Snell to John Walker, 1976 Gold Medalist. Bob Charles in golf, probably the finest left-hander in the world. World champion rowers, Grand Prix drivers, yachtsmen and, the toughest of them all, the New Zealand rugby players.

Then there's a long list of champion horses starting with Phar Lap.

Maybe it *is* the lime in the grass.

Driving

You drive on the left hand side of the road.

It is no bother. After ten minutes on the road, you don't think about it.

If you have a rental vehicle without an automatic transmission, the left hand stick shift might give you pause, as it did us in the Chilly Bin going up steep hills. But you get the hang of it fairly quickly.

International rules of the road apply in New Zealand.

We have driven thousands of miles in the country. Never been stopped by a policeman and have never seen a serious accident.

It is a great way to see the country.

The Lady Navigator: "Particularly if you have a careful and patient driver."

Driver: "And if you have a gorgeous, gentle Lady Navigator."
The Lady Navigator: "I love you."
Driver: "Thanks. I love you, too."
The Lady Navigator: "Thanks. Watch out for that truck."

Hand Kissing and Genuflections

So many kind people!

The fear of saying thanks is that we will miss someone. Risk it, we must.

First, to Mike Hoy of the THC for making our accommodations so easy—and luxurious—and to all the managers who took such kind care of us on the road. To Bill Newton of THC Marketing for filling in the blanks in the industry picture.

To Paul O'Ryan of Newmans and his North American associate, John Honeycombe, for "Ten-Ton Chilly Bin" which gave us freedom on the road, reliable transportation and flexible shelter.

To all the troops of the New Zealand Tourist and Publicity Office, starting with Jim Monahan and including George Swofford, Phil Robinson, Graham Walker, Geoff Dillon, Kevin Gough, Roman Herbst, Charlie Ives, Mark Vial, Mike Damiano, Roger Rowe, and Colin McAnnalley for tons of information and reams of data.

And to the city and regional information officers: Lydia Allen at Turangi, Merrylyn Corcoran of Greymouth, Christine Griffin in Timaru, Peter Heath in Nelson, Joseph Lane at Taupo, Annette Main in Wanganui, Brigette Molyneaux in Blenheim, Murray Pinfold in Hastings, Dennis Rigby in Palmerston North, Tom Ross in Dunedin, Kathy Saunders of Auckland, Gene Saunders in Wellington, and Noreen Young in Napier.

A special thanks goes to Dick Williams of Air New Zealand in Auckland and Barry Turner in Christchurch for getting our bodies—and our luggage—where they were supposed to be, when they were supposed to be.

Index

What The Critics Wrote About The First Book:

How to Get Lost and Found in New Zealand: You'd enjoy this one if you have no intention of ever going. But there's a real danger that John McDermott's delightful prose will start you making travel plans." *Chicago Sun-Times*

"If New Zealand wasn't already one of my favorite spots on earth, it would be after reading John McDermott." *Galveston Daily News*

"I would not leave for New Zealand before reading *How to Get Lost and Found.*" *The Federal Quarterly*

"For a change, a first class travel book about New Zealand—and written by an American at that . . . It is easily the best travel book about New Zealand that has made its appearance for some years." *Christchurch Star*

"An excellent book on the country." *The Sacramento Bee*

"A very funny travel book." *Western Regional Newspapers Magazine*

"A travel book with a difference . . . a bright staccato style that grows on one . . . written wittily, tongue in cheek. I consider it is a more accurate assessment of New Zealanders than some sociological interpretative books about us." *Dalgety News*

ORAFA Publishing Company, Inc.
1314 South King Street, Suite 1064
Honolulu, Hawaii 96814

Please send me the following *HOW TO GET LOST AND FOUND* books. I understand that I must send cash, check or money order with this order.

Name_____

Address_____

City/State_____ Zip_____

Shipping Address *(See Below)*

TITLE	PRICE	P&H	QNTY	AMOUNT	Shipping Address ** GIFTS
AUSTRALIA	9.95				1 2 3
CALIFORNIA	9.95				1 2 3
COOK ISLANDS	9.95				1 2 3
FIJI	9.95				1 2 3
OUR HAWAII	9.95				1 2 3
JAPAN	9.95				1 2 3
NEW ZEALAND	9.95				1 2 3
TAHITI	9.95				1 2 3

Hawaii Resident add 4% Sales Tax
Outside USA, add $1.50 per book for additional P&H

TOTAL

Postage and Handling:
Book Rate: Add $2.00 for first book and $1.00 for each additional book. (Allow 4-6 weeks.)
Air Mail: $3.00 per book
****For gift shipments:*** Specify address below and circle appropriate number on the order form above in the last column next to the title to be shipped. Items *not* so marked will be shipped to your address.

1st Address_____ 2nd Address_____ 3rd Address_____

_____ _____ _____

_____ _____ _____

A GIFT FROM:_____
Message will appear on label